History and Modernity in the
Thought of Thomas Hobbes

History and Modernity in the Thought of Thomas Hobbes

ROBERT P. KRAYNAK

Cornell University Press

Ithaca and London

First published 1990 by Cornell University Press.

International Standard Book Number 0-8014-2427-5
Library of Congress Catalog Card Number 90-36301
Printed in the United States of America
*Librarians: Library of Congress cataloging information
appears on the last page of the book.*

⊗ The paper in this publication meets the minimum requirements
of the American National Standard for Permanence
of Paper for Printed Library Materials Z39.48–1984.

Contents

v

Acknowledgments

This study of Thomas Hobbes builds on the work and insights of Leo Strauss. Two generations ago Strauss led the way in revitalizing the study of Hobbes by uncovering the prescientific moral basis of Hobbes's thought and explaining its significance for modern political philosophy. Inspired by his scholarship, I have tried to develop it further through an examination of Hobbes's neglected historical writings and their importance for the origins of modernity. My greatest debt, therefore, is to Strauss for providing the model of unsurpassed excellence in scholarship and human wisdom.

Unfortunately, I never had the privilege of studying under Strauss; but I was lucky enough to have the next-best thing: he was the teacher of my teachers, Werner J. Dannhauser and Harvey C. Mansfield, Jr. They introduced me to political philosophy, encouraged my work, and made a lasting contribution to 'the architecture of my soul.' I also thank Abe Shulsky, whose class at Cornell University first sparked my interest in Hobbes, and Michael Walzer, whose seminar on Hobbes at Harvard University stimulated many of the thoughts that led to this book. Several friends and colleagues provided the indispensable intellectual and moral support for the completion of this project: Arthur Melzer and Jerry Weinberger of Michigan State; Cifford Orwin of the University of Toronto; William Fuller, Jr., of the Naval War College; and Joseph Wagner of Colgate University. Finally, I thank the Earhart Foundation for its generous financial support.

ROBERT P. KRAYNAK

Hamilton, New York

vii

History and Modernity in the
Thought of Thomas Hobbes

Introduction

As the twentieth century comes to a close, we are faced with serious questions about the worth and future course of modern civilization. For some observers the economic and technological problems of modern life are the primary concern: How can the growth of advanced and developing societies continue in a world of finite resources and environmental hazards? For others the central questions are political: Will the nations shaped by the dominant ideologies of the modern age—liberal democracy, communism, and nationalism—undergo dramatic changes in the next century and produce a new balance of power in the international world? Still others see the fate of modern civilization as a religious issue: Can the spiritual emptiness of modern secular society be overcome through religious revival or a return to fundamentalism or an injection of Eastern mysticism?

In academic circles such issues are part of a larger debate about 'modernity' and 'postmodernity' which has produced a great deal of soulsearching (along with a fair amount of posturing) and elicited a sharp divergence of views. As far as one can tell, the majority of intellectuals continue to believe, somewhat defensively, in what one recent scholar has called 'the legitimacy of the modern age.'[1] But a

1. Hans Blumenberg, *The Legitimacy of the Modern Age*, trans. Robert M. Wallace (Cambridge, Mass.: MIT Press, 1983).

significant minority looks forward to a 'postmodern' consciousness of new and exotic forms of thought or looks back to the premodern ideas of classical and medieval philosophy.

Engaging in such reflection, of course, requires a clear understanding of what constitutes 'modernity' or 'modern civilization.' Although one can scarcely find a person today who does not have some awareness of what it means to be 'modern'—as the questions above suggest—this notion grows more elusive when its philosophical foundations are sought. To a certain extent the difficulty we face in understanding our own civilization is inherent in all attempts at self-knowledge. We are so deeply immersed in the modern world and so profoundly influenced by modern categories of thought that finding the right perspective from which to view and judge ourselves is almost impossible. But this problem, common to all ages and cultures, is more difficult for us because of the peculiar character of modernity.

For most people the term 'modern' is defined negatively, in opposition to what is ancient or traditional. The pride and self-confidence of an age that calls itself modern arises from its awareness of how far it has progressed or moved beyond the past. But understanding oneself in this way conceals as much as it reveals because it leads one to forget about the past as soon as it has been overcome or to see the past only in caricatures. Viewed through the lens of progress, the past becomes the 'dark ages,' and although we may occasionally feel nostalgia for how people might have lived in those benighted times, we are all but incapable of taking seriously, or even accurately identifying, their world of ideas and beliefs. Because modern self-understanding involves forgetting the past, it tends to lose sight of its own origins and to take its existence for granted, obscuring instead of revealing its animating principles. Small wonder, then, that we 'moderns' find genuine self-knowledge so difficult to attain.

If this analysis is correct, our only hope for arriving at an adequate understanding of ourselves and our world is through exercises in the history of philosophy, conducted with renewed seriousness that derives from our doubts about modernity and directed to the goal of recovering the forgotten presuppositions of the modern path. For this purpose it is particularly useful, even imperative, to take a fresh look at the thought of Thomas Hobbes. For Hobbes was one of the leading participants in the intellectual revolutions of the sixteenth and seventeenth centuries that shook the established traditions of thought and began a new order of things, the order we now call the modern age, or modernity. That Hobbes understood himself to be a founder of a new order is evident from the way he described himself—as someone who was convinced of the failure of the tradition he inherited and eager to proclaim the novelty of his thought, especially in political science. Moreover, Hobbes describes with unusual boldness, clarity, and detail the new form of political or civil society he sought to create and, more important, provides an elaborate historical account of the past forms of civilization he sought to overcome.

Hobbes, in other words, stands out among the founders of modernity because he was not only a political scientist but also a historian. Throughout his life he combined scientific and mathematical pursuits with an intense interest in the discipline of "civil history" (as he called it). He translated Thucydides, studied classical and preclassical civilization in the works of Tacitus, Diodorus, Strabo, Josephus, and other ancient historians, and composed historical works of his own, including a lengthy history of the English Civil War, *The Behemoth*. Moreover, Hobbes saw an intimate connection between his scientific and historical studies. In the historical writings he presents a view of the past that explains why it is necessary and how it is possible to begin anew and to transform the world with a new political science. If one were to judge thinkers solely by the types of writings they produced, one might be inclined to say that modernity achieved its moment of greatest self-awareness in the historical works and scientific treatises of Thomas Hobbes.

By raising this point we immediately see the most serious deficiency in the prevailing approaches to Hobbes. Surveying the scholarly literature, we find interpretations that feature Hobbes the methodologist, Hobbes the mechanistic scientist, Hobbes the linguistic philosopher and rhetorician, Hobbes the social-contract theorist, even Hobbes the moralist and theologian. But Hobbes the student of history, the investigator of the rise and fall of civilizations, is rarely mentioned or given systematic treatment. In the few cases where Hobbes's study of history is discussed, as in C. B. Macpherson's important work, its role is misunderstood: history is treated not as an intellectual discipline that Hobbes consciously pursued but as a social and ideological context (the emergence of bourgeois society) that his arguments unconsciously expressed. In other cases, such as Strauss's influential book, Hobbes's interest in history is treated as an early phase of his career when he first began to think about the practical application of moral precepts. In no instance do we find history thematically treated as the source or spring of Hobbes's political science and its self-conscious effort to create a new foundation for civilization.

To be sure, Hobbes himself is largely responsible for this over-sight. His political treatises, such as *Leviathan* and *De Cive,* are in-tended to be scientific works, modeled on geometry, that present political science as a strictly deductive system. Historical knowledge is denigrated as mere experience and excluded as much as possible from the treatises, replaced by logical deductions from postulates about sensation and the passions which are supposed to stand on their own as self-evident truths. It is only natural, then, that most interpretations of Hobbes have focused on his theory of science and neglected his views of history.

But such interpretations tell only half the story because Hobbes's science does not stand entirely on its own, independent of historical knowledge. Consider the sweeping historical thesis that underlies *Leviathan* and the other political treatises: civilization in its past and present forms, from antiquity to seventeenth-century England, has been radically defective because it has never been free from "disor-ders of state and change of government by civil war." This thesis defines the very problem that the treatises are designed to solve; yet it is never proved in the treatises. Nor can it be deduced from Hobbes's abstract postulates about human nature, according to which the passions for security, profit, and glory render men "apt to invade and destroy one another" and create the need for an absolute sovereign. For how could Hobbes know that this is *the* problem of civilization or that no previous civilization had found a satisfactory way of restraining the destructive passions? Clearly, Hobbes presup-poses detailed knowledge of the defective institutions and imperfect structures of authority in the civil societies of the past, which re-quires not only an abstract science of human nature but also a the-ory of civil history. One might even infer that Hobbes's historical theory, which defines the fundamental problem of civilization, must be temporally and logically prior to his political science, which ex-plains the solution.

This argument provides a glimpse of the complicated relation of history and science which lies at the heart of Hobbes's thought. It suggests that Hobbes begins with comprehensive reflection on the history of civilization and designs his political science in response to such reflection. But then, for unstated reasons, he reverses the pri-ority of history and science in his political treatises and asserts the strictly scientific character of his doctrine. What he leaves to us is a pattern of thought which is hard to explain but easy to recognize as the typical attitude of the modern mind toward history: he studies the past to see what must be overcome and then erases or obscures the past by presenting a new scientific outlook that seems to stand on its own. The purpose of this book is to explain how Hobbes arrives at this view of history and science and to show that his pattern of reasoning underlies the most important intellectual movement of the modern age, the scientific enlightenment.

In the first half of the book, I examine Hobbes's various historical works, with a special emphasis on *Behemoth,* in order to demonstrate that they form a coherent and comprehensive theory of history. This theory, I argue, encompasses the development of civilization from the ancient kingdoms of the Near East to the republics of Greece and Rome to the monarchies of feudal Europe and reveals the character and defects of all preexisting political authority. Hobbes's thesis, stated succinctly, is that civilization emerges from barbarism when men acquire sufficient leisure to cultivate the arts and sciences and when the rule of brute force is replaced by authority based on opinion. Hence the defining trait of civilization has been the development of a leisured class of intellectual authorities, such as priests, philosophers, and scholars, who have been honored and revered for their presumed wisdom and learning. They have become the arbiters of civilization by using their arts and sciences to control opinions and to proclaim their views of the divine and natural order as true doctrine. At the same time they have caused the dissolution of civilizations because their claims of knowledge lead to a special kind of civilized warfare: the conflict of doctrines for recognition as the authoritative wisdom of society. This phenomenon—which I call 'doctrinal politics'—is the central problem of preexisting civilization that Hobbes uncovers through his study of history.

In the second half of the book I analyze Hobbes's search for a solution. Since he has shown that the development of the arts and sciences in one form or another is responsible for the problems of civilization, one should not be surprised that he looks for a solution in a change in thinking. But it is precisely here that Hobbes confronts his deepest dilemma: How can he solve the problem of doctrinal politics by creating yet another doctrine? Is there a new doctrine that will end rather than perpetuate doctrinal warfare? In presenting Hobbes's solution I focus on this dilemma as the source of his views on the relation of history and science.

The search for a doctrine that will end doctrinal warfare motivates Hobbes to build a new kind of science, one that overcomes the conflicting claims of authoritative wisdom which have endangered civilization and frustrated the search for true knowledge. Accordingly, Hobbes seeks a foundation for science that is wholly free from trust in authority or trust in received opinions. Instead of relying on such trust, and thereby repeating the mistakes of the classical and medieval philosophers, Hobbes dismisses the whole mental attitude of trusting in received opinion as a vain belief in the harmony of mind and reality. By rejecting this harmony Hobbes exposes the human mind to an experience of fear that is humbling but also exhilarating. For it leads to the discovery of reason's autonomy, its capacity to stand on its own self-evident foundations without reliance on external authority.

This notion of autonomous or self-reliant thinking is the basis of Hobbes's project for scientific enlightenment. It enables him to construct a new edifice of science—a strictly deductive system that includes a formal method of logic, a natural science of mechanistic materialism, and a political science of absolute sovereignty. By building in this fashion he is able to claim that his doctrine is self-evident and indisputable and hence is history's final doctrine: the one that will make all doctrinal conflicts disappear and advance mankind to "immortal peace" in the last stage of civilization.

In presenting this interpretation I hope to show that Hobbes's thought provides valuable insight into the scientific enlightenment and the peculiar problems of modern politics and culture. The claim I make is not that Hobbes is the first or the only enlightenment philosopher (comparisons with Descartes will reveal important variations) but that Hobbes's pattern of thinking is the most illuminating example of this phenomenon. For Hobbes enables us to see the many unstated assumptions about history that are necessarily presupposed by enlightenment science but just as necessarily forgotten by us, the children of the enlightenment.

Hence he helps us to see why the political doctrines that grow out of the enlightenment, such as modern liberalism, produce a peculiar mixture of freedom and dogmatism—the independent thinking of self-reliant individuals combined with mental enslavement to a new type of mass conformity. Hobbes also helps us to understand how the great critics of the enlightenment, such as Edmund Burke, could be so resolutely opposed to the new politics. For the enlightenment's attempt to overcome the past and to abolish the realm of authoritative wisdom creates the potential for a new kind of doctrinal warfare—the revolutionary violence of ideological utopianism. Some of these criticisms, advanced in the conclusion of this book, will sting a little because there are few people in the modern world who are not inspired by the enlightenment and its promise of bringing a more reasonable and peaceful world. But they must be faced if we are to understand the principles of modern civilization and honestly assess its problems.

The History of
Barbarism and Civilization

Civil History and Political Science

Hobbes's political science rests on the sweeping historical claim that all past and present civil societies are radically defective because they have never been free of "disorders of state and change of governments by civil war" (*Leviathan*, ch. 31, p. 357).[1] Although this claim underlies Hobbes's entire political enterprise, it is never empirically proved or systematically examined in his scientific treatises on politics. In these works Hobbes begins by examining the faculties and passions of men in the state of nature, the condition of anarchy and brutish warfare which occurs when civilization dissolves. Moving from this point, he proceeds to his main task, constructing the mighty Leviathan state, a new form of government that will establish a secure and lasting foundation for civil society. By following this procedure Hobbes excludes from the outset a systematic analysis of the traditional forms of political authority and the historical causes of civil war. His scientific treatises, therefore, are incomplete statements of his political teaching: they present the solution to the historic failures of civilization, but they take for granted an understanding of the problem.

A brief reflection on Hobbes's method supports this conclusion. In the study of politics Hobbes employs the resolutive-compositive

---

1. References to *Leviathan* are to vol. 3 of *The English Works of Thomas Hobbes of Malmesbury*, ed. Sir William Molesworth, 11 vols. (London: John Bohn, 1839–1845). All citations of Hobbes's works are to the Molesworth edition of the *English Works* (*EW*) or the *Opera Latina* (*OL*) unless otherwise specified.

method, a method that divides the process of reasoning into three distinct stages: (1) an understanding of the defective forms of political authority as encountered in past and present civil societies; (2) the resolution of these forms of political authority into their constituent elements, or the state-of-nature teaching; and (3) the reconstruction of the constituent elements into a new whole, or artificial sovereignty (*De Cive*, Preface).[2] From this account of Hobbes's method, one can see that the first stage of his thinking is omitted from the scientific treatises, which open at the second stage and move to third. As Watkins points out, Hobbes has made a fundamental distinction between the process of "invention or discovery [and that] of teaching or demonstration. The process of discovery is not presented in a didactic work of exposition . . . [such as] the *Leviathan*, which opens with an account of the premises and not with an account of how Hobbes arrived at them."[3]

This procedure has created difficulties for Hobbes scholars, who have drawn their interpretations primarily from the scientific treatises. In these works the original view of defective politics survives only in bits and pieces—in brief polemical remarks scattered throughout the texts or in a single summary chapter on "the dissolution of commonwealths." In conformity with the resolutive-compositive method, Hobbes has reduced his original understanding of political phenomena to a simple psychological teaching, according to which the passions for security, profit, and glory render men "apt to invade and destroy one another" and create the need for an absolute sovereign. Yet this teaching does not explain why the civil societies of the past have been unable to restrain these passions, either by the external restraints of laws and institutions or by the internal restraints of habit and conscience. Nor does this teaching identify precisely the immediate causes of civil war, such as class conflict, economic competition, political faction, religious war, dynastic struggles, racial strife, military rivalry, or any of the other historical causes of human conflict. Because the historical record has been expunged from the state-of-nature teaching, most scholars have been in the difficult position of attempting to understand Hobbes's solutions without fully understanding the problem.

2. See also J. W. N. Watkins, *Hobbes's System of Ideas: A Study in the Political Significance of Philosophical Theories* (London: Hutchinson, 1965), p. 47; Leo Strauss, *The Political Philosophy of Hobbes*, trans. E. M. Sinclair (Chicago: University of Chicago Press, 1936), p. 2.

3. J. W. N. Watkins, "Philosophy and Politics in Hobbes," in *Hobbes Studies*, ed. Keith C. Brown (Cambridge, Mass.: Harvard University Press, 1965), p. 245.

This predicament has led a number of scholars to reconstruct Hobbes's view of the fundamental political problem, either by referring to independently known historical information or by searching throughout Hobbes's political treatises for precise models of human conflict. Macpherson, for example, analyzes the social and economic conditions of seventeenth-century England, claiming that an unstated "social assumption" underlies Hobbes's political treatises. He argues that the psychological postulates of the state-of-nature teaching refer to the acquisitive desires and competitive instincts of an emerging "possessive market society."[4] Richard Peters also maintains that a historical context is needed to understand Hobbes's fear of anarchy and concern for security. He states that Hobbes's system is a response to the post-Renaissance dissolution of feudalism and rise of individualism; these developments produced "the greatest gains in the field of individual liberty. . . . But the cost was loss of security. The economic, social, and religious ties of a traditional society cannot be shaken off without a threat to security."[5]

In addition to historical reconstructions, philosophical ones have been presented. F. S. McNeilly offers a "formalized" version of Hobbes's state-of-nature teaching. He claims that it is designed to show the problem of "value competition," that is, the logical impossibility of realizing all of one's values without denying the same opportunity to others.[6] Harvey Mansfield argues more substantively that Hobbes's concern is with the conflict of opinions about the good, the just, and the useful as described by Aristotle. The focus of Mansfield's interpretation, therefore, is the problem of political partisanship which arises when men dispute the "direct questions" about the ends or purposes of the state.[7] Sheldon Wolin and others contend that Hobbes sees the primary political problem as a linguistic one: the description of the natural condition of mankind refers to the "anarchy of meanings" or the conflicting definitions that men give to words.[8]

Such interpretations, while not wholly incompatible with each other, indicate the range of possibilities that scholars have presented

4. C. B. Macpherson, *The Political Theory of Possessive Individualism* (London: Oxford University Press, 1962), pp. 46, 54–59.
5. Richard Peters, *Hobbes* (Baltimore: Penguin, 1956), p. 180.
6. F. S. McNeilly, *The Anatomy of "Leviathan"* (London: Macmillan, 1968), pp. 254, 239.
7. Harvey C. Mansfield, Jr., "Hobbes and the Science of Indirect Government," *American Political Science Review*, 65 (1971), 98–99.
8. Sheldon Wolin, *Politics and Vision* (Boston: Little, Brown, 1960), p. 257; Frederick Whelan, "Language and Its Abuses in Hobbes's Political Philosophy," *American Political Science Review*, 75 (1981), 59–74.

in reconstructing Hobbes's view of the fundamental political problem. Yet in all cases something obvious has been overlooked: Hobbes himself analyzes the defects of past and contemporary civil society in his extensive set of writings on civil or political history. These writings form a significant part of Hobbes's work, although they are presented in a variety of books, essays, and statements. The most important are *The Behemoth,* Hobbes's history of the English Civil War, and *A Dialogue between a Philosopher and a Student of the Common Laws of England,* his analysis of the English common law system as well as his most detailed exposition of the origin of England's political institutions. In addition to these major works, there are important short histories, such as "An Historical Narration on Heresy," a work on "Ecclesiastical History" in Latin verse, and the introduction to Hobbes's translation of Thucydides. Finally, Hobbes's thoughts on history can be found in the political treatises proper, in many observations scattered throughout the texts, and in extended statements appearing in the Preface to *De Cive* and in parts III and IV of the *Leviathan.* Although these writings are presented in a variety of contexts and were composed at different times in Hobbes's career, they are all part of the intellectual discipline that Hobbes calls "civil history" and are the most important sources for understanding his view of past and contemporary civil society.[9]

In the argument that follows I shall attempt to piece together these writings into a whole and show that they form a coherent theory of history, the subject of which is the evolution of man from barbarism to civilization. This theory of history, to be sure, is not a philosophy of history in the manner of Hegel. It lacks the idea of

---

9. Scholars who have called for an interpretation of Hobbes's historical writings without providing it themselves are Gordon Schochet, "Thomas Hobbes on the Family and the State of Nature," *Political Science Quarterly* 82 (1967) 445, and Richard Ashcraft, "Ideology and Class in Hobbes' Political Theory," *Political Theory,* 6 (1978), 28.

The only scholars who argue that Hobbes's thought not only is influenced by history but also contains a historical dimension or "eschatology" are J. G. A. Pocock, "Time, History, and Eschatology in the Thought of Thomas Hobbes," in *Politics, Language, and Time* (New York: Atheneum, 1971), pp. 148–201, and Eldon Eisenach, *Two Worlds of Liberalism: Religion and Politics in Hobbes, Locke, and Mill* (Chicago: University of Chicago Press, 1981). Their claim is that the "prophetic" history presented in pts. III and IV of *Leviathan* is actually a Hobbesian version of Protestant millennialism which restores the realm of faith to politics. But, as Jeffrey Barnouw points out in an insightful critique, their argument is misleading because it is precisely Hobbes's intention to "take the messianic dimension out of politics": Jeffrey Barnouw, "Persuasion in Hobbes's *Leviathan,*" *Hobbes Studies,* 1 (1988), 19. What is needed, then, is a systematic interpretation of Hobbes's writings on civil history which takes note of parallels with other historical theories but does not impose an alien theoretical framework on his thought.

inevitable development toward an end or final stage; and it is, for the most part, a story of retrogression rather than of progress. Nevertheless, Hobbes's account qualifies as a genuine theory of history because it outlines a definite pattern of development from barbarism to civilization and traces the development of world civilization through three distinct stages. Moreover, it identifies precisely the defect of past and contemporary civilization and shows that the construction of a new foundation for civil society is both necessary and possible.

From Barbarism to Civilization:
The Rule of Force Replaced by Opinion

A survey of Hobbes's historical writings reveals that Hobbes investigated the condition of civil society from the time of ancient Egypt to seventeenth-century England. His sources for these investigations (at least those he identifies by name) were the great historians, poets, and philosophers of antiquity and the lesser-known historians of contemporary Europe. From the works of Diodorus Siculus, Caesar, Strabo, and Josephus, as well as from the Old Testament, Hobbes acquired a knowledge of the ancient kingdoms of the Near East, such as Egypt, Israel, Persia, Assyria, and India (*Behemoth*, pp. 277–283; *De Cive*, XVI.9). From the works of Thucydides, Tacitus, Plutarch, Seneca, Cicero, as well as from historical observations in Aristotle's *Politics*, Hobbes acquired an understanding of the republics of ancient Greece and Rome (*Behemoth*, p. 233; *De Cive*, XII.3; *Opera Latina*, v, 359). And from the works of contemporary historians, such as Selden, Heath, and the common law historians, as well as from the writings of Tacitus, Hobbes developed his views on the origins of feudal Europe and the institutions of monarchy, gentry, and church (*Leviathan*, ch. 10, p. 84; *Dialogue on the Common Laws*, p. 167; *Behemoth*, Epistle Dedicatory).[10] Judging from these sources and writings, one can infer that for Hobbes the known civilized world consisted of three types of societies: the ancient kingdoms of the Near East, the republics of ancient Greece and Rome, and the monarchies of Christian Europe.

In addition to studying the kingdoms and republics of the civilized world, Hobbes investigated the historical condition of those people

10. References to *A Dialogue between a Philosopher and a Student of the Common Laws of England* are to the edition by Joseph Cropsey (Chicago: University of Chicago Press, 1971). References to the Epistle Dedicatory of *Behemoth*, which is not included in the Molesworth edition, are to the second Tönnies edition (New York: Barnes and Noble, 1969).

he calls savages, barbarians, or heathens. His knowledge of such people appears to be derived from many of the same sources, although in this regard his citations are less explicit. In any case, there are at least three distinct peoples or conditions that Hobbes refers to as savage or barbaric: "the savage people of America" and "those that live near the Poles" (that is, the Indians and Eskimos of North America) (*Leviathan*, ch. 13, p. 114; ch. 30, p. 324; ch. 46, p. 655; *De Corpore*, 1.7); the Germanic tribes of prefeudal Europe and their descendants who became the Saxon tribes of early England (*Leviathan*, ch. 10, p. 83; *Dialogue*, pp. 162–163); and the period of barbarism before the founding of the Greek city-states, when men lived by plunder and rapine (*Leviathan*, ch. 10, p. 81; *De Cive*, v.2). These tribes and peoples are the source of Hobbes's thoughts on the condition of savagery or barbarism.

As this overview suggests, the primary theme of Hobbes's studies in civil history is the distinction between barbarism and civilization. To understand Hobbes's criteria for distinguishing the two conditions, we may begin with a brief reflection on his terminology. In speaking of the societies of the past, Hobbes sometimes uses terms that emphasize their *political* characteristics—"commonwealths," "cities," "polities"—and at other times uses terms that emphasize their *civilized* qualities—"civil society," "civil life" (*Leviathan*, ch. 9, p. 71; *De Cive*, x.1; *De Corpore*, 1.7; *De Homine*, x.3).[11] Hobbes uses both sets of terms interchangeably because he regards civilization as a condition that combines a certain level of political development and a certain manner of living. Wherever government was sufficiently strong and well established to provide peace and leisure, men began to cultivate the finer things of life; above all, they began to cultivate philosophy or the arts and sciences. Thus, Hobbes observes, it is a general rule of history that "commonwealth is the mother of peace and leisure; and leisure, the mother of philosophy. Where first there were great and flourishing cities, there was the first study of philosophy" (*Leviathan*, ch. 46, p. 666). Civilization, in other words, has been a condition in which government has provided the leisure for intellectual cultivation. In a condition of savagery or barbarism, by contrast, political authority has been so little developed that no one has had the leisure to cultivate the arts and sciences (*Leviathan*, ch. 13, p. 114; ch. 46, p. 665). According to Hobbes, then, civilization has been distinguished from

11. References to *De Homine* are to the translation in *Man and Citizen*, ed. Bernard Gert (Garden City, N.Y.: Doubleday, 1972).

barbarism by the power and sufficiency of political authority, by the enjoyment of leisure, and by the development of the arts, sciences, and philosophy.

Using this standard, Hobbes traces the evolution of men from barbarism to civilization. He maintains that in the most primitive condition the only form of authority was that of fathers or conquerors who ruled by "natural force" over families and tribes. Hence, Hobbes says, "the beginning of all dominion amongst men was in families; in which, the father . . . was absolute lord of his wife and children . . . [and of those] enemies they took and saved, [who] were their servants" (*Dialogue*, p. 159; *Leviathan*, ch. 17, p. 159).[12] In this condition a continuous struggle for survival occurred, as the various families and tribes waged war on each other for territory, scarce goods, and servants. Accordingly, plunder or piracy was not regarded as dishonorable; indeed, it was "a manner of living, and as it were a certain economy, which they called *lestriken,* living by rapine." The harshness of life was mitigated only by a primitive code of military honor which required magnanimity in victory and abstention from cruelty, and by the "economy" of plunder, which counseled victors to spare the people, animals, and instruments that were useful for production (*De Cive*, v.2; *Leviathan*, ch. 17, p. 159). As for the cultivation of the arts and sciences, only the practical arts—the "arts necessary for man's life"—were ever developed in the condition of barbarism. For the most part, Hobbes says, primitive men lived by "gross experience"—that is, by observations derived from immediate sense experience—because they lacked the leisure to cultivate speech (except for the most rudimentary kind), to develop writing, or to acquire systematic knowledge (*Dialogue*, p. 162; *Leviathan*, ch. 46, p. 665).

Of the various historical peoples from which this general description is drawn, the ones that Hobbes discusses in greatest detail (and seems to regard as the paradigm of savage people) are the Germanic and Saxon tribes of prefeudal Europe (*Leviathan*, ch. 10, p. 82). He elaborates upon their life and evolution in recounting the origins of England's political institutions in the *Dialogue of the Common Laws.* There he traces England's beginnings to a prehistoric era, when the island was inhabited by Saxon families and tribes whose ancestors came from Germany. As "a savage and heathen people," Hobbes says, they lived "only by war and rapine . . . written laws they had little, or none, and very few there were in [that] time . . . that could write or read." Among such savages authority

---

12. See also Schochet, "Thomas Hobbes on the Family," p. 445.

was either "paternal or by conquest," and the "succession of lands was determined by the pleasure of the master of the family . . . [or by] natural descent, [which] was held for the law of nature, not only amongst the Germans, but also in most nations before they had written laws." The prehistoric era was followed by a period in which the Saxon tribes came under Roman domination and England developed written laws and customs. Although this period saw the beginning of political consolidation, England remained divided into many petty kingdoms, each of which developed the custom of meeting with a council of advisers to design laws. The third period began with the conquest of the Saxon kings by William the Conqueror, who established a great monarchy and brought England to the stage of civil society. As king, William maintained the custom of meeting with advisers or parliaments; but he changed the title to property by taking it from the petty kings and distributing it to his generals in exchange for oaths of loyalty and military service (*Dialogue*, pp. 158–168). Thus England evolved from barbarism to civilization in several stages, as political power was consolidated by force and written laws and customs were developed.

In the *Dialogue* and in *Behemoth*, Hobbes indicates that this general pattern was followed in the historical origins of all civilized nations. He remarks that "great monarchies have proceeded from small families . . . [which were extended] by war, wherein the victor not only enlarged his territory, but also the number and riches of his subjects. . . . [And in this] manner, *which is by war, grew up all the greatest kingdoms of the world*, viz., the Egyptian, Assyrian, Persian, and the Macedonian monarchy; and so did the great kingdoms of England, France, and Spain" (*Dialogue*, p. 161; emphasis added). As for the republics of ancient Greece and Rome, their development was a variation on this theme. In the earliest times of Greece, before the founding of the city-states, men lived by plunder and rapine. Thereafter "the Greeks had for a while their petty kings, and then by sedition came to be petty commonwealths [that is, small republics]; and then growing to be greater commonwealths, by sedition again became monarchies" (*Behemoth*, p. 252). Similarly, Rome began with primitive tribes consolidated into monarchy; then, "in Rome, rebellion against Kings produced Democracy, upon which the Senate usurped under Sylla, and the People again upon the Senate under Marius, and the Emperor usurped upon the People under Caesar and his Successors" (*Dialogue*, p. 161). In short, the ancient republics emerged in stages, after barbarism, monarchy, and the rebellion against kings. They differed, however, in being "cemented by human wit"—that is, by human agreement—rather than by conquest and hereditary succession (*Elements*, ii, 2.5.3).[13]

As a general rule, then, the evolution from barbarism to civilization followed a typical pattern: families, tribes, and petty kingdoms were consolidated by war or agreement into commonwealths, which were either great monarchies or small republics. This political development was accompanied by a certain peace and leisure, which allowed for intellectual development in various spheres, from the cultivation of speech and writing to the development of arts and sciences.

To this point Hobbes's historical analysis seems to indicate that the evolution from barbarism to civilization is a kind of 'progress.' But is this really the case? Which condition is superior with regard to human felicity and misery? According to Aristotle, civilization as such is superior to barbarism. In his classic statement in Book I of the *Politics*, Aristotle argues that the growth of political society constitutes progress toward human perfection: the evolution from families to tribes to cities or commonwealths improves men by making them increasingly self-sufficient and civilized. In prepolitical societies, preoccupation with the satisfaction of basic needs prevents men from developing their moral and intellectual abilities. In political societies, however, they rise above "mere life" and attain the "good life," understood as a life of leisure devoted to the exercise of the moral virtues in political activity and the cultivation of the mind in the study of philosophy. For Aristotle and other classical philosophers, the good life is the end or purpose of civilization. As a self-sufficient existence that includes all the elements of happiness or felicity, it is superior to all other conditions.

Now Hobbes agrees with Aristotle to a certain extent. Political consolidation into small republics or great monarchies does indeed constitute progress because it brings a measure of relief from the wars among clans and tribes (although Hobbes is more 'realistic' than Aristotle in describing the process of consolidation as a violent conquest rather than a natural growth). In addition, the increase in leisure and the advancement of the arts (by which Hobbes means the practical arts or technical sciences as opposed to the liberal arts or speculative sciences) bring increased freedom from necessity and

13. References to Hobbes's political treatise *The Elements* are to the *English Works*, which divides the work into pt. i, "Human Nature or the Elements of Policy" (thirteen chapters), and pt. ii, "De Corpore Politico or the Elements of Law" (subdivided into a first part with six chapters and a second part with ten chapters). Hence the citation II, 2.5.3 means pt. II, the second part, fifth chapter, third section.

scarcity. By virtue of the practical arts, Hobbes says, civilized people enjoy some of the "commodities of mankind" (*De Corpore*, I.7; *Elements*, 1,13.3). In these respects civilization provides greater felicity or happiness and is superior to precivil life.

But Hobbes stops here in his agreement with Aristotle about the superiority of civilization. Hobbes ultimately concludes that civilization as previously constituted is not better than savagery and in certain respects is a more miserable and more degraded condition. Hobbes's reversal of the traditional judgment is based on the following consideration. The political evolution of cities and commonwealths has been accompanied by leisure for intellectual development, not only in the practical arts but also in the speculative and moral sciences. As men acquired freedom from necessity, they turned their minds to higher things, to thoughts about the divine and natural order and to definitions of justice and right which went beyond immediate experience to the formulation of general principles; eventually such thoughts led to the development of philosophy, theology, jurisprudence, and other intellectual disciplines. As a result, a new type of authority arose: the rule of patriarchs and conquerors was replaced by the authority of priests, philosophers, orators, lawyers, and intellectuals of all types who sought to rule not by natural force but by *opinion*. The replacement of force by opinion, however, has not made men more "civil" or increased their felicity. Instead, it has produced a new type of warfare that primitive men were spared by their ignorance: in civilized societies, the wars among tribes for territory and plunder have been superseded by wars among intellectuals over opinions and doctrines.

The cause of this historic development, in Hobbes's view, was the change that occurred in men's desires and passions as they were freed from the harsh struggle for survival. In the condition of barbarism men were motivated primarily by an appetite for necessary things and secondarily by a desire for honor and glory. Even in their pursuit of honor and glory, they measured their esteem by necessary things: honor was recognition for possession of goods, children, servants, or military command and led to displays of self-sufficiency, such as abstention from cruelty and sparing of the vanquished. In a word, honor was magnanimity for primitive men (*De Cive*, v.2; *Elements*, II, 1.6.2). By contrast, civilized men, feeling secure from want, seek honor and glory in unnecessary things—in titles, in symbols, and above all in opinions or claims to knowledge. In civilized societies magnanimity degenerates into vainglory, which is a false sense of sufficiency, measured not by possessions and command but by flattery and agreement. The most powerful form of vanity among civilized men is the desire to be esteemed wise and learned by having one's opinions and doctrines recognized as the ruling or authoritative opinions of society. This desire for intellectual recognition is the cause of civilization's misery and degradation. For, as Hobbes observes, "man is most troublesome, *when he is most at ease; for then he loves to show his wisdom,* and control the actions of them that govern the commonwealth" (*Leviathan,* ch. 17, p. 157; emphasis added). Moreover, intellectual vanity causes men "to hate and be hated by reason of the disagreement of opinions"; the result is malice and cruelty of a kind unknown to savages (*De Cive,* x.9; *De Homine,* x.3). Hobbes's conclusion (later developed by Rousseau) is that the very government, leisure, and intellectual cultivation that traditionally were thought to mark the superiority of civilization have made it as miserable as savagery and in certain respects more cruel.

The Stages of Civilization: From Prephilosophic Opinion to the Age of Doctrinal Politics

This critical insight provides the theme of Hobbes's history of civilization. According to Hobbes, all civilized societies hitherto have sought to replace the natural force of patriarchs and conquerors with the authoritative opinions of intellectuals, derived from speculative and moral philosophy (including everything from prophetic arts and divinity science to classical philosophy and modern jurisprudence). While each of the civilized nations of the world has been independently founded, a general development of world civilization has occurred from the ancient kingdoms to the classical republics to the monarchies of contemporary Europe—a development characterized by the ever-diminishing influence of coercive powers and the ever-increasing influence of philosophy or science. Accordingly, the history of civilization can be divided into three periods, defined by the level of intellectual or philosophical development. This periodization underlies all of Hobbes's writings on civil history, although it is presented and most succinctly in the preface to *De Cive* and in chapter 46 of the *Leviathan.*

Before examining the three stages in detail, it will be helpful to summarize them and to give each an appropriate label (these labels, it should be emphasized, are mine, although the historical divisions are made by Hobbes). The first stage of civilization arose in the ancient kingdoms of the Near East; it might be called the 'prophetic age' because intellectual cultivation took the form of prophetic arts and divinity science. Hobbes describes this period as a kind of golden age, when opinion was essentially prephilosophical and the power of kings was not threatened by priests and prophets, or the threats to royal power could be repelled by the skillful management of opinion. The second stage arose with the republics of ancient Greece and Rome; it might be called the 'philosophical age' because philosophy was secularized and political philosophy was invented by Socrates. In this period philosophical disputation of laws and customs became the pastime of learned men, who kept the ancient republics in a state of constant turmoil. The third stage, feudal and contemporary Europe, might be called the 'doctrinal age' because, as Hobbes observes, philosophy has become academic doctrine and widely diffused among all kinds of people. In this highest stage of historical civilization, everyone has become the owner of a doctrine and a pretender to scientific knowledge, so that it has become the most artificial and unstable period in human history. Thus, for Hobbes, the advent and popularization of philosophy has been the ruin of civilization.

In the Preface to *De Cive,* Hobbes describes the earliest stage of civil society as an era of obedience to law and acceptance of received opinion. At that time there were priests, poets, and prophets who sought knowledge of the divine and natural order. Yet, surprisingly, they were generally obedient to authority, even apologists for their political sovereigns. As Hobbes remarks, "the most ancient sages" delivered their opinions "either curiously adorned with verse, or clouded in allegories, as a most beautiful and hallowed mystery of royal authority." He then speculates about why they did so:

> I suppose the ancients foresaw this, who rather chose to have the science of justice wrapped up in fables, than openly exposed to disputations. For before such questions began to be moved, princes did not sue for, but already exercised the supreme power. They kept their empires entire, *not by arguments, but by punishing the wicked and protecting the good.* Likewise, subjects did not measure what was just by the sayings of private men, but by the laws of the realm; nor were they kept in peace by disputations, but by power and authority. Yea, they reverenced the supreme power as a certain visible divinity. . . . Whereof, *it was peace and a golden age. (De Cive,* Preface; emphasis added)

This passage describes the condition of the ancient kingdoms as one in which the political rulers were automatically supported by the religious and poetic authorities, who created fables and myths about the divinity of kings in order to promote obedience. With their support kings were able to maintain royal authority without resorting to rational argument or disputation, solely by the exercise of power in "punishing the wicked and protecting the good." Hobbes seems to look back at these times with nostalgia, as a period of naive obedience and belief, as a "golden age" of civil peace.

An examination of Hobbes's other historical writings, however, suggests that the account in *De Cive* is somewhat idealized. In *Behemoth* Hobbes devoted a lengthy narrative to the observations of Diodorus Siculus, a Roman historian of the first century B.C., who sheds much light on the question of "how philosophy, together with divinity, have much conduced to the advancement of the professors thereof . . . next to the authority of kings themselves, in the most ancient kingdoms of the world" (p. 276). Hobbes's commentary on Diodorus discusses the relation of kingship and divinity science in Egypt, Israel, Persia, Assyria, India, and other civilizations of the ancient world.[14] Of them all, the cases of Egypt and Israel are most illustrative of the tension and harmony that existed at that time between kings and priestly-philosophical authorities.

The Egyptians, Hobbes remarks, are thought to be "the most ancient kingdom and nation in the world, and their priests had the greatest power in civil affairs, than any subjects ever had in any nation." The power of the priesthood was derived in part from its status as a hereditary class in a hierarchical society. However, the real source of its power was its control over opinions, about the gods, natural events, and legal questions. The priests, Hobbes observes, quoting Diodorus, " 'had most credit with the people, both for their devotion toward the gods, and also for their understanding gotten by education.' " In addition, they were influential in the greatest affairs of state as counselors to the king, " 'partly executing and partly informing and advising; foretelling him, by their skill in astrology and art in the inspection of sacrifices, the things that are to come,

14. Hobbes's references to Diodorus Siculus are to his long and famous work titled *The Library of History of Diodorus of Sicily* (c. 56 B.C.). This work appears to have been Hobbes's most important model for his own history of world civilization, a debt that Hobbes acknowledges by calling Diodorus Siculus "the greatest antiquary perhaps that ever was" (*Behemoth*, p. 276).

One can infer that Hobbes admired Diodorus for his ambitious aim of writing a common or universal history (*koinai historiai*) of the world (*Diodorus of Sicily*, trans. C. H. Oldfather, 10 vols., Loeb Classical Library [London: William Heinemann, 1933] I, 4.6). Laid out in forty books (fewer than twenty of which have survived), Diodorus's work covers universal history from the creation of the world to his own times. It surveys myths of creation, the emergence of the first men and their primitive condition, all the known civilized nations from Egypt to Ethiopia to Assyria to India to the Greeks and Romans of his day. It focuses on human development from barbarism to civilization, with special emphasis on opinions of the gods and the relation of priests to kings. All of these themes have been picked up and developed by Hobbes.

and reading him out of their holy books, such actions . . . as are profitable for him to know.' " Their power in civil affairs extended to adjudication and expertise in legal procedure. The judges in Egypt were chosen from the priestly class because of their reputation for knowing the truth, as symbolized by the medallions worn by chief justices which were inscribed with the word "truth" (*Behemoth*, pp. 278–279). Hobbes's description of ancient Egypt indicates that, in fact, the authority of kings was virtually usurped by the priestly-philosophical authorities, whose knowledge of divinity science, prophetic arts, and legal science gave them control over the minds of kings and subjects. Nevertheless, Hobbes's description suggests that this ancient civilization was generally stable because the intellectual authorities did not engage in public disputation of the laws and established opinions.

The kingdom of ancient Israel, by contrast, was frequently disrupted by conflicts of opinion, as Hobbes reveals in *Behemoth* and *De Cive*. To dramatize its problems, he compares the period of rule under Moses with the period from Joshua to Saul. Under Moses the Jewish nation was unified because Moses was both the civil sovereign and the foremost prophet. Nevertheless, as Hobbes points out, because authority resided partly in coercive power and partly in the right to interpret the Word of God, Moses was challenged by a number of rivals in his lifetime: by the "conventions or synagogues" of Corah and his accomplices, by Aaron the high priest and Miriam his sister, and by other prophets. Each of these groups disputed Moses' claim to exclusive knowledge of the Word of God and raised the threat of sedition.

Yet Moses was able to repulse these challenges because, as a civil sovereign and skillful statesman, he successfully used a special method of inflicting punishment on his rivals. Instead of disputing the doctrines of his rivals, Moses exposed the ambition behind their doctrines, thereby discrediting their claim to speak for God and inciting the people's anger and vengeance against them. Moses defended himself, Hobbes says, by showing that "the conventions of Corah . . . and of Aaron with his sister against Moses, were raised not for the salvation of their souls, but by reason of their ambition and desire of dominion over the people" (*De Cive*, xvi.13). By using this technique—a technique that resembles Hobbes's recommendation of demanding *Cui bono?* or "Who benefits?" from any doctrine—Moses was able to punish his rivals without engaging in doctrinal disputes.

After Moses the Jewish nation became a "priestly kingdom," in which the interpretation of divine law and the Word of God belonged to Eleazar the high priest, who was also the king. The experience of the Jewish people in this period was more troubled than in the preceding one. The high priests were continually challenged by the prophets for the right to interpret the law and Word of God; but they lacked the political skill of Moses and thus were unable to punish their rivals. As a result, the nation was in a continuous state of turmoil; "the rights of inflicting punishment depended wholly on private judgment; and it belonged to a dissolute multitude and each single person to punish or not to punish, according as their private zeal should stir them up." Of the post-Mosaic period, Hobbes draws the following conclusion: with regard to "the *right* of kingdom, the supreme civil power and authority of interpreting God's word were joined in the high priest"; but with regard to "the *fact,* they were in the prophets who judged Israel" (*De Cive,* XVI.15).

In sum, life in the ancient kingdoms of Egypt and Israel was not quite the golden age described by Hobbes in the Preface to *De Cive.* Authority was based on the coercive power of kings as well as on the opinions of priests and prophets, a combination that diminished the influence of civil sovereigns and created a source of continuous conflict. In both Egypt and Israel, however, as well as in Assyria and India, the priesthood was a hereditary class or family, which provided a natural basis for its authority and limited the scope of private opinion. Furthermore, Hobbes indicates that the experience of ancient Israel, the most unstable nation, was the exception rather than the rule. The Israelites, Hobbes says, were "a people greedy of prophets," implying that the peculiar problem of the Jewish people was the appeal of independent prophets (*De Cive,* XVI.15). Yet even this problem, Hobbes shows, could be managed by civil sovereigns such as Moses who skillfully used the technique of discrediting and punishing seditious prophets. With these qualifications, Hobbes's view of the "prophetic age" as a period of relative stability (though perhaps not a golden age) can be sustained.

Further support for this view is provided by Hobbes's account of the republics of Greece and Rome, which reveals that they were far more unstable than the ancient kingdoms of the Near East. Hobbes's harsh judgment of the classical republics may seem unusual at first glance because the priestly class was much weaker in Greece and Rome than in other ancient civilizations, for several reasons. In the first place, the priesthood was not a hereditary class or family: "In Greece, one man and one woman had the priesthood" (*Behemoth,* p. 278). In fact, the poets rather than an official priesthood or clergy were the "principal priests" among the Greeks and Romans; they delivered tales about gods and spirits to the people

(*Leviathan*, ch. 45, p. 638). Furthermore, as Hobbes observes in his commentary on Diodorus, the Greeks were the first to free philosophy from religion. Previously "philosophy" was equated with the explanation of natural events by the arts of prophecy, such as astrology, inspection of sacrifices, and magic (although Hobbes notes that the Egyptian priests and the Chaldean sect in Assyria also practiced astronomy and mathematics). It was "philosophy after the manner of the Greeks," however, that finally separated the study of Nature from the prophetic arts and weakened the power of priests (*Behemoth*, p. 281). As a result, the ancient republics never suffered from a division of sovereignty between political rulers and priests: their "civil laws were the rules whereby not only righteousness and virtue, but also religion and the external worship of God, were ordered and approved" (*Elements*, II, 2.6.2). Nor did the ancient republics suffer from disputes among various priests and prophets, as in ancient Israel. In short, the ancient republics of Greece and Rome were highly secularized: both philosophy and politics were emancipated from religion and took precedence over religion.

Nevertheless, the ancient republics, like the ancient kingdoms, were based on authoritative opinions that were inherently unstable. These opinions were derived not from divine and customary laws, interpreted by priests and prophets, but from notions of distributive justice and political prudence, interpreted by legislators, orators, and political philosophers. As a result, the problem endemic to the ancient republics was political faction caused by demagogues and philosophers. They aroused the common people and corrupted noble youths with two novel kinds of intellectual discourse: the art of rhetoric and the science of dialectics. Compounding these problems was the invention of political science or civil philosophy by Socrates and his followers, who made the disputation of established laws and opinions the pastime of idle intellectuals. These developments marked the beginning of a new age of civilization, the 'philosophical age' of disputative politics.

Hobbes's early thoughts on Greek civilization are presented in the introduction to his translation of Thucydides. Here Hobbes explains why Thucydides is "the most politic historiographer that ever writ": his subject is the political in the strict sense, the public life of the Greek city-states, where government was exercised by citizens in the assembly and forum. In recording the history of the Greek cities, Thucydides shows that the inherent defect of political or public life was the instability of opinion caused by public deliberations about justice and prudence. These deliberations were vitiated by "demagogues [contending] for reputation and glory of wit." In domestic

affairs the demagogues created factional strife, while in foreign and
military affairs they encouraged hazardous adventures, all for the
sake of intellectual honor and glory, that is, for the sake of seeing
their opinions preferred before others. The only hope for stability,
Hobbes adds in this early essay, was for sober statesmen to oppose
and discredit the demagogues. But this was an exercise in futility
because the people preferred flatterers or men who captivated their
imaginations with bold enterprises. Most honorable men, such as
Thucydides himself, simply retired from public life with a sense of
resignation about the self-destruction of Greek political life.[15]

The instability of opinion in ancient Greece was heightened by a
historic event that changed irrevocably the civilized world: Socrates
invented civil philosophy or political science. Hobbes describes the
effect of this innovation in the Preface to *De Cive* as follows. In the
ancient world, philosophy first appeared as *natural* philosophy when
the explanation of natural events by the prophetic arts was superseded by investigations into "the faces and motions of things" (physics) and "their natures and causes" (metaphysics). Similarly, the
study of justice and right was originally part of divinity science; as a
rational inquiry it existed only in embryo, barely "glimmering forth
as through a cloud of fables and myths." After the founding of natural philosophy, Socrates invented civil philosophy, because he "set
so great a value on this, that utterly abandoning and despising all
other parts of philosophy, he wholly embraced this [civil science]."

15. Introduction to Thucydides, *EW*, VIII. Although Hobbes refers to Thucydides
as "the most politic historiographer that ever writ," he says that Diodorus Siculus is
"the greatest antiquary perhaps that ever was." Thus it is difficult to determine who
is Hobbes's favorite historian; but the two superlatives suggest that the conventional
view, which gives the prize unequivocally to Thucydides, needs to be qualified. See
Strauss, *Political Philosophy of Hobbes*, p. 59; and Miriam Reik, *The Golden Lands of
Thomas Hobbes* (Detroit: Wayne State University Press, 1977), ch. 2.

Perhaps we can explain Hobbes's praise for both Thucydides and Diodorus in the
following way. Thucydides deserves credit as the "most politic" historian because he
shows the rise of the Greek city-states from barbarism and the self-destruction of the
city-states. In other words, he portrays most vividly the fragility of a civilization whose
essential activity is politics (although see Clifford Orwin, "Stasis and Plague: Thucydides on the Dissolution of Society," *Journal of Politics*, 50 [1988], 843–846, for the
differences between Hobbes and Thucydides on the dissolution of civil society). But
Hobbes regards Diodorus as "perhaps the greatest" of historians because his theme is
greater: Diodorus was one of the first historians to write a universal or world history.
He studied the ancient kingdoms of Egypt, India, and Assyria as well as Greek and
Roman civilization and treated the relation of kings and priests or religious politics.
Hobbes seeks a combination of the two: a synthesis of Thucydides' concern with the
fragility and self-destructiveness of civilization with Diodorus's interest in universal or
world history.

However, Hobbes remarks, while the beginning of natural philosophy was "to the advantage of mankind," the invention of civil philosophy produced nothing but misery and civil strife. No longer could the political sovereigns of the world rely on protective myths and the skillful punishment of rivals; henceforth they had to base their authority on rational doctrines of right and uphold them by argumentation. The golden age of naive obedience was finally and irrevocably over, and the philosophical age of disputative politics had begun.

The precise reason for this historic development was the mode of rational inquiry introduced by Socrates and his followers: dialectics or disputation, which consisted of reasoning from opinion to knowledge. In order to know the definition of justice or right, it was necessary to dispute the conventional opinions of justice and to discover a standard of natural justice. The Socratic revolution thereby called into question all established laws and opinions and made the appeal to higher standards of justice the accepted practice of philosophers and intellectuals. Henceforth all politics became disputative. Thus when Hobbes attacks the troublesome men of antiquity who loved "to dispute," he does not mean that they simply liked to argue or happened to disagree with established opinions; he means they were practicing dialectics or disputation, whose very method was to dispute "received opinions" (*De Cive*, Epistle Dedicatory and Preface; *De Corpore*, Epistle Dedicatory).

The philosophical mode begun by Socrates and other classical philosophers eventually transformed the civilized world. As Hobbes records, "men were so much taken by this custom [of disputing opinions] that in time it spread itself over all Europe, and the best part of Africa; so as there were schools publicly erected and maintained, for lectures and disputations, almost in every commonwealth" (*Leviathan*, ch. 46, p. 667). With the advent of Christianity it became part of divinity science and was institutionalized in universities, schools, and churches. The result was a new stage of civilization—the 'doctrinal age'—characterized by the institutionalization and popularization of disputative philosophy. In this age the most casually educated men, even the common people, became practitioners of disputative science and owners of scientific doctrines. As Hobbes observes, "Now at length, *all men of all nations, not only the philosophers but even the vulgar,* have and do still deal with this as a matter of ease, exposed and prostitute to every mother wit, and to be attained without any great care or study" (*De Cive*, Preface; emphasis added). In Hobbes's age the practice of philosophy or science, and hence the disputation of established laws and opinions, has become the ideal of civilized living for men of education and leisure, as well as for the common man. It has produced the most advanced stage of civilization, in which the passion for intellectual honor and glory, previously confined to a few priests and philosophers, has become a universal desire.

To understand fully the problem of civilization in the doctrinal age, we must turn to Hobbes's history of the monarchies of Christian Europe. In explaining their origins and foundations, Hobbes follows his usual procedure of focusing on the development of political institutions out of conquest and hereditary succession and the development of rival institutions based on opinion and learning. Hobbes's purpose is to show that these political and intellectual institutions have produced the most artificial and unstable civilization in human history: all actions and thoughts are derived from academic doctrines, and the civilized passion of vainglory has reached its most ridiculous and destructive level.

According to Hobbes, the political and social institutions of Western Europe—its monarchies and gentry—have their origins in the precivil state, in the Germanic tribes that roamed the continent and the Saxon tribes that inhabited England. As we noted earlier, these tribes and clans originally were ruled by warlords and petty kings; eventually they were consolidated by conquest into great monarchies, forming the nations of Europe. The warring tribes and clans were thereby transformed into a civilized "gentry"—a class of aristocratic families who distinguished themselves by symbols of honor, such as "heralds" and hereditary titles. The heralds were originally the coats of arms used by the Germanic warlords to identify their soldiers; later, when they were forced to lay down their arms, the designs were kept by families as signs of honor or distributed by monarchs as honorific rewards for service. Similarly, hereditary titles, such as duke, count, marquis, and baron, were once the designations of military offices in the German militia and other armies; later, in more peaceful times, they were made into mere titles of honor, without power or command. In the evolution from warlords to gentry, the code of honorable conduct was also transformed, from one of military prowess and magnanimity, acquired on the battlefield, to one of gallantry and vanity, derived primarily from reading romances (*Leviathan*, ch. 10, pp. 81–84; ch. 6, p. 46). In describing the origins of monarchy and gentry, Hobbes shows that the emergence of civil society by political consolidation brought peace among warlords, accompanied by the redirection of honor from recognition of possession and command to the vanity of titles, symbols, and gallantry.

Accompanying the growth of political and social institutions in Europe was the development of the church and the universities. They were shaped by the philosophical and academic tradition begun in ancient Greece and modified by Christianity. The distinguishing feature of this tradition, as we have seen, was the dialectical or disputative method of reasoning. When this method was developed into a general mental habit, it formed the entire intellectual horizon of Christian Europe, for two reasons. First, it implied that knowledge was acquired by reasoning from "authority," which among the classical philosophers meant the authority of common opinion and among the Scholastics meant the authority of the Bible and the classical authors, as well as traditions and customs. An appeal to authority was virtually equated with true knowledge. Second, and more precisely, the search for knowledge was equated with the analysis of words or speech, on the assumption that speech provides access to the natures and causes of things. According to Hobbes, the Greeks were the first to develop this view of knowledge; they invented rhetoric and dialectics, the original arts and sciences of speech. Indeed, Hobbes says, "the Greeks had but one word, *logos*, for both reason and speech; not that they thought there was no speech without reason, but no reason without speech." Surprisingly, this view of knowledge was not fundamentally changed by the advent of Christianity, despite the fact that it appealed to faith rather than to reason as the highest form of knowledge. For the study of Scripture consisted of analyzing "the Word of God . . . [which in Latin is] *sermo*, in Greek *logos*, that is, some speech, discourse, or saying" (*Leviathan*, ch. 4, p. 25; ch. 36, p. 407). The synthesis of classical philosophy and scriptural studies simply turned dialectics into academic disputation: instead of reasoning solely from common speech, like the Greek philosophers, the Scholastics reasoned from Scripture and authoritative texts to define the meaning of words. Similarly, they transformed the classical art of rhetoric into a more stylized form of public preaching, involving dramatic gestures and indoctrination through repetition of words (*Behemoth*, p. 193). University disputation and public preaching thereby became the most highly honored activities in the Christian world, creating an entire civilization of academic speech.

This stage of civilization has produced the greatest human misery. For the priests, scholars, and preachers of the Western world not only cultivated the arts and sciences of speech; they also popularized or democratized them. By endorsing the idea of the Protestant Reformation, that everyone could interpret Scripture for himself, they made every individual the owner of a doctrine and an amateur practitioner of disputation. The result, according to Hobbes, was a phenomenon unprecedented in the history of civilization: religious sectarian warfare. In the ancient kingdoms and republics, the established opinions on religion and politics were always open to challenge by prophets and demagogues who held contrary opinions. Yet kings and civil sovereigns never allowed private men as much freedom to dispute and to preach publicly as they are allowed in the nations of Christian Europe. As Hobbes observes,"there was no such [public preaching] permitted in all the world outside of Christiandom, *nor therefore any civil wars on account of religion"* (*Behemoth*, pp. 243–244; emphasis added). Such wars cause the greatest human misery because disputes over doctrines and words multiply the number of sects almost infinitely, and because disputes between sects of the same religion call forth the greatest malice and cruelty. In the doctrinal age, when disputative science pervades all aspects of life, Western civilization inevitably degenerates into bitter wars and revolutions over doctrines, exemplified above all by the English Civil War (*Behemoth*, pp. 166–169).

Hobbes's conclusion, then, is that the long march from barbarism through the prophetic, philosophical, and doctrinal ages of civilization has had the effect of replacing savage wars over territory and plunder with 'civilized' wars over doctrines and words.

The Final Stage of Civilization:
Enlightenment and Everlasting Peace

In presenting Hobbes's account of world history, I have tried to emphasize the deep ambivalence Hobbes feels about the development of civilization. On the one hand, he acknowledges the superiority of civilization in its original impulse and ongoing attempt to develop the highest human capacities—to cultivate the mind or intellect through the study of the arts and sciences. He shows that civilization emerges from barbarism when patriarchs and conquerors who rule by brute force are replaced by cities and nations founded not only on force but also on opinion. Hence the distinguishing feature of civilized life has been the formation of society by authoritatively established and received opinions—about the divine and natural order, justice and political right, and legal or customary procedures. Such a condition is made possible by the historic achievement of civilization, the discovery of philosophy or science and the discovery of justice, right, and law. In describing the history of this achievement, Hobbes expresses many reservations but never seems to doubt its ultimate worth. In Strauss's words, "Hobbes was indebted to the tradition for a single, but momentous idea: he accepted on trust the view that political philosophy or political science is possible and necessary."[16] In this respect Hobbes accepts the superiority of civilization to barbarism, particularly as it developed in the West, and thereby continues the work of the philosophical tradition begun by Socrates, Plato, and Aristotle.

On the other hand, one cannot fail to detect the bitter disappointment of Hobbes, often expressed in contemptuous and indignant remarks, at the almost willful perversity civilized men have shown in betraying their claim of superiority over barbarism. The so-called wise and learned men, who have cultivated the arts and sciences, have undermined and destroyed civilization, jeopardizing their own work. The honor and reverence they have received for their claims of authoritative wisdom have raised them above kings and generals, but the competition for such honor has also divided them into factions, sects, and schools as each has sought to have its own opinions established (by the state and other institutions) as orthodoxy or true doctrine. As a result, the very activity of civilization—the rule of opinion over brute force and the cultivation of the arts and sciences—has been the cause of its dissolution. This historical analysis is the evidence for Hobbes's sweeping claim that civilization hitherto has been a condition as miserable as and possibly more degraded than barbarism. In this respect Hobbes sounds like Rousseau and other radical critics of civilization, scorning its presumptuous claims of superiority over more naive or primitive ways of life.

Despite this ambivalence, Hobbes sides with the defenders of civilization against its critics and ultimately delivers an affirmation of civilization. But his affirmation entails the belief that civilization can and must be refounded on principles that its earlier defenders would have thought impossible or undesirable. Hobbes's fundamental claim is that the realm of received opinion and authoritative wisdom which hitherto defined civil society can be transcended and abolished—relegated, as it were, to the past and deleted from the historical record. At the same time, he contends that science or philosophy, the rational articulation of truth about the natural order and the right ordering of society, can be preserved. A new doctrine of science can be discovered which does not begin from received opinion but stands on its own autonomous foundations. This new doctrine, which I shall refer to (adapting later terminology) as

16. Leo Strauss, *Natural Right and History* (Chicago: University of Chicago Press, 1953), p. 167.

Hobbes's 'science of enlightenment,' can be the foundation of a new and modern form of civilization which will enable man to enjoy "immortal peace" in an "everlasting commonwealth" (*De Cive*, Preface; *Leviathan*, ch. 30, p. 325). By articulating this doctrine and disseminating it among the people, Hobbes hopes to fulfill, once and for all times, the promise of civilization.

Hobbes is aware that his project is both a continuation of and a radical departure from his intellectual predecessors. In a well-known passage in *Leviathan* (ch. 31, p. 357), he compares himself to Plato in asserting that the troubles of cities will never cease until philosophers become kings or kings become philosophers (*Republic*, 473d). Plato's claim is that political or civil society is like a cave where men live in the dark, unable to see anything but the shadows of artificial things reflected on the walls (515c). These shadows are the authoritative opinions of society—the ideas about the divine and natural order which are taken on trust from authorities without ever being questioned or examined. They determine the way members of particular cities or civil societies conceive of right and wrong and perceive reality, although they are for the most part false or, at best, secondhand reflections of reality. According to Socrates, Plato, and other classical philosophers, political and civil life is defective because its wisdom is prephilosophical: it rests on mere opinion rather than on philosophical or scientific knowledge. This struggle against "opinion" in the name of true knowledge and the need for a philosophic ruler to enlighten society is the common ground on which Hobbes stands with Plato.

At first glance the Hobbesian and Platonic understandings of the task of philosophy may appear to be the same. Plato's image of the cave corresponds to Hobbes's image of the kingdom of darkness. Like Plato, Hobbes uses this image to indicate that preexisting civil society is an empire of authoritative opinion (*Leviathan*, ch. 44, p. 604). And like Plato, Hobbes seems to define philosophy or science as the replacement of opinion with true knowledge. But Hobbes's understanding of the empire of opinion and the realm of true knowledge differ radically from that of Plato as a consequence of his historical approach.

In the first place, Hobbes views the empire of opinion as a phenomenon that has been historically created and altered. For Hobbes the advent of classical philosophy—the very philosophy begun by Socrates, Plato, Aristotle and later modified by the Scholastics—has changed irrevocably the civilized world. He is aware that he and his contemporaries live in a different age than did the classical philosophers, an age dominated by university learning and the widespread diffusion of academic doctrines. In this academic age of doctrinal politics, the opportunity exists for an altogether new kind of political science which would not merely permit the chosen few philosophers to ascend from the darkness of the cave to the light of true knowledge but bring light to the cave itself—enlightening the whole of society by making everyone a practitioner of true philosophy.

Such a possibility, Hobbes contends, was not conceived of or was not available to the classical philosophers. He emphasizes, even exaggerates, the degree to which the philosophers of ancient Greece were bound by the conventional political and religious opinions of their times. Hobbes acknowledges that they appealed to abstract standards of natural justice and thereby called into question established laws and opinions. But he also claims that, instead of attempting to change such opinions, they were content to be spokesmen for the popular religious beliefs and political conventions of their times (*Leviathan*, ch. 46, pp. 668–675; ch. 21, p. 202). In other words, the classical philosophers never sought to make radical changes in the nature of civil society; they thought that the cave or kingdom of darkness would always exist, and that one would be foolish to try to change it.

In contrast to the classical philosophers, Hobbes sees himself living in an age when the conventional opinions of society have already been changed by the influence of the philosophical tradition itself. The claim of philosophy or science to discover true knowledge is recognized by almost everyone. The philosophical tradition has been established in the universities, and what was once the preserve of the elite has been popularized so that "all men of all nations, not only the philosophers but even the vulgar, have and do still deal with this as a matter of ease" (*De Cive*, Preface). It has become extremely popular in the Western world to practice philosophy because the claim of knowledge is so appealing to one's vanity and confers so much honor and power. In addition, philosophy has become popular because the traditional method of dialectics or disputation is easily imitated: one borrows opinions from authority or invents a new opinion by making verbal distinctions and then proclaims the conclusion to be true knowledge. Accordingly, once the claim of philosophical knowledge was introduced to Western civilization, it was only a matter of time before everyone learned to make such claims and the democratization of philosophy occurred.

In this advanced stage of civilization, a new kind of political science becomes necessary and possible. It is necessary because one can no longer enter the traditional debates about the true religion or the just regime or the nature of things and hope to resolve them by a dialectical analysis of opinions. Such an attempt would merely create another doctrinal dispute and perpetuate the failure of traditional politics and science. But Hobbes realizes that a new alternative is available to him. At this moment in history a unique opportunity exists because the claim of philosophy to discover true knowledge has been established and universally recognized, while the method of reasoning from received opinion has been discredited by the multiplicity of doctrines.[17] This is a privileged moment in the history of civilization. Without abandoning the aspiration of reaching scientific knowledge of justice or right, one can rebuild the human mind on a foundation free from opinion and even hope to find a receptive audience among the general population.

This new type of philosophical enterprise is Hobbes's science of enlightenment. It seeks to transform the nature of civil society by abolishing the historical realm of authoritative opinion and replacing it with a universally recognized doctrine of science that stands on its own evident foundations. Such a doctrine, Hobbes claims, will be indisputable; indeed, it will be the 'final' doctrine of history because it will end all doctrinal disputes and bring mankind to the next and last stage of civilization. Before examining Hobbes's vision of the future, however, let us turn to his major historical work, *Behemoth*, for a deeper understanding of the phenomenon of doctrinal politics.

17. Hobbes sometimes describes the condition of his age as a kind of infinite sectarianism, in which "this opinion [of private knowledge of good and evil] hath spread itself so largely through the whole Christian world, that the number of apostates from natural reason is almost become infinite" (*De Cive*, xii.6).

» 2 «

The Behemoth:
Doctrinal Politics
and the English Civil War

The Peculiarities of Hobbes's History

The *Behemoth* is Hobbes's longest and most systematic work of civil history. It presents a comprehensive analysis of the English Civil War as well as general reflections on the origins and foundations of Western civilization. In the entire corpus of Hobbes's writings, no other work provides so much insight into the problems of past and contemporary civil society. All the same, Hobbes scholars have treated it as a companion piece to the political treatises rather than as a work to be studied in its own right.[1] The prevailing scholarly view is that *Behemoth* is a work of secondary importance because, as one of Hobbes's late writings, it simply applies principles previously articulated in *Leviathan* and the other political treatises to the analysis of a particular political event.[2]

This view, however, is based on an inference from the chronology of Hobbes's writings which fails to grasp the true relationship between Hobbes's histories and scientific treatises. As I argued in chapter 1, Hobbes's histories are logically prior to his treatises be-

1. As Ashcraft recently observed, "In the scores of considerations of Hobbes's political theory extent, virtually no attention has been paid to *Behemoth*." Richard Ashcraft, "Ideology and Class in Hobbes' Political Theory," *Political Theory*, 6 (1978), 28.

2. See, for example, Maurice M. Goldsmith, Introduction to Thomas Hobbes, *Behemoth or The Long Parliament*, ed. Ferdinand Tönnies, 2d ed. (London: Frank Cass, 1969), p. xiv.

cause they present the problem of traditional politics and science, whereas the treatises present the solution. Thus, regardless of its place in the chronology of Hobbes's writings, *Behemoth* is a work of primary importance. It elaborates and completes the history of civilization which is the logical beginning point of Hobbes's thought. More specifically, it reveals the defect of contemporary Western civilization by showing how the rise of doctrinal politics and disputative science inevitably led to the English Civil War.

At the beginning of *Behemoth* Hobbes states that his purpose is not merely to describe the events of the recent civil war, as other historians have done, but to explain the "causes and artifices" that brought them to pass (p. 220).[3] By this remark Hobbes indicates that his civil history is designed to be not a mere chronical of events but a didactic work on politics. Its purpose is to teach the reader lessons about the defect of contemporary political authority and to explain specifically why King Charles I was incapable of maintaining his power and preserving civil peace. These objectives determine the structure of *Behemoth,* which Hobbes outlines in the Epistle Dedicatory as follows.[4] Part I examines the causes of the rebellion, "certain opinions in divinity and politics." Part II exposes the artifices of the rebels, specifically the techniques of indoctrination and rhetoric by which they incited the people against the king. Parts III and IV narrate the events of the war from 1640 to 1660, focusing on the role of opinions about taxation, the conscription of soldiers, and military strategy on the outcomes of battles and shifts of sovereignty. The continuous thread throughout the book is the effect of opinions and the arts of persuasion on the exercise of sovereign power.

As this summary indicates, *Behemoth* is a distinctive kind of history. Maurice Goldsmith astutely observes that it differs from the 'Thucydidean' history of the civil war written by Clarendon, which simply records the speeches and deeds of the principal actors, and from the 'Marxist' history written by Harrington, which analyzes the social and economic causes of the war.[5] In contrast to these accounts, Hobbes shows that the civil war was caused by opinions and doctrines of right which were created and exploited by ambitious intellectuals solely for the purpose of displaying their wisdom and learning. This distinctive view is succinctly expressed in Hobbes's remark about the folly of the civil war: "It is a hard case that there should be two

---

3. All references to the text of *Behemoth* in this chapter are to vol. 6 of *The English Works* and will cite only the page number.
4. The epistle dedicatory to *Behemoth* is included in the Tönnies edition but not in the *English Works.*
5. Goldsmith, Introduction to *Behemoth,* pp. x–xiii.

factions to trouble the commonwealth, ... and that *their quarrels should be only about opinions, that is, about who has the most learning,* as if learning should be the rule of governing all the world" (p. 275; emphasis added).

In order to demonstrate this thesis, Hobbes necessarily departs from the method of other historians. Whereas the Thucydideans record the deliberations of public men and follow their outcomes, leaving prudent readers to draw the lessons for themselves, Hobbes writes in a didactic manner that exposes the hidden motive of intellectual ambition behind all opinions.[6] And whereas the Marxists expose the use of opinion or ideology for class domination, Hobbes reveals that opinions are a force in their own right, independent of social privilege and economic interest, because they are the means for demonstrating intellectual superiority. According to Hobbes, the purpose of civil history is to expose the folly of traditional forms of authority which make opinions of justice and right the foundation of power; for this practice turns the title to rule into a claim about wisdom and learning and creates factions or sectarian disputes that eventually lead to civil war.

In presenting this analysis in *Behemoth,* Hobbes employs an unusual form of writing. Instead of adopting the narrative style of conventional historians, he uses the dialogue form, or, more precisely, a conversation between two unnamed interlocutors, A and B. This form of writing appears to be a variation on the "doctorstudent" dialogue that Hobbes uses in other works, such as the *Six Lessons in Mathematics* and *A Dialogue between a Philosopher and a Student of the Common Laws of England.*[7] The utility of the dialogue form in these writings is obvious. Hobbes's purpose is essentially polemical; he is concerned primarily to attack the doctrines of his opponents rather than to demonstrate his own teaching. Dialogues, as opposed to narratives or demonstrative arguments, are especially suited to polemical writing because they allow for the exchange of thesis and antithesis or statement and rebuttal. Another, less obvious advantage to the dialogue form may be inferred from the unusual construction of Hobbes's dialogues. In setting up exchanges between interlocutors, Hobbes does not simply present a spokesman for his opponents and one for himself. Both the doctor *(A)* and the student *(B)* appear to speak for Hobbes, with the student usually asking naive questions and the doctor responding. This format removes the

---

6. Introduction to Thucydides, *EW,* VIII, xviii–xxix.

7. See Royce MacGillivray, "Thomas Hobbes's History of the English Civil War: A Study of *Behemoth," Journal of the History of Ideas,* 31 (1970), 179.

drama of polemical argument and confrontation but adds a deeper dimension to the exchanges. It enables Hobbes not only to refute his opponents but also to comment on their hidden motives, especially the learned folly and intellectual vanity that lie behind their doctrines.

Such exchanges are especially suited to the purposes of *Behemoth*. As the doctor *(A)* says in the opening lines of the work, the goal of this history is to expose the "hypocrisy and self-conceit" that produced the recent events in England. Or, as the epigraph on the title page of *Behemoth* announces: "We are discussing the wars which spread over the plains of England, *where the name of right was given to crime*.[8] These statements point to the moral purpose behind Hobbes's use of the dialogue form: the exchange of naive question and cynical response enables him to uncover the deceit and to puncture the illusions that lie behind all high-sounding claims of justice and right. In Hobbes's hands, then, the dialogue is not used, as it is by Plato, to present a dialectical argument that analyzes the content of opinions and shows the movement by questions and answers from opinion to knowledge. Instead, Hobbes uses the dialogue in the manner of an enlightenment philosopher: to discredit the whole empire of opinion or doctrine by exposing it as an artificial creation of ambition and intellectual vanity.

These remarks on the writing of civil history help us to understand the title of Hobbes's work on the English Civil War. That title, *Behemoth*, has puzzled scholars because it calls to mind *Leviathan*, the title of Hobbes's most famous political treatise. In *Leviathan* Hobbes says that he named his political treatise after the mythical monster or beast in the Book of Job because it is an apt metaphor for his mighty sovereign, "the king of all the children of pride" (ch. 28, p. 307). Not surprisingly, scholars have wondered if Behemoth, the name of another monster described in the Book of Job, is not also a metaphor for a political sovereign—perhaps for Charles I or Charles II or some ideal sovereign who might have prevented the civil war. Although Hobbes offers no explanations about the meaning of *Behemoth*'s title, the parallel to *Leviathan* appears to be misleading. For, as Royce MacGillivray points out, the word *behemoth* in Hebrew is a plural form: "monsters" or "beasts"; thus it would be inappropriate for a sovereign because Hobbes insists on the unity of sovereignty.[9] The title *Behemoth*, therefore, probably refers to the

8. Quoted in Latin on the title page of *Behemoth*, without translation or citation (my translation and emphasis; I could not find the source of this quotation).
9. MacGillivray, "Thomas Hobbes's History," p. 178.

leaders of the rebellion. Supporting this suggestion is the subtitle that is sometimes affixed, *The Long Parliament*, and a comment in the Preface to *De Homine*, where Hobbes refers polemically to his enemies as "the beasts."[10] The most convincing evidence for this suggestion, however, is the subject of *Behemoth* itself; its focus is the ambitious men who used seditious doctrines to overthrow King Charles I. An examination of Hobbes's history leaves little doubt that they are the monsters or beasts of the title.

The Analysis of Doctrinal Warfare

The dialogue in *Behemoth* opens with a naive question: Why was King Charles I, ruling by descent from a long-established royal line and possessing adequate abilities of body and mind, incapable of maintaining his power and preserving civil peace? In response to his question the speakers present a teaching about political realism which is based on two simple premises. The first premise, repeated many times throughout the book, is that sovereign power consists in control of the militia: "He that is master of the militia is master of the kingdom, and consequently is in possession of a most absolute power" (pp. 285, 166, 290, 344). The second premise is that any king with enough money should be able to form a mercenary militia of 60,000 men, a size sufficient to defend a nation such as England. The implication is that money or revenue is the sufficient condition of absolute power (p. 167).[11] With this simple statement of political realism, Hobbes sets the stage for the drama of a king who was genuinely desperate: Charles I lost control of his kingdom because he could not even maintain a mercenary militia.

In explaining the king's predicament, Hobbes points not to any particular deficiencies in Charles himself but to the general problem of political authority in the contemporary age of doctrinal politics. To maintain an adequate militia, a ruler must draw upon the resources of the people; for "ambition can do little without hands," and the "hands" of a ruler are the people who become his soldiers and supply him with revenues (p. 252). In principle, Hobbes asserts, it should not be difficult to draw on these resources because the vast majority of people are indifferent to political causes and partisan opinions: "There were very few of the common people that cared

---

10. The subtitle to the Tönnies edition, *Behemoth or The Long Parliament*, is not included in the *English Works* and apparently did not appear in the original edition.

11. See also *De Cive*, xii.5, "Monies are the sinew of war and peace."

much for either cause, but would have taken any side for pay or plunder" (p. 166); and "The common people, whose hands were to decide the controversy, understood not the reasons of either party" (p. 308; also p. 319). Given the apolitical nature of the people, King Charles should have been able to recruit and support a mercenary militia. But "the people were corrupted," Hobbes says, and would neither pay their taxes nor allow themselves to be bribed into service or obedience.

To understand this statement, one must remember that when Hobbes speaks of the corruption of the people, he means the reverse of what is today meant by corruption—a compromise of principles for the sake of private gain. For Hobbes corruption has exactly the opposite meaning. The people were "corrupted" because they abandoned their natural indifference to partisan opinions and ignored their natural preference for private gain; their corruption consisted in acquiring an artificial concern for general or abstract principles in the form of opinions and doctrines of right. In *Behemoth* corruption is the process by which the people are indoctrinated by intellectual authorities (priests, scholars, and political demagogues) in the literal sense of being filled up with doctrines and turned into zealous partisans. As a result, the raising of armies depended not on monetary rewards or material incentives but on the control of opinions and doctrines.

The central issue of *Behemoth*, therefore, is the question of who corrupted and seduced the people into becoming practitioners of doctrinal politics. Hobbes replies that the "seducers were of diverse sorts," and he enumerates them: Foremost were Presbyterian ministers and other religious sectarians who maintained the doctrine that spiritual authorities may intervene in politics to defend religious orthodoxy and that subjects may disobey the law if it violates their consciences. Second in importance were the "democratical gentlemen" of the Long Parliament who maintained that monarchy was tyranny and that only a democratic or republican form of government was just. A third group consisted of lawyers of the common law who opposed the idea of royal prerogative and held that taxes and armies could not be raised without the consent of the people. A fourth group was composed of merchants who opposed the taxes of King Charles and favored a republic, reasoning by analogy from the experience of the Dutch that republics were most conducive to commercial prosperity. Finally, men of wasted fortunes were in favor of civil war for opportunistic reasons, believing that if they sided with the victorious party they might have their riches restored (pp. 167–169).

Of these diverse groups Hobbes states explicitly that the Presbyterian ministers and democratical gentlemen were the chief conspirators and that their motivation was intellectual vanity:

> Yet certainly the chief leaders were ambitious ministers and ambitious gentlemen; the ministers envying the authority of the bishops, *whom they thought less learned;* and the gentlemen envying the [king's] privy-council, *whom they thought less wise than themselves.* For it is a hard thing for men, *who do all think highly of their own wits, when they have also acquired the learning of the university,* to be persuaded that they want any ability requisite to the government of a commonwealth. (P. 192, emphasis added; also pp. 198, 212, 363, 405)

In this passage Hobbes develops his distinctive teaching about political authority in the age of doctrinal politics: the motivation of public men is not a matter of interest or power per se but a desire to be recognized as intellectually superior, as the wisest and most learned of men. This desire, Hobbes notes, is latent in all men but is most prevalent in those with a university education. For it is there that ministers and gentlemen acquire their opinions and doctrines as well as the vain belief that their superior knowledge in matters of right entitles them to rule. From this observation Hobbes draws the general conclusion that "the core of the rebellion, as you have seen by this and read of other rebellions, are the Universities" (p. 236).

Given such statements, it is simply incorrect to argue, as several prominent scholars have done, that Hobbes places greatest emphasis on the London merchants or that he views the English Civil War as essentially a bourgeois revolution driven by the demands of a "possessive market society." This thesis, first developed by Macpherson and later modified by Frank Coleman and Richard Ashcraft, is based on several of Hobbes's observations about the economic factors of the war, which they have expanded into Marxist or quasi-Marxist readings of *Behemoth.* As evidence for this thesis Macpherson points to Hobbes's observation that the London merchants were among the leaders of the rebellion and that they deprived the king of vital financial resources by delivering to the rebels "the purses of the city of London . . . and other corporate towns." Macpherson also notes that Hobbes traces the wealth of the merchants to the buying and selling of labor and describes both merchants and common people as believing in the inviolability of property rights. From these observations Macpherson draws the conclusion that Hobbes attributed the English Civil War "to the new strength of market interests and market-made wealth."[12]

Despite the ingenuity of this and similar interpretations, a Marxist reading of *Behemoth* is seriously misleading, in two important respects. In the first place, it fails to acknowledge that doctrines take precedence over social and economic factors in Hobbes's analysis. Hobbes says explicitly that the causes of the civil war were "opinions in divinity and politics" and traces them to institutions of opinion and learning but not to material bases. There is simply no class analysis in *Behemoth*.

In the second place, Hobbes treats economic factors independently of any demand for a bourgeois social order or "possessive market society." He argues that ordinary people were opposed to taxation because they accepted the rules of "precedent and custom" supplied to them by the lawyers of the common law; this was a case of simple selfishness turned into arrogant self-righteousness by authoritative doctrines (p. 169). In the case of the merchants, Hobbes says, "their grievances are but taxes, to which citizens, that is merchants, whose profession is private gain are naturally mortal enemies; *their only glory being to grow excessively rich by the wisdom of buying and selling*" (p. 320; emphasis added). Hobbes's view is that the London merchants joined the rebellion (they did not *lead* the rebellion) because they felt oppressed by taxes, as commercial men have felt throughout history. This view implies that the merchants had no "market" ideology, although they may have acquired their wealth by buying and selling labor. Moreover, even in the pursuit of private gain, Hobbes argues, their primary motivation was not possessiveness, acquisitiveness, or greed, as Macpherson would have it. Their motive was "the glory . . . [of growing] excessively rich by the wisdom of buying and selling." In other words, Hobbes attributes the

---

12. Macpherson, *Political Theory of Possessive Individualism*, pp. 65–66. In developing this thesis Coleman and Ashcraft add a neo-Marxist element by recognizing not only economic but also cultural factors in Hobbes's analysis, such as religion and ideology. According to Coleman, Hobbes views the civil war as the revolution of "commercial Protestantism," which combined the commercialism of London merchants with the private inspiration of Protestant ministers to produce a new type of energetic individualist who sought to throw off the shackles of the traditional order; Frank M. Coleman, *Hobbes and America: Exploring the Constitutional Foundations* (Toronto: University of Toronto Press, 1977), pp. 57–66. Ashcraft goes a step further by arguing that *Behemoth* is based on a complex theory of ideology and class which traces the seditious doctrines of the civil war to the shift of socioeconomic forces from the feudal aristocracy to the Protestant middle class; Ashcraft, "Ideology and Class," pp. 44–50. The problems with these interpretations will be discussed below.

merchants' love of gain to intellectual vanity—to a desire to prove their wisdom by making shrewd deals, for which the accumulation of riches serves as a tangible sign. This analysis accords with Hobbes's general view, expressed in other works, that "the glory of wisdom is greater than riches; for the latter are usually had as a sign of the former" (*De Homine*, xi.8). The irony of the Marxist reading of *Behemoth* is that Hobbes is so far from reducing doctrines to economics that he actually treats economic behavior as an outgrowth of intellectual vanity.

Hobbes's account of the English Civil War in *Behemoth* is truly distinctive and cannot be fitted into the mold of other histories or political philosophies. Its central feature is a historical account of the religious, political, and legal doctrines that caused the civil war and the techniques by which they were manipulated to corrupt the people and overthrow King Charles. In developing this argument Hobbes turns first to the Presbyterian ministers and uncovers the source of their doctrine about priestly intervention in politics. This investigation leads to a lengthy disquisition on the papacy and the Protestant Reformation which shows how Christianity became a religion of doctrines and doctrinal disputes.

According to Hobbes, Christianity in its original and primitive form under Jesus and the Apostles was little more than a teaching about a moral life and a pure heart, with almost no concern for speculative opinions, rules of worship, or church government. But this ethical religion of Jesus, which stressed actions and intentions, was soon transformed into a dogmatic religion of priests, which stressed opinions and doctrines prescribed by the clergy and upheld by the church. In Hobbes's words, the clergy of the early church made "rightness of opinion, [rather] than of action and intention," the test of salvation, and thereby acquired control over the minds and consciences of believers which surpassed the influence of coercive powers (p. 243). With this innovation they set out to conquer the world by controlling the definition of opinions and doctrines.

The key to this strategy was the distinction between "orthodoxy" and "heresy." Hobbes places such emphasis on the development of these notions that he treats them in four separate works: in *Behemoth* (pp. 174–176); in the *Dialogue of the Common Laws* (pp. 122–132); in a separate essay, "An Historical Narration on Heresy and the Punishment Thereof" (*EW*, iv, 385–408; also attached to the Latin *Leviathan*); and in his *Ecclesiastical History* (*Opera Latina*,v, 341–408). In these accounts Hobbes argues that the notion of heresy originated among the Athenian schools of philosophy and was later borrowed by the Christian clergy, who transformed it into an instrument for intellectual domination. Among the Greeks, Hobbes says, the notion of heresy arose because the greatest philosophers of the day—Pythagoras, Plato, Aristotle, Epicurus, and Zeno—failed to agree in their philosophical speculations, so each developed his own set of doctrines and his own school or sect. At the time, "heresy" was simply "the doctrine of a sect, . . . taken upon trust of some man of reputation for wisdom, that was the first author of the same." Hence heresy was originally seen as nothing more than "a private opinion." And even though the various sects disputed and reviled one another, none was condemned as heretical because "they were all equally hereticks" (*Dialogue*, pp. 123–124; *Behemoth*, p. 174; "On Heresy," p. 387).

This understanding of heresy was changed fundamentally by the advent of Christianity. The most zealous of the early Christians applied themselves to learn Greek philosophy and rhetoric in order to defend the faith to the Gentiles. In so doing they inherited the quarrels of the Greek sects, which they sought to overcome by transforming "heresy" from a neutral term, signifying a private opinion, to a term of opprobrium which meant wrong or false opinion, requiring censure and punishment. Henceforth, Hobbes asserts, the mission of Christianity became the defense of orthodoxy (right opinion) and the punishment of heresy (wrong opinion) through the device of ecclesiastical censure or excommunication. By claiming the sole authority to define orthodoxy and to excommunicate, the early clergy proclaimed the one, universal church and asserted its claim against all others. In the general councils it condemned the great heresies and expelled their proponents from the church. In defense of orthodoxy it intervened in politics and subordinated the Roman emperor and the princes of the Western world. And by teaching the people that one is damned if "he die in a false opinion in an article of Christian faith," it captured the minds of the common people (*Behemoth*, p. 173; *Dialogue*, p. 126; and *Leviathan*, ch. 46, p. 684).

As the papacy grew, however, it decided that stronger weapons than the threat of excommunication were needed to maintain its hold on the minds of the people. Hence in the twelfth century it developed two new institutions, the universities established at Oxford and Paris and an order of traveling preachers. Hobbes calls this development "the second polity of the Pope" to distinguish the early from the medieval church and to emphasize the political purpose of the new institutions. The second polity surpassed the first by "turning religion into an art": it defined Christian orthodoxy by drawing upon Aristotelian philosophy and Scripture, producing that brand of divinity science known as Scholasticism; and it developed the arts of disputation and .rhetoric to defend this doctrine. According to Hobbes, the papacy also trained an army of traveling preachers to disseminate the doctrine of the schools to the people and to direct their allegiance from their political sovereigns (*Behemoth*, p. 184).

In tracing the growth of the papacy from its earliest days to the Middle Ages, Hobbes reveals both the strength and the weakness of doctrine as a means of domination: the first polity of the pope transformed Christianity into a doctrinal religion and used the threat of excommunication to gain ascendancy over emperors and princes; but it was vitiated by heresies and schisms. The second polity established the universities and solidified its hold on the minds of subjects; but it was vitiated by fierce academic disputes about such issues as God's essence and attributes, man's soul and free will, and the nature of political and moral duties. Nevertheless, these intellectual controversies did not lead to actual rebellion and civil wars because they were confined largely to priests and scholars.

It was not until the Protestant Reformation that the Christian world experienced outright sectarian warfare. In explaining this phenomenon Hobbes presents an interpretation of the Reformation which emphasizes both continuity and radical change in the evolution of Christian doctrine. On the one hand, he treats the Reformation as just another doctrinal dispute, comparable to the great heresies of the early church and the academic disputes of Scholasticism. From this point of view, the Reformation was simply another challenge to the established doctrine in the name of a new Christian orthodoxy. On the other hand, Hobbes acknowledges that it was different in principle from all previous disputes: the Reformation proclaimed the radical ideal that every man could interpret Scripture for himself in order to determine his own beliefs (and even had the Bible translated into the vulgate to make it accessible to the common people) (p. 191). This idea was not simply a disagreement about how to define orthodoxy, as previous heresies and disputes had been, but a challenge to the very notion of orthodoxy: the Reformation denied in principle the idea of orthodoxy by affirming the private inspiration of every individual. From this point of view, the Reformation marked a radical departure from the past because it made the central point of controversy not the *content* of orthodoxy but the *authority* to determine orthodoxy as such.

By presenting both views of the Reformation, Hobbes is able to teach what he regards as the most important lesson about the notion of doctrinal orthodoxy: it tends to unravel of its own accord as heresies and reformations generate more and more controversies about the definitions of orthodoxy; eventually the multiplication of disputes calls into question the very existence of orthodoxy, and the warring sects argue more and more about authority (about who should decide rather than what to decide).

Hobbes contends that when the power of the popes was broken in England by the intrigues of Henry VIII, the bishops simply arrogated to themselves the old methods of the popes—such as excommunication, disputation, and rhetoric—to impose their views of orthodoxy and to become the established Church of England. It did not take long, however, for the bishops to receive the same treatment at the hands of the Presbyterian ministers, who sought to take church government away from the episcopate and give it to the presbytery, a national assembly of their own church elders. They, in turn, were attacked by Independents and more radical sects (Nonconformists) who sought to place church government in each independent congregation and to allow liberty of religion for private inspiration. From these events Hobbes draws the conclusion that the conflict among Catholics, Anglicans, Presbyterians, and Independents was not over orthodoxy or the essential dogma of religion but over church government: "I confess I know very few controversies amongst Christians, of points necessary for salvation. They are questions of authority and power over the Church, or of profit, or of honour to Churchmen, that for the most part do raise all the controversies" (p. 243). Although Hobbes sometimes says that the Presbyterian ministers opposed the bishops because they "disliked their Canons and Common-prayer book," he insists that the controversies over specific points of doctrine were secondary to disputes over religious authority itself (p. 192).

Using this analysis of the Protestant Reformation, Hobbes explains how the Presbyterian ministers fomented the rebellion. The key to their success was their charismatic preaching, which was so powerful that Hobbes asserts: "The mischief proceeded wholly from the Presbyterian preachers, who, by a long-practised histrionic faculty, preached up the rebellion powerfully" (p. 363). In analyzing the extraordinary effect of these preachers, Hobbes points to the coincidence of several factors.

First, the Presbyterian ministers inherited the tradition of free and autonomous preaching begun by the papacy. As a means of influencing the people, Hobbes says, this tradition was without parallel in the kingdoms of the civilized world: "I do not remember that I have read of any kingdom in the world, where liberty was given to any private man to call people together, and make orations frequently to them, . . . except only in Christiandom. I believe the heathen Kings foresaw, that such a few orators would be able to make a great sedition" (p. 183). The Presbyterian ministers, in other words, were favored by a unique freedom of operation to influence the people.

Second, Hobbes argues, the natural mentality of the common people was especially suited to influence by personal preachers: "For the common people [were] . . . ignorant of their duty to the public, as never meditating on anything but their particular interest; in other things, to following their immediate leaders; which are either their preachers or the most potent gentlemen that dwell amongst them; as common soldiers for the most part follow their immediate captains, if they like them" (p. 212). The mentality of the common people is a kind of parochial loyalty, which arises from a trust in the familiar and from an indifference to anything but private and particular interests. In addition, the people place greater emphasis on the personal qualities of a leader than on the content of his teachings and principles: "For men of age and quality are followed by their inferior neighbors, that look more upon the example of those men whom they reverence, and whom they are unwilling to displease, than upon [their] precepts and laws" (p. 231). The common people follow a leader out of familiarity, reverence, or respect for his apparent integrity and wisdom, and from fear of displeasing him. A trusted leader therefore enjoys almost limitless freedom to indoctrinate his followers: trusting the man, the people adopt whatever doctrines he happens to hold. The Presbyterian ministers were the beneficiaries of this kind of trust.

Third, the Presbyterians made the central issue of their teaching the question of church government. During the exile of the Protestants to Calvinist Geneva in the time of Queen Mary, they acquired a preference for the presbyterian form of church government (the rule of presbyters, literally elders) established in that city. Upon returning to England, Hobbes says, they sought to tear down the episcopacy or bishopric and "endeavored, to the great trouble of the Church and the nation, to set up that [Presbyterian] government here, wherein they might domineer and applaud their own wit and learning" (p. 333). In observing this conflict, Hobbes formulates a general maxim, which might well be taken as his summary view of Christian politics, that "neither the preaching of friars nor of parochial priests, tended to teach men *what*, but *whom* to believe" (p. 184; emphasis added). The Presbyterians followed this maxim by cultivating allegiance to their ministry rather than understanding of their doctrine.

Finally, the Presbyterian preachers cultivated a unique style of preaching. They used dramatic rhetoric and vehement pronunciation, in the manner of tragedians, and spoke extemporaneously, instead of reading from the *Book of Common Prayer,* as the Anglican clergy did. This dramatic preaching was the most effective means for cultivating their authority because it appeared to be a sign that their words were directly inspired by God. It also confirmed their Reformation teaching that men must testify to their salvation by feeling "their own private spirit, meaning the Holy Ghost dwelling within them." Moreover, Hobbes says, they flattered the people by not criticizing their acquisitive habits, thus endearing themselves to the merchants of market towns; and they opposed "vain-swearing" and lust, thus asserting control over the guilty consciences of frustrated young men. In all of their dramatic rhetoric and manipulation of the passions, the Presbyterian ministers aimed primarily at indoctrinating the people against the bishopric and acquiring authority over their minds and behavior. The effect was so extraordinary, Hobbes claims, and "the doctrine of the Presbyterians has been stuck so hard in the people's heads and memories (I cannot say into their hearts; for they understand nothing in it, but that they may lawfully rebel) that I fear the commonwealth will never be cured" (pp. 193–196).

Thus, Hobbes traces the rebellion of the Presbyterian ministers to institutions established by the papacy for the control of opinions and to a distinctive brand of preaching. Reflecting generally on his analysis, one might think that it does not differ much from those of other philosophers and historians of the modern age. It is a critique of Christian politics which attempts to explain in entirely secular terms (political and psychological rather than providential) how Christianity conquered the Western world and then unraveled itself in the Reformation and its sectarian wars. In essence, it treats the doctrines of Christianity as artifices of the clergy for establishing an earthly empire and seeks to expose their hidden desires for power and glory. Interpretations of Christianity with these principal themes have been developed before and after Hobbes by such thinkers as Machiavelli, Rousseau, and Nietzsche. We may well ask, then, if there is anything that distinguishes Hobbes's analysis and points to the special features of his political science.

Hobbes's analysis is indeed distinctive, for a reason that usually goes unnoticed. Most modern interpreters of Christianity who look for 'secular' explanations of Christian politics emphasize the effects of doctrines that are unique to Christianity. Machiavelli, Rousseau, and Nietzsche, for example, make a sharp distinction between pagan religions and Christianity because the latter is defined by special teachings about meekness and compassion, asceticism, universal brotherhood, and otherworldliness. Their writings attempt to show how the specific opinions and doctrines of Christianity have decisively changed the political and psychological character of the Western world. They particularly emphasize the way Christianity has destroyed the pagan virtues of martial valor and patriotism, while making men pacific and self-denying on the one hand and domineering on the other.[13]

Hobbes, by contrast, shows that the problem of Christian politics has little or nothing to do with the doctrines that are peculiar to Christianity. He argues that all religions and sects tend toward a common pattern of behavior, despite doctrinal differences, because the content of the doctrine is irrelevant to the reasons that lead men to believe it. Thus paganism, Judaism, and Christianity, as well as the various Christian sects (Catholicism, Anglicanism, and Presbyterianism) are virtually identical in actual practice because all religions are empires of opinion built by clergymen who teach their followers "not *what*, but *whom* to believe." To sustain this thesis, Hobbes begins with the observation that all religions are sectarian movements led by clergymen who use obscure or incomprehensible doctrines about supernatural mysteries in order to appear wise and learned, so that people will trust blindly in their authority. Hobbes further observes that polytheism and monotheism tend to resemble each other because the monotheistic religions, such as Christianity, absorbed and continued pagan demonology. Also, Christianity, despite its teaching about meekness and an otherworldly "Kingdom of God," became an earthly empire like other religions. And the Protestant Reformation, which sought to purge Christianity of idolatry and worldliness, eventually wound up adopting all the stratagems of the pope for domination (*Leviathan*, ch. 45, p. 637; ch. 44, pp. 606, 617). The distinctiveness of Hobbes's historical analysis, in other words, lies in deemphasizing the distinctiveness of Christian politics or, more generally, in treating opinions and doctrines as mere instruments of domination regardless of their content.

Hobbes's position is therefore radical and unusual. He thinks that both leaders and followers are actually indifferent to the content of

---

13. Machiavelli, *The Discourses*, ed. Bernard Crick, trans. Leslie J. Walker (Baltimore: Penguin, 1970), II.2, p. 278; Rousseau, *Of the Social Contract*, ed. and trans. Richard W. Crosby (Brunswick, O.: King's Court), IV.8, pp. 94–99; Nietzsche, *Beyond Good and Evil*, trans. Walter Kaufmann (New York: Random House, 1966), nos. 62, 202, 260.

opinions and are impressed only by the authority of the man who espouses the opinions—by his appearance of wisdom, learning, inspiration, or other privileged knowledge, which others take as a sign of divine election. Because the goal of all religion is to gain recognition for its authority, Hobbes believes that Christian politics can be understood without reference to special or unique doctrines of Christianity. This view reflects Hobbes's general teaching about historical civilization: that the human mind hitherto has been captivated by the claim of authoritative wisdom per se and the differences among creeds, opinions, and doctrines are mere pretexts for asserting intellectual superiority over others.

Insofar as distinctions exist among religions, however, they lie in the different techniques for gaining recognition of authority or in degrees of intransigence in claiming authority. In this respect Hobbes's analysis in *Behemoth* does reveal something distinctive about Christian politics: Christianity was decisively influenced by classical philosophy, which introduced formal notions of orthodoxy and heresy to distinguish authoritative from nonauthoritative wisdom and sewed sectarianism into the fabric of Christianity. Eventually this historical development led to the Protestant Reformation, which disputed the very notion of orthodoxy and allowed every individual to seek recognition for his own doctrine, thereby raising the struggle for recognition to maximum intensity. Thus, although Hobbes argues that all religions follow a common pattern of behavior, he also claims that only Christianity in the doctrinal age of Western civilization produces sectarian wars over religion.[14]

After treating the seditious religious opinions in *Behemoth*, Hobbes turns to the political opinions responsible for the civil war. For the rebellion was fomented by an alliance of Presbyterian ministers who rejected the orthodoxy of the established church and a group of "democratical gentlemen" who challenged the legitimacy of monarchy. The latter group championed the cause of the Long Parliament by accusing King Charles of tyrannical behavior and declaring that only democracy or a republic was a just form of government. In uncovering the source of this opinion, Hobbes shows that it did not arise spontaneously from the political arena or from the interests of the gentlemen as an economic class; rather, it arose from the tradition of political philosophy established in the universities. He claims that the idea of distinguishing between just

14. Rousseau, too, claims that doctrinal wars of religion were unknown in the pagan world and are peculiar to the Judaeo-Christian world. But he attributes this phenomenon to the peculiar doctrines of the Bible—to the monotheism and universalism implied in the idea of a "jealous God" (*Social Contract*, IV.8, p. 93).

and unjust regimes, like the idea of distinguishing orthodoxy and heresy, was invented by learned intellectuals and spread by the universities for the purpose of domination. In examining the origin and influence of the idea of justice, Hobbes illustrates once again the problems caused by philosophical doctrines in the development of Western civilization.

His discussion of the Western tradition of political philosophy and its connection with the civil war is unusual for several reasons. In the first place, Hobbes claims that the most important works of the tradition, such as Aristotle's *Politics* and *Ethics*, achieved their influence by historical accident. In the early days of Christianity, the clergy used Aristotle's natural science, as well as his logic and rhetoric, to defend the faith and convert the heathens; these intellectual disciplines were useful for explaining Christian doctrines about God and spiritual bodies and for developing techniques of argumentation. But political and ethical science were largely ignored at that time. Nevertheless, the Christian clergy preserved the writings of the classical authors on all subjects and generally esteemed classical learning, eventually making Greek and Latin the official languages of the church. Thus, Hobbes claims, the natural philosophy and rhetoric of the pagans became part of the Western tradition in the service of Christian doctrine, but their political philosophy became influential only by accident: "For men, grown weary at last of the insolence of priests, . . . began to search the sense of Scripture, as they are in the learned languages; and consequently, studying Greek and Latin, became acquainted with the democratical principles of Aristotle and Cicero, and from love of their eloquence fell in love with their politics, and that more and more, till it grew into the rebellion we now talk of" (p. 218). According to this account, the political writings of the Greeks and Romans were preserved by the Christian tradition and accidentally discovered by scholars who were searching not for a political doctrine but for clerical abuses in the interpretation of Scripture. Upon reading the politics of Aristotle, Cicero, and other classical authors, the scholars were seduced by the eloquence of their writings to a love of democratic principles. However fanciful Hobbes's account may be, it implies that democratic opinions are not a natural part of political life but an artificial product of an academic or literary tradition.

The most striking feature of Hobbes's account, however, is not his reduction of the Western tradition of political philosophy to a historical accident but his characterization of that tradition as democratic. This characterization is strange because its most influential representative, Aristotle, is not obviously a partisan of democracy—

a fact that Hobbes explicitly acknowledges in other passages. In the *Leviathan*, for example, he says: "I know that Aristotle in the first book of his *Politics*, for a foundation of his doctrine, *makes men by nature, some more worthy to command, meaning the wiser sort such as he thought himself to be for his philosophy, others to serve,* meaning those who had strong bodies but were not philosophers as he; as if master and slave were not introduced by consent but by difference of wit" (ch. 15, p. 140; emphasis added). Hobbes thus acknowledges that Aristotle, "for a foundation of his doctrine," maintains that by nature it is just for the wise to rule over those who are less wise. Hobbes admits, in other words, that Aristotle is in principle a defender not of democracy but of aristocracy—an aristocracy of the wise. How, then, can Hobbes characterize Aristotle as a teacher of democracy?[15]

A plausible answer to this question can be found in Hobbes's history of civilization outlined in chapter 1. Hobbes's contention is that Socrates and his followers transformed Western civilization by requiring political rulers to base their authority on rational arguments about natural justice. The Socratic tradition thereby displaced the poetical-religious authorities, establishing the philosopher as the judge of politics and making philosophical wisdom the title to rule. Hobbes refers to this new challenge as submitting the laws and established opinions to the judgment of "private men" (*De Cive*, Preface). He calls these new judges private men rather than wise men because the classical philosophers, by the term "wise men," were referring to themselves, as was Aristotle when he called for the rule of the wise over the (physically) strong. They were using the claim of wisdom as a pretext for appointing themselves judges and critics of the laws in order to satisfy their intellectual vanity. Thus the advent of political philosophy introduced the appeal to natural justice, which allowed self-appointed wise men to criticize the laws.

But the effect of this innovation was different from the intention. As Hobbes sees it, everyone who studied the classical authors appointed himself a wise man and an expert in civil knowledge:

> And now at length all men of all nations, not only philosophers but even the vulgar, have and do still deal with this [civil philosophy] as a

15. Joseph Cropsey, in "Hobbes and the Transition to Modernity," in *Ancients and Moderns*, ed. Cropsey (New York: Basic Books, 1964), pp. 227–228, also puzzles about this contradiction. He says: "Hobbes [holds the] view that Aristotle's teaching is republican, libertarian, and democratic and that it is also based on the belief in natural inequality . . . [a] connection which is truly implausible." Without attempting to resolve the problem, Cropsey simply observes that if Aristotle can be considered a libertarian-republican, so can Hobbes, with less distortion of his teaching.

matter of ease, . . . [and] those who suppose themselves to have it, . . .
do so wonderfully please themselves in its idea, as they easily brook the
followers of other arts to be esteemed and styled ingenious, learned,
skillful, what you will, except prudent: for this name, in regard to
civil knowledge, they presume to be due to themselves only. (*De Cive*,
Preface)

Although Hobbes acknowledges the distinction in principle between
serious and casual philosophers, he contends that this distinction
can no longer be maintained in actual practice because everyone has
become a self-appointed wise man. Thus the Socratic tradition of
political philosophy, which is elitist in principle, has become democratic in practice. Using the classical philosophers as authorities in a
casual and cavalier manner, everyone with a university education ap-
points himself judge and critic of the laws, and thereby makes a
claim to rule.

In Hobbes's eyes the presumption of judging, criticizing, and ruling is what men call liberty, which for so many who presume themselves to be wise and able can be satisfied only in a democracy:

. . . which Aristotle confirmeth in these words: 'For men ordinarily say
this, that no man can partake in liberty, but only in a popular commonwealth.' . . . But if the [claim] be construed according to the intention
of him that claimeth, then doth he claim no more than this, *that the
sovereign should take notice of his ability and deserving. . . . And as one
claimeth, so doth another, every man esteeming his own desert greatest.*
Amongst all those that pretend to, or are ambitious of such honor, a
few only can be served, unless it be in a democracy. (*Elements*, II, 2.8.3;
emphasis added)

This passage shows how Hobbes is able to treat an apparently pro-
democratic statement by Aristotle as identical to other statements by
Aristotle which endorse the rule of the wise and able. The trick is
that Hobbes sees the democratic claim of liberty as a pretext for
ambitious men—who actually believe that wisdom and ability should
rule and that they themselves are the wisest and most able—to dominate and rule. In other words, the claim of liberty (a merely negative claim) is transformed by ambition and intellectual vanity into a
desire for dominion by the wise and able alone. For as Hobbes observes, "every one apart considereth it [liberty] as in himself, and
not in the rest; by which means, liberty appeareth in the likeness of
rule and government over others" (*Elements*, II, 2.5.2). Hence "when

private men or subjects demand liberty, under the name of liberty they ask not for liberty, but for dominion" (*De Cive,* x.8).

From these statements we can infer that Hobbes characterizes the classical philosophers as democrats for two paradoxical reasons. First, the elitist claim of wisdom to rule is one that all will claim. Second, the democratic claim of liberty becomes a demand for exclusive dominion by the wise and able. In both cases the principle turns out to be the same: the liberty of private men, believing themselves wisest, to criticize and rule. And the effect is the same: everyone demands to rule, believing he alone is wisest. Thus the apparent inconsistency of Hobbes's view of the classical authors is reconciled by his understanding of intellectual vanity, which makes the elitist claim of philosophical rule indistinguishable from the democratic claim for political liberty.

The difficulty with this view of Aristotle and the classical philosophers is to determine whether Hobbes sees them as truly democratic or as democratic only in their influence. Hobbes certainly wishes to see them as genuine democrats, even as apologists for their own democratic regimes:

> Aristotle, Cicero, and other Greeks and Romans, that living under popular states, derived those rights, *not from the principles of nature, but transcribed them into their books, out of the practice of their own commonwealths, which were popular.* . . . And because the Athenians were taught, to keep them from desire of changing their government, that they were free men, and that all who lived under a monarchy were slaves; therefore, Aristotle puts down in his *Politics,* 'In democracy LIBERTY is to be supposed: for it is commonly held, that no man is FREE in any other government.' (*Leviathan,* ch. 21, p. 202; emphasis added)

According to this passage, Aristotle is a democrat, supporting the custom or convention of Athenian democracy. But this view is in tension with Hobbes's other statement that Aristotle makes wisdom the title to rule and with Hobbes's own distinction between serious and casual philosophy. Hobbes reconciles this tension by saying that the claims of wisdom and democracy are the same in principle—that self-appointed wise men may criticize and rule—and the same in practice because they lead to a universal clamor to rule. This reconciliation is sufficient for Hobbes to call Aristotle and the classical philosophers genuine democrats and to present them as mere apologists for their regimes.

Yet Hobbes does not quite say that Aristotle actually believed that democracy is just by nature, only that Aristotle defended democracy to stabilize political opinion.[16] It appears, then, that Hobbes admits that the classical authors are not genuinely democratic, but democratic only in their influence. To be more precise, what Hobbes shows is that the classical philosophers may have been antidemocratic in principle, but they became authorities for democratic opinion in the academic tradition of the West. In *Behemoth* it is quite evident that Hobbes's primary concern is the use of classical philosophers as authorities for liberty and democracy, rather than their actual beliefs. The gentlemen's education, Hobbes says, "furnished [them] with arguments for liberty out of the works of Aristotle, Plato, Cicero, and Seneca, . . . for their disputations against the necessary power of their sovereigns" (p. 233). What is remarkable about this statement is that Hobbes even includes Plato among the sources of democratic opinion—Plato as a spokesman for liberty and democracy?! Surely this indicates that Hobbes's real concern is with the influence rather than the actual beliefs of the authors.

Similarly, in *Leviathan* he speaks of the classical philosophers primarily in their capacity as authorities for democratic opinion:

> It is an easy thing, for men to be deceived, by the specious name of liberty. . . . And when the same error is confirmed by *the authority of men in reputation for their writings* on the subject, it is no wonder if it produce sedition, and change of government. In these Western parts of the world, we are made to receive our opinions concerning the institutions and rights of commonwealths, from Aristotle, Cicero, and other men. . . . And by the reading of these authors, men from their childhood have gotten a habit, under false show of liberty, of favoring tumults. (*Leviathan*, ch. 21, p. 202; emphasis added)

As authorities the classical authors produce democracy and anarchy. Therefore, Hobbes seeks to portray them as genuine democrats so he can claim that all democratic opinions are unnatural—derived not "from the principles of nature" but from the conventions of a particular historical period that has long since vanished. Hobbes does not want to portray the classical authors as antidemocrats who were misread or misused because he wants to discredit all claims of liberty—the philosophical criticism of the laws as well as demands

16. In fact, as Cropsey also points out, "This passage (1317a 40 ff) from the *Politics* that Hobbes quoted to indicate Aristotle's democratic tendency does nothing of the sort. It is a statement of the general opinion . . . with respect to the relation of democracy and liberty; and it would not imply Aristotle's approbation or disapprobation of either democracy or liberty" (ibid., p. 228).

for popular government. The best way to do so is to reduce them to conventions and historical accidents, in order to show that all private criticism of the laws is a mere pretext of intellectual vanity rather than a part of natural justice. To maintain this view consistently, however, Hobbes must renege on his earlier admission about the elitism of the classical authors and portray them as genuine apologists for democracy.

Despite such distortions, Hobbes's argument about the origin of democratic opinions presents a coherent view of the history of civilization, which can be summarized as follows. Most governments throughout human history have been monarchies, either paternal or despotic in origin. The democracies or republics of ancient Greece and Rome were transient interludes in the otherwise monarchical history of mankind and should be regarded as unnatural accidents. These democracies, however, gave birth to Socratic political science, which developed the idea that private men have the liberty to criticize the laws. Unfortunately, the works of this school were preserved by the Christian tradition and preserved in the universities of the Western world. Without this accident, no one today would ever dream of philosophical rule or political liberty. The presumption of contemporary democrats would not exist if Socrates and his followers had not painted such pretty pictures of the private criticism of the laws, which are so appealing to intellectual vanity. Without these authors and their acceptance as authorities, political life would have remained free (as it has in the East) of the tyranny of philosophy and of such emotionally charged words as "liberty," "democracy," "the rule of law," "justice," and "the common good." For these words and ideas are not a natural or inevitable part of political life; they arise from philosophical doctrines, created by Aristotle and other intellectuals, that distinguish just from unjust regimes and cause political factionalism in the Western world. Without such words, monarchical government, supported by beautiful fables, might have lived happily ever after, free from the discords of doctrinal politics.

The rebellion of the gentry thus arose from their education in classical literature, which meant that their democratic partisanship was inseparable from a presumption of wisdom; in fact, as paradoxical as it may sound, their democratic claims and their pretensions to political wisdom were identical. For the study of classical literature turned the gentlemen into instant philosophers and instant statesmen, who sought to set up a republic governed by themselves. They believed that facility in classical learning actually gave them the competence to rule: "For it is a hard matter for men, who do all think highly of their own wits, when they have also acquired the learning of the university, to be persuaded that they want any ability requisite for the government of a commonwealth, especially having read the glorious histories and sententious politics of the ancient popular governments of the Greeks and Romans" (p. 193). As Hobbes indicates in this passage, the attitude of the democratical gentlemen was characterized by a kind of intellectual amateurism: they were inspired by the foolish belief that reading a few books on politics qualified them to rule and that mere knowledge of justice or right is sufficient to make justice or right effective. In criticizing the educated gentlemen for intellectual amateurism, however, Hobbes implies that they were basically sincere; only a few acted out of cynical ambition, without believing in the democratic doctrines they espoused. Their fault was not iniquity but "learned folly."

Such folly, of course, had grave consequences, as the events of the democratic revolution quickly demonstrated. The democratical gentlemen sought to overthrow the monarchy of King Charles I and replace it with a republic, whose power was concentrated in the House of Commons. To achieve this goal, they employed the artifices of political rhetoric, equating monarchical government with tyranny and inciting the people against the king through the use of accusations and calumnies. The most effective accusation, made in collusion with the Presbyterian ministers, was that the king conspired to restore Catholicism in England and to suppress the Scottish presbyters. In addition, the parliamentary rebels accused the king of treason for subverting "the laws of the realm" and exercising arbitrary powers in raising armies and revenues (pp. 239–275). After making such accusations and inciting the people to rebel, however, the democratic party was incapable of establishing effective rule. The control of the democratic revolution quickly passed from the learned and eloquent gentlemen of the Long Parliament to the generals of the parliamentary army. From among the generals Cromwell emerged as the supreme commander and replaced the republic with a protectorate under his control. Commenting on the behavior of the democratical gentlemen, Hobbes draws the general lesson that "all men are fools who pull down anything which does them good, before they set up something better in its place" (p. 357).

At the root of this folly was an illusion about the power of political opinion that typified the thinking of the gentlemen because it arose from their classical education. The philosophers to whom they appealed built their whole political doctrine on the rule of wisdom and prudence and therefore vastly overestimated the power of reason in politics, while underestimating the need for physical force. As Hobbes asserts, Aristotle teaches that justice can be established on mere words and opinions, or on the impersonal rule of law, "without the hands and swords of men." Aristotle himself betrays a lack of appreciation of coercive power and invites intellectual amateurs to meddle in politics. Indeed, Aristotle's legacy in the Western world is the amateur statesman, whose intellectual vanity leads him to believe that one can rule merely by possessing a doctrine of justice or the arts of persuasion without wielding the sword. It was Aristotle, then, who was responsible for the rise and the fall of the democratical gentlemen.

The *Behemoth* thus reveals that the English Civil War was set in motion by ministers and gentlemen whose opinions and artifices were remarkably similar. Both appealed to doctrines of right developed by the academic tradition, the former to a notion of religious orthodoxy, the latter to an idea of natural justice. Both carried the doctrines of the university and the vanity of learning into the public arena: "As the Presbyterians brought with them into their churches their divinity-science from the university, so did many of the gentlemen bring their politics from thence into Parliament" (p. 192). Together they formed a "democratic" conspiracy against the papacy, episcopacy, and monarchy. To acquire a following, they used preaching and political rhetoric to arouse the anger and vengeance of the people against the alleged heresies and injustices of the established authorities. The result was an explosion of religious sectarianism and political factionalism which destroyed the traditional order but failed to replace it with a viable alternative.

To complete his analysis of the civil war, Hobbes turns to the third leading group of rebels, the lawyers of the common law. At first glance their role in the rebellion appears to be more limited than that of other groups. They joined the opposition to King Charles not for the purpose of overthrowing him but to check his excesses—to limit his arbitrary use of power. Unlike the Presbyterian ministers, who sought to subordinate the state to the church, and the democratical gentlemen, who challenged the very legitimacy of monarchy, the legalists sought merely to limit the king's prerogatives. To do so, they appealed to the authority of custom, as embodied in the precedents and judgments of the common law. They maintained that the English monarchy, by custom and historical evolution, was not an absolute but a "mixed-monarchy," which required the sharing of power among king, lords, and commons. And they held that the king could not raise an army or tax the people without the consent of Parliament.

Despite the more moderate and limited goals of the lawyers of the common law, Hobbes condemns them as harshly as the Presbyterian ministers and the democratical gentlemen. Although they did not attack directly the sovereignty of the state or the legitimacy of monarchy, they destroyed the king's capacity for self-defense during the conduct of the civil war. By imposing legal restraints on the exercise of royal power, the lawyers were more to blame for the king's defeat than any other group.

To understand the devastating effect of their doctrines, we need only recall the statement of political realism at the beginning of *Behemoth:* that an adequate militia is the necessary and sufficient condition of absolute power. The legal restraints imposed by lawyers on the conscription of soldiers, on the raising of revenues, and in the conduct of the war itself were direct attacks on the king's military power and undermined his ability to defend the monarchy. Indeed, as the argument of *Behemoth* unfolds, we see the ever-increasing role of the lawyers in the downfall of King Charles: part I shows how the religious doctrines of the Presbyterians subordinated the state and generated sectarian strife; part II shows how the political doctrines of the democratical gentlemen brought about the ascendancy of Parliament over king; and parts III and IV, which narrate in chronological fashion the events of the civil war, show how the king was defeated on the battlefield by his own legal advisers, who prevented him from marshaling and exercising the extraordinary powers required for victory.

The lawyers were distinguished from other intellectual authorities by their belief in "mixed-monarchy," a form of government based on the principle that all political power should be limited by the division of governmental functions among several bodies. The doctrine of mixed monarchy was a product of the common law and should not be confused with the classical notion of the mixed regime, which is not a mere division of functions but a mixing of classes and principles of justice. Aristotle and other classical philosophers frequently praise the mixed regime as the best possible form of government in most circumstances because it moderates class conflict and political factionalism (*Politics*, bk. IV, chs. 8–9). But the classical philosophers were not authorities for mixed monarchy. Hobbes is emphatic in claiming that the classics were authorities for radical democracy, whatever their prudential teachings may have been. The doctrine of mixed monarchy was based on an appeal to the historical evolution of England's political institutions as interpreted by the legalists. In their view the English monarchy had evolved into a form of government whereby "the naming of magistrates and arbitration of war and peace should belong to the King; judicature to the Lords; and the contribution of monies to the people, and power of making laws to all together" (*De Cive,* XII.4).

Mixed monarchy expresses the spirit of legalism in political affairs: it is a doctrine of proper procedure, derived from custom and usage, rather than a doctrine of natural justice, expressing a partisan claim to rule. The goal of such legalism is to place impersonal and impartial law above all substantive claims of justice, which seem to be nothing more than the partisan opinions of interested men. This is the meaning of the maxim, proclaimed by all legalists, that the best polity is "a government of laws, not of men." To create a government based on the impersonal rule of law, the legalists appeal to the authority of custom. For custom is thought to exist from time immemorial and appears to have no human author, unlike the claims of justice, whose authors (monarchists, democrats, oligarchs, etc.) are visible everywhere, clamoring to have their partisan views prevail. According to Hobbes, the English system of common law is precisely such an attempt to create a government of laws rather than of interested party leaders.

Although legalism originates in the general desire to transcend partisan justice and to replace the rule of force with customary laws, legalism in the West has been raised to the status of science. It not only codifies customary laws but also gives them the stamp of scientific knowledge. For this reason Hobbes ultimately traces the doctrines of the lawyers to the authority of Aristotle, to his statement praising the rule of law and to his influence in turning all naive opinions into scientific doctrines (*Leviathan,* ch. 46, p. 683). Hobbes's claim is that legalism and legal science have become another facet of public life in the age of doctrinal politics. Like divinity science and political science, legal science "hath great props: Aristotle and others; who, by reason of human infirmity, suppose the supreme power to be committed with most security to the laws only" (*De Cive,* XII.4). And like the other sciences of the academic tradition, legal science or jurisprudence employs disputation and rhetoric to define the meaning of legal terms and to indoctrinate the people. Thus the lawyers, no less than the ministers and democratic leaders, brought their university education into politics and imposed their doctrines on English society.

In discussing the influence of legal doctrines, Hobbes remarks that they were most in favor among the House of Lords. The members of this body were the leading advocates of mixed monarchy because they stood on principle against all forms of arbitrary power and extreme partisanship, whether it was found in the prerogatives of King Charles or in the radical democracy of the Long Parliament (pp. 205, 303, 306, 309). Nevertheless, in practice the lords sided with the radical democrats against the king, especially at the beginning of the rebellion. Because their goal was to moderate partisanship in any form, the lords were easily fooled by the arguments of the democratic party which made the king's prerogatives seem tyrannical. But this alliance with extremists undermined the lords' authority as moderates. When they finally recognized the radical turn of the rebellion and saw that they were being manipulated, they were powerless to defend themselves. Out of desperation they shifted sides to the monarchical party against their former democratic allies (pp. 319–320). Their behavior, Hobbes suggests, reflected the weakness and shifting loyalties of moderates in an extreme situation and the confusion of the legal mind in a lawless condition.

More important than the desperation of the lords was the effect that legalistic opinions had on the nation as a whole, including the king's most trusted advisers. The king's counselors at court and in the privy council were loyal to him, but they repeatedly advised him to seek a limited victory in the civil war out of fear of his excessive power. In criticizing this advice, Hobbes blames

> that fault, which was generally in the whole nation . . . [of thinking] that the government of England was not an absolute but a mixed-monarchy and that if the King should clearly subdue this Parliament, then his power would be what he pleased, and theirs as little as he pleased: which they counted tyranny. This opinion, though it did not lessen their endeavor to gain the victory for the King in a battle, when a battle could not be avoided, yet it weakened their endeavor to procure him an absolute victory in the war. (P. 306)

In counseling against absolute victory, the advisers encouraged the king "upon all occasions to offer propositions of treaty and accommodation . . . [which] took off the courage of the best and forwardest of his soldiers, that looked for great benefit by their service out of the estates of the rebels." This strategy also had the effect of diminishing the king's stature among the civilian population. For instead of producing aggressive military campaigns, it led to what Hobbes contemptuously calls a "paper war"—a continuous flow of written declarations about the illegality of Parliament's activities and the publication of treaties outlining terms of peace. This strategy damaged the king because "the people understood not, nor troubled themselves with controversies in writing, but rather went away with an opinion that Parliament was likely to have the victory in war." Hobbes's point is that the moderation and legalism of the king's supporters were incompatible with the necessities of war, which require extraordinary power and decisive action, aimed primarily at inspiring the troops with visions of plunder and impressing the people with prospects of victory. Such necessities, Hobbes asserts, are as pressing in his time as in the days of "Augustus and Antonius of Rome"; for "a civil war never ends by treaty" but only by military conquest (pp. 307, 319).

Hobbes also sees the hand of lawyers in more direct restrictions on the king's power. By drawing on doctrines of the common law, the lawyers convinced the people, as well as many gentlemen, that no one could be taxed without the consent of Parliament, and that "ship-money and other extra-Parliamentary taxes" were illegal. Their indoctrination was so effective, Hobbes says, that the people were averse to all public payments and, in matters of property, knew no other "rules of equity, but precedents and custom" (pp. 309, 169, 209–210). Moreover, the lawyers opposed the king's right to recruit troops by his "commission of arrays." According to Hobbes, this practice began under William the Conqueror, who exchanged land in return for promises of military service; William established the commission of arrays as a king of recruiting board, sent out to call his men to arms (p. 312). The lawyers opposed this method of recruitment, despite its basis in custom, because it allowed too much to the king's prerogative. They argued instead that custom required an act of Parliament to raise troops, which implied that the royalist army was unlawful and that Parliament's army was the only legitimate fighting force. The collective effect of these legal doctrines— about mixed monarchy, limited victory, taxation by consent, and conscription by act of Parliament—was to destroy the king's capacity for self-defense.

In the *Dialogue on the Common Laws* Hobbes discusses many of the same doctrines in greater detail and further exposes the defects of the lawyers of the common law. Their improper and often arbitrary appeals to custom and their belief that "right reason" is what makes any given custom or precedent binding create the illusion that law comes into being when lawyers declare what is right in their written reports. Yet, as experience shows, the pronouncements of judges and lawyers always require statutes and the arms of the sovereign before they can take effect. Common law, therefore, is essentially unrealistic: customary procedures and the pronouncements of right reason are not self-enforcing. Laws are made not by the author who "pens" them but by the sovereign who enforces them (*Dialogue,* pp. 55, 59). In addition to overestimating the power of reason in politics, the lawyers are guilty of a more general kind of wishful thinking. Like many people, the legalists seek to follow a moderate course, limiting taxation and the exercise of power by a reasonable interpretation of custom. But the necessities of political life require extraordinary power, which cannot abide the independent authority of custom and lawyers. A reconciliation of extraordinary power and political moderation is possible, therefore, only when custom ceases to be an authoritative standard for the law.[17]

Hobbes's critique of the legalists completes his analysis of the causes and artifices of the English Civil War. When viewed as a whole, his analysis reveals not only the predicament of King Charles I but also the general crisis of political authority in the age of doctrinal politics. The monarchies of Western Europe, originally founded by conquest and hereditary succession, have come to depend on academic doctrines of right for their legitimacy and power. The state is required to uphold a notion of doctrinal orthodoxy developed by the Christian clergy, to conform to a standard of natural justice elaborated by the classical philosophers, and to exercise power in accordance with legal procedures determined by lawyers of the common law. While these doctrines appear to have the 'civilizing' effect of replacing the primitive rule of brute force with the rule of learned opinion and rational persuasion, they actually have sewn civil discord into the fabric of Western civilization. The dependence of the state on doctrines of right has created a division of sovereignty between the intellectual authorities, who claim final authority in the determination of doctrines, and the political sovereign, who is obliged to enforce them. In addition, it has produced sectarian wars among the intellectuals, as each competes to have his own doctrine established by the state as orthodoxy. Even the common people have been forced to take sides in the wars over doctrines, contrary to their natural disposition. For the divinity science, political science, and jurisprudence established in the universities and disseminated to the public have made doctrinal politics the preoccupation of everyone in "these Western parts of the world."

At the root of doctrinal politics is the passion of intellectual vanity. In *Behemoth* Hobbes repeatedly points to this passion as the underlying or hidden motive of the rebels and of everyone else who was

17. As Cropsey suggests, this is precisely the intention of the *Dialogue:* Hobbes seeks to reconcile royal prerogative with parliamentary assent by removing Parliament's independent basis in common law; law would then possess the force required by necessity, as well as the moderation required for durability. Introduction to *A Dialogue between a Philosopher and a Student of the Common Laws of England,* pp. 14, 47–48.

infected by their doctrines. Their intellectual vanity was evident in two characteristic patterns of behavior. On the one hand, each presumed that he alone knew what was right and good for the rest of society, by virtue of his superior wisdom and learning. This presumption led each individually and all collectively to claim superiority to the king and to dictate which doctrines should be established as authoritative. On the other hand, the rebels committed the folly of overestimating the power of opinion and rational persuasion in politics. They assumed that if they merely declared what is right and used the arts of persuasion (dialectics, disputation, rhetoric, analysis of legal terminology, and other traditional forms of logic employed in the declaration of right reason), their doctrines would be recognized by everyone. In this expectation, Hobbes shows, they were utterly deluded. After overthrowing the established notions of justice and orthodoxy, they saw their own doctrines rejected in turn by other factions and stood by helplessly as control of the revolution passed into the hands of military commanders. Their doctrines were impotent, and it was left to brute force to settle the matter. The fault of the revolutionaries was both the presumption and the impotence of overintellectualism—the learned folly of believing that correct doctrine without coercive power was a sufficient basis of authority. In sum, the lesson of Hobbes's history is that the English Civil War was no accidental event; it was the inevitable outcome of the doctrinal politics and intellectual vanity of Western civilization.

The Alternative to Doctrinal Politics in Behemoth

Is there an alternative to doctrinal politics in the contemporary age? Or has the advent of philosophical doctrines made political revolution and sectarian warfare an inescapable feature of Western civilization? These questions are raised obliquely at the end of *Behemoth*. In the concluding remarks the student *(B)* asks whether anything fundamental has changed as a result of the civil war. After all, he observes, the shifts of sovereignty from 1640 to 1660 resembled a kind of circular motion: sovereignty revolved from the monarchy of Charles I, to the republic under the Long Parliament, to the Protectorate under Cromwell and his son, to a republic once again under Parliament, and finally to the Restoration of the Stuart monarchy under Charles II. Will not a new cycle of rebellions and change of regimes follow the Restoration?

To this momentous question the doctor *(A)* responds with a statement that is so bland and brief that the reader is hardly reassured about the prospects for lasting peace. He claims that the civil war has effected one crucial change in opinion: the right of the king to raise a militia without the consent of Parliament is now acknowledged by everyone; it has even been declared by Parliament itself. This acknowledged right, the doctor asserts, will be the basis of lasting peace because it impresses the people far more than any doctrine or argument and thus will "disarm the ambition of all seditious haranguers for the time to come" (p. 418). Yet one must wonder if this right really frees the new king from dependence on authoritative doctrines and removes the possibility of challenges by ambitious intellectuals. Is not the right to raise a militia without the consent of Parliament also a "doctrine of right," open to dispute by seditious haranguers? Can one really avoid doctrinal politics, now that men have advanced from barbarism to civilization and from prephilosophical civil society to the philosophical or doctrinal age?

Complete answers to these questions must await an analysis of the *Leviathan* and the other political treatises. But a partial answer may be given on the basis of Hobbes's argument in *Behemoth*. Hobbes asserts that the right of the king to raise a militia without the consent of Parliament provides a foundation for lasting peace; it will establish the authority of Charles II more firmly than that of his father and may even inaugurate a new era of perpetual peace. In making this assertion, however, Hobbes is not counting solely on a declaration by Parliament recognizing the Restoration of Charles II and his royal prerogatives. Hobbes knows better than anyone else how unreliable such declarations can be; human ambition is so resilient that recent events may soon be forgotten and new doctrines may arise to challenge the king. The only lasting solution is to reform the universities:

> B: For aught I see, all the states of Christiandom will be subject to these fits of rebellion, as long as the world lasteth.
> A: Like enough; and yet the fault, as I have said, may be easily mended, by mending the Universities. (P. 252)

In proposing to reform the universities, Hobbes seeks to rid contemporary civil society of the religious, political, and legal doctrines that inspired the recent civil war and to establish the authority of Charles II on a lasting foundation.

In this proposal we see the fundamental paradox of Hobbes's entire political enterprise. In order to bring about an end to doctrinal politics, Hobbes does not call for the abolition of the universities or for the "end of ideology" (as some present-day political scientists might have done). Instead, he calls for the reform of the universities and the introduction of his own political teaching, which he claims is the "true science of equity and justice." The paradox of Hobbes's enterprise, then, is that he introduces his own "doctrine" in order to bring an end to doctrinal politics. This doctrine, Hobbes must claim, is somehow qualitatively different from those of the past: it will not be exploitable by ambitious intellectuals for the purpose of rebellion and domination, nor will it provoke another doctrinal dispute. In *Behemoth* Hobbes attempts to meet the requirements of a 'nondoctrinal doctrine,' so to speak, by introducing a new title to rule for King Charles II, based on two notions: the right of conquest and the right of popular consent.

In introducing this new title to rule, Hobbes must follow a subtle rhetorical strategy. For he knows that the claim traditionally used by the Stuart monarchy to justify its rule was neither conquest nor consent but the divine right of kings. Yet Hobbes opposes this claim, not because it is too presumptuous or self-serving or absolutist but because he knows that it will weaken the new king. Such a claim will make Charles II too dependent on priests and scholars, who inevitably become the final arbiters in determining which doctrines and laws are in accordance with divine right.[18] Hobbes thus faces the dilemma of supporting the Restoration of the Stuart monarchy while opposing its claim of divine right. He resolves this dilemma in *Behemoth* by remaining silent about divine right in order to avoid open criticism of the Stuart claim and to avoid another doctrinal dispute.[19] At the same time he points to other foundations for the rule of Charles II, which he hopes will escape the usual problems of doctrinal politics.

One such alternative is the right of conquest, the most natural form of rule, which establishes sovereignty on force and actual might rather than on doctrines of right. In *Behemoth* Hobbes points to this foundation in several subtle ways. At the very beginning of his history, he reminds the reader that in the year 1640 King Charles I held "the sovereignty by right of descent continued above six hundred years." The implication is that the Stuart monarchy,

18. See J. N. Figgis, *The Theory of the Divine Right of Kings*, 2d ed. (Cambridge: Cambridge University Press, 1914), pp. 205–212.

19. Hobbes's failure to reassert the claim of divine right on behalf of Charles II was undoubtedly the reason the new king denied Hobbes permission to publish *Behemoth*. Hobbes complied with the command of his sovereign to the extent of not permitting the book to be published while he (Hobbes) was alive. Thus *Behemoth*, which was probably written around 1668, was published posthumously in 1682. See the discussion of this controversy in *EW*, IV, 411.

while descendant from a Scottish line of kings, held the sovereignty in England by succession from William the Conqueror, who founded the English monarchy by invasion and conquest six hundred years earlier (pp. 165–166). More important, Hobbes traces the right of King Charles I to raise a militia to the "commission of arrays," the practice begun by William the Conqueror whereby land was exchanged for promises of military service. He also reminds the reader that the Restoration of Charles II was accomplished by military conquest, not simply by a declaration of Parliament. The very last sentence of *Behemoth*, presented almost as an afterthought, is a somewhat cryptic remark in praise of General Monk, who won the decisive battle for the Royalist cause by a shrewd maneuver. Hobbes calls this maneuver "the greatest stratagem that is extant in history"—an exaggeration, no doubt, but one that emphasizes the role of bold military campaigns in the establishment of political sovereignty (p. 418).

In addition to defending the Stuart monarchy by appealing to the right of conquest, Hobbes attempts to bolster the courage of political and military rulers against clergymen and lawyers who intimidate them with their divinity and legal science. Hobbes is aware that kings, conquerors, and generals are motivated primarily by the passion of magnanimity or desire for "greatness," which needs to be educated in order to meet the challenge of doctrinal politics. In the past this passion made rulers and conquerors too high-minded to follow the intrigues and devious plots of the clergy: "For the greatness of Kings makes them that they cannot easily descend into the obscure and narrow mines of an ambitious clergy" (p. 180). This statement is an illustration of Hobbes's distinction between magnanimous men, who pursue glory by open and direct action, and vainglorious men, who pursue glory by devious and indirect means (*Elements*, I, 9.1, 9.20). Hobbes attempts to teach the kings of the world to descend a bit from their high-mindedness in order to understand the plots of clergymen, which involve indirect means to power through the manipulation of opinions rather than the exercise of force. Hobbes also demonstrates that the "greatness of kings" requires them to be courageous and ruthless in the suppression of rebellious priests and meddlesome lawyers. In *Behemoth* he cites examples of kings who acted decisively and ruthlessly to defend their lives and power. The most striking example is the Ethiopian king who sought to abolish the strange custom of his nation which gave the priests of Ethiopia the right to elect the king, as well as to order him to die, whenever they were so commanded by the gods. This custom was accepted for centuries, until King Ergamenes arose who, "having his breeding in philosophy after the manner of the

Greeks, . . . took heart as befitted a King; came with soldiers to a place called Abaton, . . . killed all the priests, abolished the custom, and rectified the Kingdom according to his will." To this lesson in history Hobbes suggests a parallel in modern times. Reflecting on the 100,000 deaths in the English Civil War, he asks rhetorically: "Had it not been much better that those seditious ministers, which were perhaps 1000, had been killed before they preached? It had been, I confess, a great massacre; but the killing of 100,000 is a greater" (pp. 281–282). By these remarks Hobbes seeks to revive not only the right of conquest but also the passion for great and resolute action, which has been repressed by the overintellectualism of the doctrinal age.

Such advice, however, cannot provide a complete solution to the problem of doctrinal politics, because a revival of the right of conquest and the "greatness of Kings" is tantamount to a return to barbarism. Yet no pure and simple return to barbarism is possible in the most advanced stage of civilization, where doctrines of right have become an established force in politics. Hope as Hobbes may, doctrines will not simply disappear, although their influence can be diminished by exposure as the creations of ambitious intellectuals. The right of conquest, therefore, is an inadequate basis for rule in the contemporary age: might without right or the simple equation of might with right cannot provide a lasting basis for rule in an advanced civilization where men expect to be governed in accordance with principles of right.

As proof we may cite Hobbes's discussion of Cromwell in *Behemoth*. At first glance Cromwell seems to be exactly the kind of ruler that Hobbes admires: he rose to sovereign power by military conquest and with ruthless courage established the Protectorate, a dictatorial regime that was not beholden to the clergy and that even allowed a limited type of religious toleration. Yet Hobbes's judgment of Cromwell is negative, and his reasons are most revealing. Hobbes's major objection to Cromwell is not that he acquired his power by force of arms but that he failed to turn military conquest into stable political rule: the Protectorate under Oliver Cromwell and his son Richard lasted only six years (1653–1659). Cromwell's problem was his inability to transform the title of conqueror and protector into the title of king, and thereby to establish a new royal line: "Cromwell, after he had gotten into his hands the absolute power of England, Scotland, and Ireland, by the name of Protector, did never dare to take upon him the title of King, nor was he ever able to settle it upon his children. His officers would not suffer it, as pretending after his death to succeed him; nor would his army consent to it, because he had ever declared to them against the government of a single person" (pp. 299, 400–402). According to Hobbes, Cromwell was forced to disavow the claim that he was a monarch and to style himself instead a "protector," in order to appease the generals and soldiers of his army. The generals resented the monarchic pretensions of a hereditary succession out of jealousy and the desire to succeed Cromwell with one of their own. And the common soldiers resented the very notion of monarchy, having been indoctrinated by Cromwell and others in the most radical ideologies of the time. As Hobbes points out, Cromwell's army was composed not only of many plunderers and opportunists but also of "fanatics" and "levellers"—the most radical Protestant sectarians and democratic partisans of the English Civil War (pp. 333, 346, 365–375). The transience of the Protectorate, therefore, was not due simply to the death of Oliver and the feebleness of Richard, although these factors hastened its downfall. It was due to the ambition of Cromwell's top generals and the doctrines of his common soldiers.

The experience of Cromwell, however, is not final proof that the right of conquest is an inadequate basis for political sovereignty. After all, as Hobbes points out, William the Conqueror founded the English monarchy by turning military conquest into stable rule. He secured the loyalty of his generals by giving them land and titles, controlled his soldiers with threats of punishment and rewards of plunder, and established a hereditary succession. But William the Conqueror was a "barbarian" prince, so to speak, who ruled by natural force and magnanimity without depending on learned opinions and doctrines. Cromwell, by contrast, had to rely on the religious and political opinions of his soldiers, which compromised his rule. Hobbes's lesson seems to be that in primitive times the right of conquest could be turned into stable political rule, but in his own times a conqueror needs a doctrine of right to legitimize his political power. Obviously the "right" of conquest, as distinguished from the fact of conquest, is itself a doctrine that Hobbes publicly proclaims as a means of bolstering the power of physical force. But is there a doctrine that can supplement the fact and the right of conquest but that cannot, at the same time, be exploited by ambitious intellectuals and cause new doctrinal wars?

To supplement conquest by an appeal to divine right would not work, because such an appeal leads to indirect rule by clergymen and eventually to sectarian warfare. To supplement conquest by a claim of virtue and wisdom would also be objectionable, because these qualities, as we have seen, are highly disputable and are readily claimed by everyone. As an alternative to traditional religious and moral claims, Hobbes introduces a novel doctrine: he combines the right of conquest and the right of popular consent into the doctrine of *"salus populi"* or "the safety of the people." This doctrine, Hobbes contends, is the only possible solution to the problem of doctrinal politics; it alone gives effective power to the political sovereign, while providing a principle of right that does not stimulate the passion of intellectual vanity.

Nevertheless, this new teaching presents many difficulties, as can be seen from the way it is introduced in *Behemoth*. At one point, while discussing Cromwell's rise to power, the student *(B)* raises the question: What was Cromwell's right to govern, as compared to that of the Long Parliament and that of King Charles II? The brief exchange that follows is the only explicit discussion in all of *Behemoth* in which the interlocutors evaluate and judge the competing claims to rule. The doctor *(A)* remarks that in 1653 Cromwell had "the supreme strength . . . as general of all the forces in England, Scotland, and Ireland"; but he lacked "the right to govern" because his title of protector was merely a disguise for military rule. Cromwell, the doctor concludes, possessed might but not right. By contrast, the Long Parliament, which established a republic from 1649 to 1651, had a partial claim to right but lacked effective power. It claimed to defend the *"salus populi"* or "the safety of the nation against a dangerous conspiracy of Papists and a malignant party at home." But the Long Parliament lacked the power of an army to secure the people's safety against these threats. Thus Parliament possessed right but not might. At this point in the discussion, the student remarks that "sovereign power is essentially annexed to the representative of the people." To this statement the doctor replies: Parliament is not "the representative of the whole nation, but of the commons only"; the king is the only authentic representative of the people because he represents all parts of the nation—not only the commons but also the lords and priests (pp. 388–389).

In this discussion the difficulties of Hobbes's new doctrine begin to appear. Hobbes wants to argue that conquest is an inadequate basis for rule and must be supplemented by popular consent or the safety of the people. But he insists that only the king can claim to represent and to protect all of the people. The irony, of course, is that in making this statement Hobbes comes close to elaborating the classical doctrine of the just regime, which defines a just political order as one that promotes the common good rather than the good of a partisan or particular group.

Thus Hobbes's attempt to find an alternative to doctrinal politics in *Behemoth* appears to be unsatisfactory. Hobbes silently rejects the claim of divine right by the Stuart monarchy and appeals to "the safety of the people"—a synthesis of conquest and popular consent which includes an unrestricted right to the means of self-defense. But Hobbes does not really explain why this doctrine is essentially different from traditional doctrines, especially from classical teachings about the just regime articulated by Aristotle. Has Hobbes failed, then, in his search for an alternative to doctrinal politics? Is it not impossible to avoid appealing to an idea of right which stands above de facto power and which invites disputation and doctrinal wars?

To these questions Hobbes would reply that he has not been defeated; he simply has reached the limits of the discipline of civil history. In this discipline one is confined to a prescientific analysis of civil society. Hence it is not possible to demonstrate the difference between the doctrines of the past, which are mere opinions (whatever they may claim), and Hobbes's own doctrine, which is the "true science of equity and justice." To understand this distinction, we must go beyond the discipline of civil history and turn to the discipline of political science in the strict and proper sense. In doing so we shall see how Hobbes reduces his prescientific history of civilization to a technical analysis of "opinion," which explains why all the doctrines of the past have never ceased to produce controversy and civil war.

» 3 «

The Methodical Analysis
of Opinion

From History to Methodical Science

The historical critique presented in *Behemoth* and other works of civil history is the beginning point of Hobbes's political science because it explains why previous civil societies are radically defective and prone to civil war. It shows that the defect of traditional forms of political authority lies not with any particular sovereign, or with the social and economic bases of authority, but with opinions and doctrines of right, regardless of who espouses them or what interests they support. Only after the defect of traditional political authority has been identified in precisely this fashion could Hobbes consider the idea of a methodical political science. For if his historical investigations had shown that the defect of previous politics was faulty leadership, Hobbes would have written treatises on the training of statesmen—as did Machiavelli. Or if they had shown that the defect was due to material conditions, Hobbes would have written treatises on social and economic revolution—as did Marx. But since history shows that the problem of traditional politics is the dependence of the state on authoritative opinions and on doctrines derived by reasoning from such opinions, Hobbes wrote treatises that methodically analyze the elements of "opinion." In turning to this analysis we see the point of contact between Hobbes's historical writings and his scientific treatises.

In the historical studies Hobbes shows that all preexisting opinions and doctrines are the artificial products of civilization. They are created by priests, philosophers, lawyers, and other intellectuals who seek to replace the rule of force with the rule of opinion. These intellectuals claim, of course, that they do not invent the opinions and doctrines that they espouse but receive them from higher authorities—from a source of knowledge or standard of appeal above the human will, such as God, Nature, or custom. It is this claim that justifies the imposition of opinions on others, especially the demand that the state officially establish certain opinions as orthodoxy and suppress others as heresy. In reality, however, such appeals to higher authorities are always mediated by *human* authorities; therefore opinions are either borrowed from men or invented by men. Whether or not the higher authorities actually exist (and Hobbes makes no determination on these matters in his historical writings), opinion stands on human authority—on an assertion by a man that a certain proposition is the only right and true one because he says it is and because his superior wisdom and learning qualify him to say so. Opinion as such is authoritative opinion in two senses: it is attributed to impersonal higher authorities, and it is pronounced by expert human authorities.

The central lesson of Hobbes's histories is that such claims have enormous appeal to the human mind but they never provide a secure foundation for civilized society. For any particular claim can be disputed by others who hold different opinions and also maintain that they speak with authority. This problem is compounded by the dialectical or disputative sciences developed in the Western world, which embrace the variety of conflicting opinions and attempt to distinguish mere opinion from scientific or true knowledge. But such a claim also requires the assertion of a man that his conclusion is the only right and true one or that his conclusion represents "right reason"—an assertion that must be made with even greater vehemence and intransigence than those made for nonscientific opinions. Opinion and reasoning from opinion thus produce a vicious circle of sectarian controversy, which cannot be settled without a contest of arms.

In sum, Hobbes's historical writings show that opinion is both powerful and impotent because it rests on authority—on a standard of appeal above the human will which requires a final and definitive interpretation by qualified experts. This characteristic explains its strength as well as its weakness throughout the history of civilization.

The historical critique outlined above leads Hobbes to consider the possibility of a new kind of political science, one based on a scientific method that overcomes once and for all times the reliance on authoritative opinion. Such a method must be one that explains in precise and technical terms why opinion and reasoning from opinion have never produced agreement, and it must provide a way of transcending opinion as such in order to provide an indisputable foundation for politics and science. It is this hope that leads Hobbes to adopt the resolutive-compositive method, the method used previously by Galileo in physics and by Harvey in physiology. The basic idea of such a method is simple. Hobbes himself compares it to taking apart a broken watch or engine, identifying the defective parts, and then reassembling the pieces into a new whole that is rationally and logically ordered. What Hobbes sees in the method of resolution and composition is a procedure for dissecting opinion into its constituent elements which identifies precisely its defective parts and suggests a way of reconstituting them into a new whole, freed of the original defects (*De Cive*, Preface; *De Corpore*, VI.7).

Hobbes's turn to methodical science, then, is not an a priori commitment or the first step in his philosophical reasoning. It presupposes prescientific or premethodological knowledge that Hobbes derives from historical observation and reflection. History shows that the disputability of opinion as such is the problem of preexisting authority, and methodical science attempts to solve this problem by logical analysis and synthesis.[1]

In addition to defining the problem, history supplies two vital premises for the application of Hobbes's methodical science to politics. In the first place, history shows that "opinion" is in fact a phenomenon susceptible to logical or technical analysis. This important point is far from obvious and requires considerable historical evidence to support it. For Hobbes the universal lesson of history is that men always appeal to higher authorities as the source of their opinions, but the higher authorities never intervene directly in human affairs to determine unequivocally which opinions should be accepted and which should be rejected. Instead, the determinations

1. This point is not adequately grasped by Watkins and others who argue for the primacy of method in Hobbes's system. Watkins seems to assume that Hobbes adopted the resolutive-compositive method simply because it was used successfully by Galileo in physics and Harvey in physiology (J. W. N. Watkins, *Hobbes's System of Ideas*, pp. 47–68). By contrast, see the insightful article of John Dewey, "The Motivation of Hobbes's Political Philosophy," in *Thomas Hobbes in His Time*, ed. Ralph Ross, Herbert Schneider, and Theodore Waldman (Minneapolis: University of Minnesota Press, 1974), pp. 8–30. Dewey specifically calls for a reexamination of the forgotten historical basis of Hobbes's thought which reveals "the troubled regime of opinion" as the motivation for Hobbes's turn to scientific politics. See also Mansfield, "Hobbes and the Science of Indirect Government," pp. 98–102, who shows that "opinions of good and bad in politics" lead Hobbes to the methodical analysis and reconstruction of political authority.

are made by human beings themselves—by human agents and mediators, who use the arts of dialectics and rhetoric to persuade others and manipulate coercive powers to enforce their prescriptions when persuasion fails. This insight permits Hobbes to draw a momentous conclusion: history justifies a posture of metaphysical neutrality regarding the existence and character of all higher authorities. In other words, God, Nature, and custom may or may not exist independently of the human will, and their existence may be immaterial or material. Whatever is the case, knowledge of higher authorities requires submission to a human authority, to a particular man whose judgment is taken on trust because of his reputation for wisdom, learning, inspiration, or other signs of privileged knowledge. As Hobbes says in reference to the problem of knowing God's will:

> For who is there differing in opinion from another, and thinking himself to be in the right, and the other in the wrong, . . . that would not be content to submit his opinions, either to the pope, or to a general council, or to a provincial council, or to a presbytery of his own nation? And *yet in all cases he submitteth himself to no greater than human authority.* Nor can a man be said to submit himself to Holy Scripture, that doth not submit himself to some or other for the interpretation thereof. (*Elements*, II, 2.6.13; emphasis added)

From such observations Hobbes can infer that the metaphysical question of whether or not higher authorities actually exist and provide support for human knowledge can be separated from the psychological question of how human authorities create opinion and belief in the minds of other men.

Thus the question of God's existence and Providence in caring for the reception of his revelation, as well as the question of Nature's existence as an ordered and intelligible whole, indeed all of the ultimate questions regarding the existence and character of higher authorities, can be set aside in the effort to explain the phenomenon of opinion or belief. Opinion can be treated as something artificial, as something caused by human agency which exists only in the minds of men. Opinion, then, is susceptible to technical analysis: it can be taken apart, its defective elements can be removed, and its parts can be reassembled, all by a purely mental exercise. The explanation of opinion and belief is thereby removed at the outset from the domain of metaphysics or theology and is reduced to a methodical analysis of the human mind (although metaphysics may return at a later point in the argument to vindicate the method).

In this way the historical critique of opinion justifies the suspension of judgment on ultimate metaphysical questions and permits method—a combination of logic and psychology—to become the first science.

Another way that history provides the presuppositions of methodical science is by showing that one can abstract entirely from the *content* of opinions in explaining why men believe or do not believe in them. As Hobbes insists repeatedly in *Behemoth*, the influence of religious sectarians (Catholics, Anglicans, Presbyterians, and Independents) as well as political partisans (monarchists, aristocrats, democrats, and levelers) was due not to the content of their opinions but to the *authority* of particular leaders. And among the leaders themselves, Hobbes argues, opinions were adopted not because of their content but because they provided pretexts for rebellion and domination. As a general rule, Hobbes observes: "to dispose men to sedition . . . [there must be a] pretense of right; for though a man be discontent, yet if in his own opinion there be no just cause . . . nor any pretense to justify his resistance and to procure aid, he will never show it" (*Elements*, II, 2.8.1). No man will show his ambition without an opinion of right. Yet, surprisingly, any opinion will suffice. Elitist claims or democratic claims serve equally well as pretenses for rebellion, as long as they are asserted to be the only right and true opinions, and the people are properly indoctrinated, by eloquence and other techniques, to believe such claims. From these observations, however, Hobbes does not conclude that men are cynical opportunists in adopting their opinions. To the contrary, he maintains that ambitious men "could not poison people with those absurd opinions contrary to peace and civil society, unless they held them themselves" (*De Cive*, XII.12). What Hobbes does infer is that the choice of opinions, by both leaders and followers, is essentially *arbitrary* because their belief, faith, or trust is not in the content of the opinion but in the authority of the person who propounds it— in his claims of authoritative wisdom and expert knowledge.

But precisely because the content of opinions is arbitrary, the dialectical science of traditional philosophers, which analyzes opinions in order to distinguish the true from the false, the just from the unjust, the orthodox from the heretical, and ultimately the apparent from the real, is impossible. This way of reasoning simply increases the arbitrariness already inherent in the adoption of opinions. While a dialectical analysis of the content of opinions is impossible, a methodical analysis of the component parts or elements is possible, because one can abstract from the content and analyze opinion *as such*.

Thus Hobbes's historical critique of civilization, by tracing the defect of traditional politics and science to their foundation on opinion and by showing both the artificial and arbitrary origins of opinion in human authority, supplies the presuppositions of his methodical science.

Opinion Resolved into Speech and Mental Thoughts

In attempting to follow Hobbes's steps in applying the resolutive-compositive method to the phenomenon of opinion, however, we face an immediate difficulty: Hobbes does not present the process of resolution in any of his writings. The historical works, such as *Behemoth*, present a view of political phenomena which is prescientific or prior to methodical analysis. They simply describe particular opinions (religious, philosophical, political, legal) and show how these opinions are created and manipulated by ambitious men for purposes of rebellion and domination. By contrast, Hobbes's scientific treatises, such as the *Leviathan*, begin with an elaborate "epistemology," in which previous opinions and doctrines already have been resolved into their constituent elements and the various errors, deceptions, and absurdities of previous thought have been neatly catalogued. Thus we never see the actual process of resolution in any of Hobbes's works; we see only the beginning point and the conclusion. What intermediary steps did Hobbes take in moving from the historical to the scientific point of view?

An important clue is provided by Hobbes's use of the term "opinion" (and related terms, such as "belief," "faith," "trust," and "doctrine") in his historical writings and scientific treatises. In the histories Hobbes uses these terms repeatedly but loosely, without attempting to define them. For example, when analyzing the problem of political authority in *Behemoth*, he formulates the general maxim that "the power of the mighty hath no foundation but in the opinion and belief of the people" (*Behemoth*, p. 184). And when he comments on the folly of the English Civil War, he says that "it is a hard case that there should be two factions to trouble the commonwealth, . . . and that their quarrels should be only about opinions, that is, about who has the most learning, as if learning should be the rule of governing all the world" (*Behemoth*, p. 275). In these statements Hobbes uses "opinion" and "belief" in one sense to mean a conviction—any idea or principle that is held to be true. He also uses them in a more sophisticated sense to mean a doctrine—a set of principles acquired by higher learning or theoretical education.

The only place in the historical writings where Hobbes actually attempts to define his terms is in the discussion of "heresy." In *Behemoth,* as we noted above, Hobbes traces the notion of heresy back to the Athenian schools of philosophy, where, he claims, the word meant nothing more than a "private opinion" (p. 175). He elaborates this definition in the *Dialogue on the Common Laws* by explaining that heresy consisted of any "opinion contrary to the doctrine of another man." Heresy simply meant "the doctrine of a sect, . . . taken upon trust of some man of reputation for wisdom, who was the first author of the same" (p. 123). With this definition Hobbes attempts to remove the stigma attached to the notion of heresy by equating it with any partisan opinion or sectarian doctrine. At the same time he points to the fundamental similarity of all such opinions: the taking of ideas on trust from a man reputed to be wise. Thus Hobbes's historical writings, while not designed to give a precise analysis of the phenomenon of opinion, repeatedly emphasize two characteristics: (1) a settled conviction or adherence to a principle that is thought to be true, and (2) trust in a man who seems to be learned and wise.

In moving from the historical writings to his scientific treatises on politics, Hobbes refines these observations; but he sometimes speaks so casually about the phenomenon of "opinion" that one can easily overlook the import of his remarks. He says in *Leviathan,* for example, that "the actions of men proceed from their opinions; and in the well-governing of opinions, consisteth the well-governing of men's actions" (ch. 18, p. 164). And in *De Cive* he makes a grand assertion sound like common sense when he says that "all controversies are bred from hence, that the opinions of men differ concerning *meum* and *tuum, just* and *unjust, profitable* and *unprofitable, good* and *evil,* . . . and the like" (vi.9; Hobbes's emphasis). Such references to the phenomenon of "opinion" in the treatises do not seem to be technical or precise, and most readers pass over them without stopping to think that herein lies the central problem of political science.

But Hobbes also draws our attention to this phenomenon in the treatises by translating historical observations into precise definitions of opinion and belief. Each of the political treatises contains a discussion of the human mind in its various states of knowing, which Hobbes distinguishes as follows. In the *Elements* he states that "opinion" in the strict and proper sense consists in thinking that a certain proposition is true without knowing that it is true, because it is actually false or because it has been admitted "from trusting to other men." After stating this definition Hobbes immediately refines it by identifying "belief" as a species of opinion: "And particularly, when the opinion is admitted out of *trust to other* men, [we] are said to *believe* it" (*Elements*, I, 6.6, 6.7, Hobbes's emphasis). In presenting such definitions Hobbes does not derive them from any prior argument; he simply asserts them as if they were self-evident. Yet it is apparent that they are distilled from historical observations that are deliberately omitted from the treatises. For they embody the foremost insight of Hobbes's historical studies: that opinion is a kind of conviction based on trust in the wisdom of a human authority.

In *De Cive* Hobbes refines his definitions by developing two additional insights. First, he observes that the primary ingredient in all opinions is language—that is, words or speech used to declare what is right or wrong or to describe things and events. As Hobbes says, the object of an opinion, "that which is believed, is evermore a *proposition*, that is, a speech affirmative or negative, which we grant to be true" (XVIII.4). Second, he argues that assent to the truth of any proposition is caused by one of the following mental actions:

> Now the propositions which we receive for truth, we always grant for some reasons of our own; and these are derived either from the *proposition itself*, or from the *person propounding*. They are derived from the proposition itself, by calling to mind what things those words, which make up the proposition, do by common consent usually signify. If so, then the assent which we give is called *knowledge or science*. . . . But when our reasons, for which we assent to some proposition, derive not from the proposition itself but from the *person propounding*, whom we esteem so learned that he is not deceived, and we see no reason why he should deceive us; our assent, because it grows not from any confidence of our own, but from another man's knowledge, is called *faith*. And by the confidence of whom we do believe, we are said *to trust them, or to trust in them*. (*De Cive*, XVIII.4; Hobbes's emphasis)

The two fundamental acts of the human mind, according to Hobbes, are *knowing* a proposition is true, which is science, and merely *thinking* a proposition is true, which he describes variously as opinion, belief, faith, and trust. The latter are distinguished from knowledge because the words that make up the proposition have been received on trust from other men without questions or demands for clear definitions.

In the *Leviathan* Hobbes presents his final version of these notions, refining them one step further. As before, he makes a fundamental distinction between knowing something is true and merely thinking it is true, and he distinguishes the two mental acts by the use of language or speech. But in describing the various kinds of assent that fall short of knowledge or science, Hobbes dwells at length on the difference between "opinion" and "conscience," on the one hand, and "belief" and "faith," on the other. He defines opinion very simply as assenting to "the truth of somewhat said, though sometimes in absurd and senseless words, without the possibility of being understood"—that is, assenting to the truth of a proposition that is obscure or incomprehensible. This, Hobbes claims, is also the proper understanding of what men currently call conscience: "[For those] vehemently in love with their own new opinions, though never so absurd, and obstinately bent to maintain them, [give] . . . their opinions also that reverenced name of conscience; as if they would have it seem unlawful, to change or speak against them; and so pretend to know they are true, when they know at most, but that they think so" (ch. 7, pp. 53–54). The gist of this somewhat complicated formulation is that conscience is also assent to a proposition that is obscure or incomprehensible, but it is held and asserted with the vehemence of a claim to knowledge, even though it is merely thought to be true. Conscience, therefore, is nothing more than a vehement opinion of the truth.

Both of these phenomena are to be distinguished from belief and faith. As Hobbes says, "When a man's discourse beginneth not at definitions, it beginneth either at some other contemplation of *his own,* and then it is still called opinion; or it beginneth at some saying *of another,* of whose ability to know the truth and of whose honesty in not deceiving, he doubteth not; and then the discourse is not so much concerning the thing, as the person; and the resolution is called BELIEF and FAITH" (ibid.; emphasis added, Hobbes's capitalization). The difference, then, between opinion and conscience on the one hand and belief and faith on the other is that the former involve assent to obscure and incomprehensible speech that is one's own, while the latter involve assent to obscure speech that is borrowed from another man, whose wisdom and integrity we have no reason to doubt. In all cases Hobbes has defined those mental states that consist of thinking without knowing as assenting to the truth of a proposition without first asking for clear definitions of words, either from love and trust in one's own wisdom or from trust in the wisdom of another man.

From these statements we may draw the following conclusions about Hobbes's steps in the methodical resolution of opinion. For Hobbes, "opinion" in the generic sense refers to all mental states that consist in thinking something is true without actually knowing it to be true. He observes that the primary element of an opinion is language, words, or speech—a proposition about something that is affirmed or denied. The defining trait of opinion and kindred phenomena (such as conscience, belief, faith, or trust) is that the speech that forms the proposition is obscure or incomprehensible and thus cannot really be *known* to be true. The implication is that assent to such propositions must occur independently of the meaning of words (because they are not understood); it must be due to trust in the authority of the speaker, either in one's own authority or in that of another man. Opinion, then, is unclear speech taken on trust in the authority of someone who seems to be wise. This is the first step in Hobbes's methodical analysis, the reduction of opinion to the speech of human authorities.

Using this insight, Hobbes is able to explain the disputability of opinion in terms of misuses of speech. In his scientific treatises he traces the immediate cause of political and philosophical controversy to abuses of speech of one kind or another. This point has been duly emphasized by Hobbes scholars, in studies by Sheldon Wolin, J. W. N. Watkins, and Frederick Whelan. Hobbes's argument is summarized most succinctly by Whelan, who catalogues the abuses as follows: inconstant signification, equivocation or metaphor, and absurdity.[2] Inconstant signification occurs when speakers use a word to mean different things. Equivocation is giving variable meanings to a word in order to deceive other people, as in the use of metaphors by rhetoricians and orators, who twist the meanings of words for the purpose of winning arguments. Absurdity is the use of words for things that are inconceivable because they do not really exist (*Leviathan*, ch. 4, pp. 20, 29; ch. 5, pp. 32–35). In all cases Hobbes explains the abuses of speech in terms of one simple problem: words are being used without clear mental thoughts or without clear ideas in the mind. The first two cases consist of using words with vague or ambiguous mental thoughts; the last case, absurdity, consists of using words "insignificantly," without any corresponding mental thoughts at all. Such vague and insignificant speech causes controversy in discourse and argument because the speaker and listener do not have the same thing in mind and hence, strictly speaking, cannot understand each other (*Elements*, 1, 13.2–4). In this argument Hobbes reveals the second step in the process of resolution: he identifies speech and mental thoughts as elements of opinion.

2. Wolin, *Politics and Vision*, p. 257; Watkins, *Hobbes's System of Ideas*, pp. 138–156; and Whelan, "Language and Its Abuses in Hobbes's Political Philosophy," pp. 61–65.

After tracing the disputability of opinion to the use of words without clear mental thoughts, Hobbes must consider the question of why the human mind inclines men to use speech in such an inexact, imprecise, or incomprehensible fashion. The problem is that men seem to be utterly indifferent to the need to have a clear mental picture to accompany their words; they seem to be wholly unaware that words must refer to some idea if they are to have life and meaning. The reason for this strange indifference, Hobbes argues, is the natural tendency of the human mind to borrow words on trust—to use words as they are received in common or conventional usage and to repeat them by habit or memory. This natural tendency is further reinforced by the philosophical and academic tradition in the Western world which has developed the arts and sciences of speech. They take as their starting point the conventional usages of words and use them either for persuasion or for the discovery and articulation of the nature of things. But this method of reasoning increases the ambiguity of common speech by deliberately separating words from clear mental thoughts.

The tendency to borrow words on authority without understanding and to separate verbal discourse from mental discourse is latent in every human being; but its influence varies according to each person's level of education and learning. Thus, Hobbes observes, "the common sort of men seldom speak insignificantly," that is, they seldom use words without mental thoughts consisting of common-sense experience unless they are corrupted by learned men. Accordingly, Hobbes claims that the "vulgate" is superior to the learned languages: English, French, and German are preferable to Greek and Latin; and Latin in the time of Cicero, Varro, and the Roman grammarians is to be preferred to its contemporary usage because language employed in daily affairs is commonsensical and down-to-earth and refers to particular things (*Leviathan*, ch. 8, pp. 69–70).

Nevertheless, common or vulgar speech has a tendency to lose touch with clear sense experience because it is often distorted by interest or used simply for intellectual display. In *De Cive* Hobbes observes that words "by vulgar use either to adorn or deceive ... are so wrested from their significations, that to remember the conceptions for which they were first imposed on things is very hard." Common speech then becomes deceitful or exaggerated, either to disguise one's interest or to gain intellectual recognition by displays of eloquence and the telling of fantastic tales ("if one relates some wonder, the rest will tell you miracles") (*De Cive*, I.2). Common speech thereby assumes a new aspect: it becomes metaphorical speech, which Hobbes defines as the use of words "in other senses than they are ordained for, which thereby deceives others" (*Leviathan*, ch. 4, p. 20). For the most part, the metaphorical speech of common people is vain but innocent. It consists in using "metaphors, tropes, and other rhetorical figures, instead of words proper, . . . as for example, in the common speech 'the way goeth,' or 'the proverb says this or that,' whereas ways cannot go nor proverbs speak" (*Leviathan*, ch. 5, p. 34). This tendency of common people to use metaphors to make inanimate things come alive explains why their colloquial speech is colorful and vivid. But colorful and vivid speech separates words from clear sense experience in fanciful animations and idle gossip about wonders and fantastic events.

The corruption of common speech is carried one step further by the rhetorical speech of political men. Rhetorical speech or eloquence develops the common use of metaphor into an art—an art of persuasion whose sole purpose is to achieve victory in argument. Hobbes examines the rules of this art in a short treatise, *The Whole Art of Rhetoric*, and in his political treatises, especially in *De Cive* (where he discusses at length the role of speech in political assemblies, crowds, and public gatherings of all types). His most revealing analysis of rhetoric or eloquence is the following statement in *De Cive:*

> Now eloquence is twofold. The one is an elegant and clear expression of the conceptions of the mind. . . . The other is a commotion of the passions of the mind, such as hope, fear, anger, pity; and derives from a metaphorical use of words fitted to the passions. That forms a speech from true principles; this from opinions already received, . . . The art of that is logic, of this rhetoric; the end of that is truth, of this victory. . . . [Using rhetoric] they can make things to them who are ill-affected seem worse, to them who are well-affected, seem evil; they can enlarge their hopes, lessen their dangers beyond reason: this they have from that sort of eloquence . . . which by moving their minds, makes all things appear to be such as they in their minds, prepared before, had already conceived them. (XII.12)

Hobbes elucidates the working of rhetoric by contrasting it to logic. Both are arts of persuasion, but rhetoric is designed to win any argument, whereas logic is used exclusively to convince men of the truth. Rhetoric or eloquence works by exaggerating through the use of metaphors in order to make anything seem better or worse than it really is. Prepared by "opinions already received," the mind connects words for good and evil, justice and injustice, benefit and harm with certain mental thoughts and passions. An apt metaphor, by drawing a false comparison or by slightly misnaming an action or event, "fits" the thing in question to the thoughts and passions of the mind as they already exist somewhat incoherently in commonly received opinions. The apt use of metaphors exploits the fact that common usages of words are not consistently applied to the same thought; this ambiguity enables the speaker to represent any action or event as identical to a conception already in the mind of the audience and to arouse the corresponding passion.

In the *Elements* Hobbes states that of all the passions, pity and indignation are most increased by eloquence (I, 9.10–9.11). Since pity is a passion caused by a conception of unjust ruin, and indignation is a passion caused by a conception of unjust success, either one can be increased by metaphorical speech that exaggerates the injustice of a given action. In his *Art of Rhetoric* Hobbes explains how this process works: "Concerning metaphors, the rules are these: He that will make the best of a thing, let him draw his metaphor from somewhat that is better. As for example, let him call a *crime an error.* On the other side, when he would make the worse of it, let him draw his metaphor from somewhat worse; as calling *error, crime*" (*EW,* VII, 489; Hobbes's emphasis). By making a false comparison or by slightly misnaming a thing, the speaker calls to mind the wrong thoughts and passions. Anger against a rich man who injures a poor man by error or miscalculation is raised to furious indignation when an eloquent speaker represents it as crime or rapacity. The polished orator is so skillful in the art of false comparisons and apt misnaming by metaphor that he can arouse pity or indignation from any received opinion of justice.

When common and rhetorical speech are further refined, the highest and most artificial type of speech emerges: dialectics or disputation. Dialectics is thought to be the highest form of speech because its goal is not mere adornment or persuasion; it is used to discover truth by reasoning from conventionally received opinions to scientific knowledge. In the philosophical and academic tradition of the West, this mode of analysis has been applied to every intellectual discipline that claims the status of "science," whether the ultimate ground of science is reason or revelation. The three most influential sciences—Aristotelian philosophy, Scholastic divinity science, and the jurisprudence of the English common law—are all dialectical or disputative in their method of reasoning. In these sciences one sees the greatest separation of words from mental thoughts.

Dialectics or disputative science is essentially a science of speech because the "received opinions" that are taken as the beginning point are the customarily used words for things, especially those words that are most general or universal. The goal of dialectics is simply to define the meanings of words, on the assumption that the proper definition of a thing in speech is identical to knowledge of the thing itself. Dialectics uses speech to define the "essence" of the thing, which states both what it is (its nature) and why it is (its cause). By collecting the customary and received usages of words and subjecting the conflicting or ambiguous meanings to critical analysis, the dialectician arrives at a final and true definition of the thing in question. This conclusion is the definition of its essence and attains the status of "right reason constituted by nature."

According to Hobbes, dialectical science develops the tendencies that are latent in every kind of speech into a formal method of rational inquiry. It thereby gives a kind of official sanction to borrowing words on trust and to reasoning from authority. It also strengthens the tendency to use words for recognition because it seeks to define words in terms of other words, usually by multiplying verbal distinctions, rather than by asking for definitions in terms of mental thoughts (*De Corpore*, 6.15). Thus the highest intellectual distinction of the dialectician is to be recognized as the "authority" or final arbiter of the meanings of words.

Hobbes's analysis of the most influential dialectical sciences in the Western tradition illustrates these points. Aristotelian philosophy, he observes, consists of logic, natural science, and moral or political science and aspires to be a comprehensive account of the nature and causes of things. But because "Aristotle . . . takes for principles those opinions which are already vulgarly received" and employs a dialectical analysis of common speech, his sciences are little more than classifications of words which confer extra honor on conventional usages by the claim that they accord with the nature of things (*Elements*, I, 13.3). Aristotle's logic, Hobbes says, is simply a classification of grammatical predicates, which Aristotle presents as a description of the actual qualities of things in order to enhance "his own authority" (*De Corpore*, 2.16). Similarly, his metaphysics and physics are attempts to define the most universal words for things, such as matter, form, and substance. But his claim that such universal names actually correspond to "abstract essences" that are the causes of natural phenomena captivates the mind and distracts it from its own thoughts. In moral and political science Aristotle reasons from conventional moral language, from what is commonly praised and blamed. The result, however, is a list of names for virtues and vices and for just and unjust regimes which reflects the conventional usages of ancient Athens and gives men "disgraceful names to express their anger in" when they dislike their government (*Leviathan*, ch. 46, p. 683). In Aristotle's hands dialectical science is simply a means for asserting his authority over the use of language.

The divinity science of the Scholastics builds upon Aristotelian dialectics by appealing not only to common speech but also to a literary tradition, which includes the works of the classical authors, the Bible and Church Fathers, as well as other sacred books and customs. Its aim is to develop definitions in speech which explain the basic tenets of the Christian faith, such as God's essence and attributes, the nature of spirits, the nature of the soul and of free will, and the causes of natural phenomena. From Hobbes's point of view, Scholasticism adds nothing new in principle to Aristotelian philosophy because it still seeks to define words in terms of other words without referring to mental thoughts and assumes that words refer to real things in the divinely created natural order. Scholasticism merely raises the philosophical analysis of speech to a more artificial or more academic level. The dialectical method is formalized in the disputative method; it becomes the "disputed question," which presents negative and affirmative opinions drawn from the books of the learned authorities and concludes with an assertion of the right answer. Metaphysics and physics are rarefied into the theory of "substantial forms" and "occult qualities," invisible causes of phenomena that are separated from material bodies. Moral science develops the habits of virtues into more rigid rules of "conscience" and more fluid notions of "infused" grace or "pouring in of souls." Hobbes's criticism of Scholastic disputative science is the same as that of classical dialectics: it takes names without corresponding mental thoughts for entities in nature in order to acquire authority over the minds of men.

Another heir to the Aristotelian tradition is the jurisprudence of the English common law. It also uses a form of dialectical reasoning to define the meanings of words, focusing specifically on legal terms. As Hobbes explains in the *Dialogue on the Common Laws,* the scholars of the common law, such as Sir Edward Coke, employ a type of dialectics because they define legal terms by drawing on three types of received opinion: the "precedents" laid down in the written reports of judges, the language of past statutes, and the unwritten usages of words in the grammar and conventions of the English language. Jurisprudence is thus a less rigorous but more technical version of classical dialectics. Although it does not employ rules of logic or systematic classification of words, it requires long familiarity with the sources and employs a kind of intuitive judgment to pick and choose among them in order to arrive at a definition that seems to fit the circumstances and to express "right reason."

In actual practice, Hobbes argues, the dialectical reasoning involved in jurisprudence is little more than a study of etymologies—a study of the origins and historical usages of "treason," "felony," "murder," and other legal terms that are disputed in judgments and cases. But "etymologies are no definitions," Hobbes says (*Dialogue*, p. 110). When a legal scholar defines a word by appealing to its etymology, he is merely affirming its conventional usage. Or, as sometimes happens, he adds to the etymology a new usage according to his fancy. Hence jurisprudence, like classical dialectics, appeals to an impersonal standard of right reason; but in doing so it interposes the judgment of a man to settle the definition of words. It thus relies on a human authority who claims to speak for the higher authority of common law and expects his pronouncements to be accepted as final.

In all cases, then, Hobbes argues that "opinion" and "doctrine" (which is opinion elevated to learned discourse) can be reduced to inexact and insignificant speech. It results from the tendency of the human mind to trust in authority or to assume that one speaks with authority without providing definitions of words in terms of clear mental thoughts.

The Passions of the Mind

Surprisingly, Hobbes does not trace this tendency to intellectual passivity, mental laziness, or lethargy. Rather, he traces it to passions that make the mind bold, active, and ready to believe that customary, conventional, traditional, and learned speech is derived from higher authorities (from beings that exist independently of the human will). This insight about the power of the passions over speech constitutes the third and last step in the process of resolution: Hobbes separates opinion into the constituent elements of words, mental thoughts, and passions. By taking this last step, Hobbes reduces the methodical analysis of opinion to a psychological problem. He seeks to identify those passions that cause men to believe that words of human authorities derive from higher authorities and do not require clear mental thoughts to be understood.

Such behavior, he contends, is the work of two powerful passions. For the majority of men who have no exposure to higher learning, fear is the cause of trust in authority. But for intellectual elites (and even for ordinary people who develop intellectual pretensions), the tendency to trust in authority is caused by intellectual vainglory. To understand this point, we must turn to a lengthy discussion of Hobbes's psychology, focusing not on the passions in general but on those that incline men to trust in authority and to use speech in an inexact or incomprehensible fashion. Let us approach this problem somewhat indirectly, by way of a comparison of Hobbes and Machiavelli. For the psychological analysis that Hobbes uses to explain the misguided trust of the human mind bears a striking resemblance to Machiavelli's political psychology.

In *The Prince* and the *Discourses*, Machiavelli divides all men into two natural classes or types, "princes" and "people." Each class has its own distinctive pattern of behavior, which is determined by its ruling passion or humor. The princes, according to Machiavelli, are the small minority of ambitious men who seek honor and glory by dominating rival princes and the people. Their ruling passion is the desire for glory. The people are the vast majority of men who simply want to be secure in their possessions and to be left alone, free from domination and exploitation. Their ruling passion is the desire for security or the fear of death and dispossession (*The Prince*, chs. 9, 19).

These passions produce a complex kind of interaction that Machiavelli views as the foundation of political power. The common people are concerned above all with avoiding oppression by domineering and rapacious princes, who are the greatest threat to their security. Although they actually prefer to be apolitical and to live private lives, the people are driven into politics because the only way to be secure is to seek the protection of one prince against those who threaten them. As a result, the people's fear of death and dispossession inclines them to trust the authority of those princes who appear to be protectors. But the people accept the rule of such a prince only when it is, so to speak, 'invisible'—only when the prince hides his love of domination and appears to be a protector rather than an exploiter, a liberator rather than a conqueror.

For princes the art of ruling, and hence the path to honor and glory, lie in the ability to inspire awe in the people but to keep their domination as indirect and invisible as possible. They do so primarily by exposing the hidden ambition of other princes through the device of a public "accusation" or indictment. By accusing a rival prince, who claims to be a protector, of merely being an ambitious exploiter, and by unmasking his schemes as mere ploys for power, the artful prince makes his own ambition invisible and makes that of his rivals visible. Such exposure of ambition arouses the people, who are normally private and passive, and causes them to demand the satisfaction of revenge against the alleged oppressors. The artful prince thereby acquires a following among the people; he is trusted and leads the people in revenge, securing their gratitude as a protector against oppressive princes. Ironically, then, a successful prince is one who dominates the people by liberating them.[3]

To explain the phenomena of opinion and belief, Hobbes develops a psychological theory that is similar to that of Machiavelli. In the first place, Hobbes divides all men into two groups, one concerned primarily with honor and glory, the other with fear and security. In the *Behemoth* this division underlies his analysis of the English Civil War, which shows how the various intellectual authorities, driven by a desire for honor and glory, competed among themselves to corrupt and seduce the credulous people. In the political treatises this analysis is reduced to a simple psychological teaching. As Hobbes says in *De Cive:*

> All men . . . have a desire and will to hurt, but not proceeding from the same cause, neither equally to be condemned. For one man . . . permits as much to others as he assumes to himself; which is an argument of a temperate man, and one that rightly values his power. Another, supposing himself above others, will have a license to do what he lists, and challenges respect and honour, as due him before others; which is the argument of a fiery spirit. This man's will to hurt ariseth from vainglory, and the false esteem he hath of his own strength; the other's from the necessity of defending himself, his liberty, and his goods, against this man's violence. (I.4)

One type of man—a fiery spirit—seeks to dominate for the sake of honor and glory; the other type simply wants to be left alone and to be secure in his possessions from the invasions of domineering men. This classification in *De Cive* corresponds to the passage in the *Leviathan* where Hobbes distinguishes between the few who seek conquest beyond security and the rest "who would be glad to be at ease within modest bounds," but who nevertheless must invade others and increase their power out of concern for self-defense (ch. 13, p. 112). In the *Elements* Hobbes also speaks of those who seek glory; he distinguishes them from the average man, of whom "there be two things that may trouble his mind, . . . the one, is loss of liberty; the other, uncertainty of *meum* and *tuum* [that is, uncertainty about his

3. *Discourses on Livy*, bk. I, chs. 11, 16, 29; see also Harvey C. Mansfield, Jr., "Machiavelli's New Regime," *Italian Quarterly*, 13 (1970), 70–74.

possessions]" (II, 2.5.2). These passages demonstrate that Hobbes, like Machiavelli, makes a distinction between "princes" and "people," between the few whose ruling passion is the desire for honor and glory and the many whose ruling passion is to be free from oppression and secure in their lives and property.

Although Machiavelli and Hobbes agree on the basic division of human types and dominant passions, they diverge on a crucial point. For Machiavelli, the struggle for domination and freedom from domination is the real dynamic of politics; this struggle creates the dialectic of glory and fear. For Hobbes the struggle for domination is not simply political; it is a contest of opinions for recognition of their truth and for recognition of intellectual superiority in those who espouse them. Accordingly, Hobbes makes a subtle but important distinction between two types of ambition: one type is vanity or vainglory, which is concerned with mental pleasures and intellectual superiority; a second type is true glory or magnanimity, which is concerned with real power and command. The first is the passion of intellectual "princes"—the scholars, philosophers, priests, lawyers, orators, and even bookish romantics like Don Quixote. The second is the passion of the political and military "princes"—the monarchs, conquerors, and patriarchs who historically have exercised actual coercive power. Hobbes's emphasis on the struggle of opinions also makes him less inclined than Machiavelli to see the differences between the common people and the elites as natural. Hobbes traces the differences in passions among men to learning and education, which have been increasingly diffused by the progress of historical civilization and have infected even ordinary people with intellectual vanity.

Ultimately Hobbes diverges from Machiavelli because Machiavelli does not take seriously the contest over opinions, beliefs, and doctrines that political actors may espouse. Machiavelli teaches the art of manipulating appearances because men care passionately about the issue of domination versus freedom and need the illusion of being free from domination. But Machiavelli does not think that men have a need to believe in the *truth* of their opinions because such belief is not the reason they hold their opinions or trust in a leader. Hence he has no technical theory of "opinion" and no real interest in the distinction between opinion and knowledge. The study of politics remains for him an art, a teaching about prudence and the manipulation of passions, rather than a "science of justice."

Hobbes is more naive and at the same time more cynical. He thinks men really do believe in the opinions they espouse: they believe that their opinions are true, that their opinions are in accordance with reality, and they seek to impose their opinions on others to make others acknowledge their truth. The irony is that men will believe anything is true or, stated differently, that their actual choice of opinions is accidental and arbitrary. What most amazes Hobbes is that politics is a life-and-death struggle about opinions that consist of incomprehensible speech (obscure religious doctrines, metaphysical abstractions, rhetorical exaggerations, legalistic terminology) that men actually think are true and take with the utmost seriousness. As he shows in *Behemoth*, it is not exploitation per se but the accusation of "heresy" or "false doctrine" or the word "tyrant" that most excites the passions and arouses men to political action. By accusing the established authorities of heretical opinions, the intellectual elites mobilize the masses against their rivals and foment rebellion. This is the tragedy and folly of doctrinal politics, in Hobbes's view.

To explain this extraordinary phenomenon, Hobbes has developed a methodical analysis of "opinion" which separates the elements of opinion into speech and mental thoughts, on the one hand, and the passions that cause men to believe that they are true, on the other. These passions, then, are not merely political passions, expressing a desire for domination and freedom from domination, but "passions of the mind," which convince men of the rightness and truth of what they say. Hobbes, of course, does not deny Machiavelli's fundamental point that the conflicting claims of parties, sects, and regimes disguise an underlying uniformity in men's passions. Hobbes simply thinks that people actually believe these claims. Hence an analysis of the passions must reflect the paradoxical phenomenon of sincere belief and utter indifference to the content of belief. This insight turns Hobbes's psychology of fear and glory into an explanation of why the mind tends to believe that opinions taken on trust in human authorities must have their origin in superhuman authorities, in authorities that exist independently of the human will.

The Metaphysical Assumptions of Opinion

Hobbes's psychology, in other words, is really an attempt to explain the metaphysical assumptions of opinion. For the vast majority of men—the "common people" or the "vulgar," as Hobbes calls them—such assumptions are caused by fear. In explaining this point, one must be careful to distinguish two types of fear; for one kind inclines the human mind to trust in authority, another leads it to distrust authority. The first kind is treated in Hobbes's discussion of the "natural seeds of religion," a classic statement of the view that religion is a form of superstition arising from fear and ignorance. When one feels anxiety about the future and gnawing fears about death or harm, and when one does not understand the causes of good and evil fortune, the mind turns to religion. It takes dreams or imaginations of ghosts and spirits to be real and supposes them to be the causes of things. In this way fear is the origin of "opinions concerning the nature of powers invisible" (*Leviathan*, ch. 12, pp. 98–99). In addition to creating the belief in powers invisible, fear and ignorance incline many men to surrender their minds to authority; for "when [a man] cannot assure himself of the true cause of things, (. . . the causes of good and evil fortune [being] for the most part invisible), he supposes causes of them, either such as his own fancy suggesteth; or he trusteth the authority of other men, such as he thinks to be his friends, and wiser than himself" (*Leviathan*, ch. 12, p. 94). Because of this tendency, religious opinions are not usually limited to the individual imagination but are the products of priests, prophets, and others with reputations for wisdom. Fear, in other words, inclines the human mind to trust not only in the reality of its mental images but also in the wisdom of other men. Fear creates trust or belief in human authorities who claim to speak for divine authorities.

Fear, however, is merely the "seed" of religion. It explains why the vast majority of men are prone to believe that invisible powers are the causes of things and to trust those who seem to have privileged insight about such powers. But why do the authorities themselves believe that they have such privileged knowledge? Why do they think that they have a superior right to proclaim what is right and true for those who trust in them? In Hobbes's view, it is not usually the cynical pursuit of power that leads the intellectual authorities to make such claims, although admittedly some have done so in the course of civil history. Most priests, philosophers, and other learned men are perfectly sincere in the claim that they are wiser than everyone else and deserve to be trusted as spokesmen for impersonal higher authorities—such as God, Nature, or custom—that exist independently of the human will. Such men may benefit from the trusting tendency of the common people, but they too are merely trusting in authorities that are higher than themselves. To explain their behavior, Hobbes uses the psychology of intellectual vanity or vainglory.

We have already seen that Hobbes alludes to the passion of intellectual vainglory in many places in his historical writings and scientific treatises as the desire to display one's wisdom and learning, usually through the arts and sciences of speech. In *Behemoth* he points to intellectual vanity as the motive of those who led the rebellion: "Certainly the chief leaders were ambitious ministers and ambitious gentlemen; the ministers envying the authority of the bishops, whom they thought less learned, and the gentlemen envying the (king's] privy-council, whom they thought less wise than themselves" (p. 192). In *De Cive* Hobbes uses this psychology to explain the motivation of demagogues, orators, and party leaders; they undertake the ordeal of public life solely for the "trial of wits . . . [which is] an uncertain trial of a little vainglory, . . . and causes them to hate and be hated by reason of the disagreement of opinions" (x.9). And the psychology of intellectual vainglory underlies Hobbes's statement in *Leviathan* that certain animals are more sociable than men because "they want the art of words, by which some men can represent to others, that which is good in the likeness of evil" and because "man is most troublesome, when he is most at ease: for then it is that he loves to shew his wisdom" (ch. 17, p. 157). Finally, it is this psychology that underlies Hobbes's entire critique of the "vain" and pernicious philosophy of Aristotle and the Schools. In order to understand Hobbes's psychology of intellectual vanity, we must first examine his general description of vanity and then consider the specific connection between vanity and speech.[4]

In his observations on vainglory or vanity, Hobbes repeatedly emphasizes two characteristics. The first is a feeling of superiority to other men, arising from a belief that one is specially favored by Providence or Nature. We may call this aspect of vanity the feeling of special election. The second characteristic is a sense of insecurity, leading to a desire for confirmation of one's superiority by the honor and esteem of other men. We may call this the need for recognition. These two characteristics are the key to Hobbes's psychology of vainglory and can be seen in the following accounts of human behavior.

Men's actions, Hobbes observes, are extremely varied in their goals and methods. Yet on closer inspection, all betray a common underlying motive: a search for signs or marks of superiority. When

4. The role of vanity in Hobbes's political philosophy is developed by Strauss, *Political Philosophy of Hobbes*, pp. 6–29. Yet Strauss has not fully elaborated the relation of vanity to Hobbes's historical analysis of political phenomena or to the illusions of speech. Strauss, therefore, tends to link vanity to imagination—to imagination of power—rather than to speech, which is "vain" precisely because it lacks mental thoughts or imagination. "On the Basis of Hobbes's Political Philosophy," in *What Is Political Philosophy?* (New York: Free Press, 1959), p. 176n.

men experience good luck, they regard it as a sign of "the secret working of God" (*Leviathan*, ch. 10, p. 74). Hence men love to watch the shuffling of cards when they gamble and to admire novelties of all kinds because they seem to portend favors from above (*Elements*, I, 9.18). Similarly, physical beauty or form usually causes "an excessive opinion of one's own self" because it seems like a kind of natural selection (*Leviathan*, ch. 8, p. 62). And laughter, Hobbes observes, is "sudden glory arising from a sudden conception of some eminency in ourselves, by comparison with the infirmity of others" (*Elements*, I, 9.13). Even in the pursuit of wealth, men are driven not by greed but by a search for signs of superiority, especially intellectual superiority; for growing rich is a testimony to unusual shrewdness. Indeed, success in all enterprises is sought not because the attainment of the ends is intrinsically desirable but because it is a mark of superiority (*De Corpore*, Preface). From these observations Hobbes concludes that the "principal defect of mind . . . [is the] imagination of some *predominancy* above the *rest*, that we have *no passion but from it*, . . . [which] is nothing else but excessive *vain glory*" (*Elements*, I, 10.9; Hobbes's emphasis). Thus Hobbes sees vainglory pervading all human endeavors as a superstitious feeling that signs or marks of distinction indicate divine or natural favor.

This feeling of superiority, however, is usually accompanied by a sense of insecurity because the signs or marks of distinction are not sufficient evidence of superiority. Hobbes remarks that laughter "is vainglory [because it is] an argument of little worth, to think the infirmity of another, sufficient matter for triumph" (*Elements*, I, 9.13). Hence hobbes defines vainglory as a "feigning or supposing of abilities in ourselves, which we know are not" (*Leviathan*, ch. 6, p. 46). He also observes that because a vain man lives by pretense, he has a compelling need for recognition—for the honor and esteem of other men—in order to confirm his own uncertain opinion of his worth. Such a man "looketh that his companion should value him, at the same rate he sets upon himself: and upon all signs of contempt, or undervaluing, naturally endeavors . . . to extort a greater value from his contemners, by damage; and others, by example" (*Leviathan*, ch. 13, p. 112). Vainglory, in sum, is a feeling of superiority based on a "false estimate" of one's abilities and sufficiency, leading to a need for confirmation by the flattery, praise, or agreement of other men.

This description explains why Hobbes makes a fundamental distinction in his treatises between vainglory on the one hand and "true glory," or magnanimity, on the other. Both passions arise from a feeling of superiority; but they differ radically in the signs of superiority and the means by which it is confirmed. As Hobbes says: "Vainglorious men, [are] such as estimate their sufficiency by the flattery of other men, . . . without assured ground of hope from the true knowledge of themselves" (*Leviathan*, ch. 11, p. 89). A vain man, in other words, relies on the recognition of others for confirmation of his worth and sufficiency; he relies on "the fame and trust of others, whereby one may think well of himself and yet be deceived." By contrast, Hobbes says, "Magnanimity is no more than glory, . . . but glory well grounded upon certain experience of a power sufficient to attain his end in an open manner" (*Elements*, 1, 9.20). A magnanimous man, in other words, does not depend on the recognition of others to confirm his sense of superiority; it is "well-grounded upon certain experience of power" and on "true knowledge of himself." The difference is one of self-sufficiency. Vainglory arises from signs that lack certain evidence of superiority, creating a need for recognition by other men. Magnanimity arises from certain experience of power, which can be confirmed simply by self-knowledge, without requiring the honor and esteem of other men. Accordingly, magnanimity is most characteristic of statesmen, kings, and military conquerors, whose sense of superiority is based on the possession and exercise of genuine command. By contrast, vainglory is most incident to intellectuals, whose sense of superiority is based on claims of wisdom and learning, especially in the arts and sciences of speech.

Intellectuals and those with intellectual pretensions are proud but insecure because their feeling of superiority is based on the cultivation of speech, which, of all the signs or marks of distinction, is the one that most captivates and beguiles the human mind. Indeed, the cultivation of speech produces defects of mind that Hobbes classifies among the forms of madness. One kind is "spiritual madness," whereby men without sufficient evidence believe that their words are inspired by God. It is most often found in "sick-brained men, who having gotten good store of holy words by frequent reading of the Scriptures, make such connexion of them . . . that their sermons, signifying just nothing, yet seem divine" (*De Cive*, x.9). According to Hobbes, the belief that one is divinely inspired arises from signs and marks that human vanity interprets to be miracles from above. Hence men do not need interruptions of the regular order of Nature to believe that they have miraculous powers, as Spinoza argues.[5] Rather, Hobbes suggests, men see the miraculous hand of

5. See Benedict de Spinoza, *A Theologico-Political Treatise*, in *The Chief Works of Spinoza*, trans. R. H. M. Elwes (New York: Dover, 1951), I, ch. 6, "Of Miracles."

God in strange and obscure speech. Such speech (without extraordinary events) seems to be the miracle of miracles; it, more than
anything else, stimulates the human mind to believe in special election. For the height of vanity is reached when a man believes that
"the first cause of the whole [universe] has spoken to him."[6]

Another form of intellectual vainglory is "learned madness,"
which is found most commonly in philosophers and Schoolmen,
"who speak in such words, as put together, have in them no signification at all" (*Elements*, 1, 10.9). For they take the emptiness of their
words to be a sign that words correspond to "abstract essences" in
Nature which are immaterial and hence do not have visible and sensible appearances in the mind. Hobbes treats men of both sorts as
mad because they take the very obscurity and emptiness of their
words to be signs of special favor—signs that their speech has supernatural or natural support and that they are intellectually superior
to others.

Hobbes describes the effect of this delusion in chapter 8 of *Leviathan*, titled "Of the Virtues commonly called Intellectual; and their
Contrary Defects." Here he says that spiritual and learned madness
issue from pride or vainglory, "the excess whereof is the madness
called RAGE and FURY. And thus it comes to pass that . . . excessive opinion of a man's own self, for divine inspiration, wisdom,
learning, form, and the like, becomes distraction and giddiness: the
same joined with envy, rage: *vehement opinion of the truth of anything,
contradicted by others, rage*" (*Leviathan*, ch. 8, p. 64; emphasis added).
In this account Hobbes maintains that those who think that they are
divinely inspired or wise are suffering from an excess of self-love,
from a feeling that they have been specially chosen by God or
Nature to reveal the truth or the right way to men. This feeling
makes them insist on having their opinions recognized by others and
drives them to rage when they are contradicted. What drives them
to impose on others, we may infer, is the very vagueness of their
speech: because it lacks evidence or corresponding mental thoughts,
it drives them to seek confirmation in the agreement of other men.

Hobbes's psychology of intellectual vainglory, therefore, is far
more than a portrait of a certain human type. It is the premise of
his entire philosophical system because it explains the fundamental
illusion of the human mind: the belief that words are derived from
higher authorities and hence do not need to be accompanied by
clear mental thoughts in order to be understood. One only needs to
trust in the authority of the speaker, either in one's own authority or

6. Strauss, "On the Basis of Hobbes's Political Philosophy," p. 181.

in that of another man, whose unclear words are themselves signs or marks of superior wisdom. When that authority is not recognized, as inevitably it is not when signs are disputable, the speaker is led to impose his words dogmatically on others in order to gain recognition and confirmation. But such behavior is vain; it overestimates the power of speech to uncover the truth and to secure agreement. The human mind is simply deluded by its own self-love into thinking that words correspond to reality and will be supported without the accompaniment of clear mental thoughts and, ultimately, without the force of arms.

With this insight we reach the conclusion of Hobbes's methodical analysis of opinion. By resolving opinion into its constituent elements, Hobbes is able to identify precisely the immediate cause (the inexact usage of words) and the underlying cause (the vanity of trusting in superhuman support for speech) that make opinion and reasoning from opinion inherently disputable. It must be emphasized, however, that this analysis in no way entitles Hobbes to make a judgment about the existence of the higher authorities that the mind is so ready to trust. The fact that men attribute their speech to entities such as God, Nature, and custom, whose signs of support are lacking, says nothing about whether they exist or do not exist, whether they are material or immaterial. It simply means that higher authorities have no observable effect in determining which opinions and doctrines will prevail in the human mind. It is a comment about the effective power of superhuman beings in human affairs rather than a judgment about the existence of such beings. But it does permit Hobbes to treat opinion as an artificial phenomenon, as something that is created and sustained by human agency.

At the same time, the methodical analysis of opinion raises a difficult problem for Hobbes. It elevates his critique of traditional politics and science to a new level, translating historical observations into timeless categories of speech and psychology. Yet it does not indicate how to overcome the disputability of opinion or the disputes of doctrinal politics. Indeed, the translation of historical observations into universal and timeless categories (such as speech, thought, and passion) seems to compound the difficulty of finding a solution. For it suggests that the root cause of the problem, the passion of intellectual vainglory, is a permanent feature of human nature. If this is the case, how can intellectual vanity and the deeply rooted tendency of the human mind to trust in authority be overcome and eventually be eliminated? To answer this question, we shall turn to Hobbes's theory of enlightenment.

»4«

The Science of Enlightenment

What Is Enlightenment?

Hobbes's political thought, I have argued, begins with historical reflection on the fragility of civilization. His central insight is the dependence of civilized life on authoritative wisdom, embodied not only in received opinions and traditions but also in the philosophical and theological doctrines of the Western world which are derived by reasoning from opinion. This development has led to the problem of doctrinal politics, the multiplicity of doctrines competing for recognition, each claiming to be the only right and true doctrine or the final expression of right reason. The lesson of civil history for Hobbes is that preexisting civilization is defective because it is continuously exposed to the doctrinal wars of intellectual authorities and their followers.

The second major step in Hobbes's reasoning is the movement from history to methodical analysis: the translation of historical observations about the problem of "opinion" into a logical and psychological analysis that abstracts from the content of particular opinions and resolves opinion *as such* into the constituent elements of speech, thoughts, and passions. In the course of this analysis, Hobbes shows that opinion and doctrines derived from opinion are inherently controversial because they consist of words borrowed on trust from human authorities without clear thoughts in the mind. The root cause of this problem is the passion of intellectual vainglory, which creates the illusion that the inexact speech of human authorities comes from higher authorities and will be supported by divine or natural powers.

The historical and methodical analysis thus outlined enables Hobbes to entertain a possibility that previous thinkers might have

95

considered an impossible dream: the possibility of refounding civilization on an indisputable basis and of creating thereby an everlasting commonwealth. Hobbes realizes, of course, that the whole project depends on the answer to a single but momentous question: Is it possible to overcome the passion of intellectual vanity and the historic tendency of the human mind to trust in the words and wisdom of authority? For Hobbes, as well as for many of his contemporaries and successors, the answer lies in a new conception of science—a kind of science that Hobbes compares to the task of "bringing light to the kingdom of darkness" and that later scholars would call (undoubtedly with Hobbes's metaphor in mind) "the scientific enlightenment." Hence we must now ask: What is enlightenment?

A preliminary answer might begin with some observations by Kant, a philosopher who in many ways is an opponent of Hobbes but who also is an heir to Hobbes's vision of enlightenment as a means to everlasting peace. Kant provides some help because one century after Hobbes he posed the question—What is enlightenment?—and answered it in unforgettable words: "Enlightenment is man's release from his self-incurred tutelage. Tutelage is man's inability to make use of his understanding without direction from another. Self-incurred is this tutelage when its cause lies not in lack of reason but in lack of resolution and courage to use it without direction from another. *Sapere aude!* [Dare to know!] 'Have the courage to use your own reason'—that is the motto of enlightenment."[1] The definition of enlightenment proposed by Kant is simple and direct: to be enlightened is to think for oneself, to use one's mind without direction from another.

In defending and encouraging this new way of thinking, however, Kant clearly recognizes that it would not be established without a change of historic proportions. The tendency of the human mind throughout history, among the philosophers as well as ordinary people, has been opposed to enlightenment. The deepest and strongest tendency of the mind has not been to think independently but to trust in authority: to defer to the judgment of those thought to be wiser or more holy than oneself, to follow received opinion hallowed by the name of tradition and made sacred by ancestor worship, or to follow the advice of experts in technical matters that laymen cannot understand. Thus, Kant acknowledges, "For any single individual to work himself out of the life under tutelage *which has become almost his nature* is very difficult. He has come to be fond

1. From the essay "What Is Enlightenment?" in Immanuel Kant, *On History*, ed. and trans. Lewis White Beck (Indianapolis: Bobbs-Merrill, 1963), p. 3.

of this state, and he is for the present really incapable of making use of his reason, for no one has ever let him try" (p. 4; emphasis added). To be sure, Kant adds, "there will always be some independent thinkers, even among the established guardians of the great masses, who, after throwing off the yoke of tutelage from their own shoulders, will disseminate the spirit of rational appreciation" to the rest of mankind. But true enlightenment requires an intellectual revolution not only for the intellectual elites; it must also bring a spirit of independent thinking to the ordinary man. And such enlightenment must be so securely established that no relapse into the old habit of tutelage, of surrendering the mind to authority, can occur. Otherwise, Kant warns, "a true reform in ways of thinking" will not be accomplished. Instead, "new prejudices will serve as well as old ones to harness the great unthinking masses" (p. 4).

Kant's statement about enlightenment—his definition of the term, his expression of hope and fear of disillusionment—is a remarkably succinct and clear account of the most important intellectual movement of the modern age. As Kant's words so clearly state, the central issue of enlightenment is a contrast between two ways of thinking: (1) the mental habit of the past, "self-incurred tutelage," or placing one's trust in the authority of others who are thought to be wiser; and (2) the mental habit projected for the future, thinking for oneself or intellectual self-reliance. This statement presents the central issue of enlightenment as a fundamental dualism, an opposition both of historical epochs (the past vs. the future) and of mental habits (trusting authority vs. self-reliance).

By stating the central issue so directly, Kant helps us to understand Hobbes, as well as a host of other modern philosophers who began or advanced the cause of enlightenment.[2] In general terms, Hobbes states the same dualism as the difference between "the kingdom of darkness," which has prevailed in the past, and his own science, which will bring light to the kingdom of darkness (*Leviathan*, ch. 44, p. 604). In more specific terms, Hobbes describes the two ways of thinking as the contrast between following "received opinions" and "the authority of books" versus beginning with one's "own

2. The term "Enlightenment" is most often applied to the philosophes of the eighteenth century. But it should not be used so restrictively. For these philosophers are heirs to the founders of modernity—Bacon, Machiavelli, Descartes, Galileo, Hobbes, Spinoza, Locke—who in the sixteenth and seventeenth centuries sought to overthrow the Aristotelian-Scholastic tradition in the universities and to redefine philosophy or science. This point is acknowledged by Cassirer, who tends to see the Enlightenment as the progressive development of "autonomous reason" which reaches full maturity in the philosophy of Kant. See Ernst Cassirer, *The Philosophy of the Enlightenment* (Boston: Beacon Press, 1955), pp. xi, 3–36.

meditation" and knowing what "we make by ourselves" (*Leviathan*, ch. 4, pp. 24–25); or as the contrast between the method of the "dogmatists" who "take up maxims from their education, and from the authority of men, or of custom, and take the habitual discourse of the tongue for ratiocination" versus the method of the "mathematicians," who "proceed evidently from humble principles" (*Elements*, I, 13.4).

Other formulations of the same dualism by modern philosophers include trust versus radical doubt (Descartes); heteronomy versus autonomy (Kant); conformity versus individuality (Mill); closed society versus open society (Popper); traditional versus rational (Weber). Even opponents of the modern enlightenment tend to use such dualisms: tradition versus abstract reason (Burke); dogmatists versus free spirits (Nietzsche). And in contemporary political language, categories expressing the same dualism are authority versus individualism; backward versus progressive; underdeveloped versus developed; prejudice versus freedom of thought; traditional versus modern. The pervasiveness and familiarity of such dualisms are tributes to the success of the modern enlightenment in changing the way we think about politics as well as the way we think about thinking.

Indeed, the easy acceptance of such categories makes it difficult to recover the preenlightenment categories of thought which the modern enlightenment rejected and sought to overcome. As we have seen from Hobbes's history of civilization, the preenlightenment world frames the whole question of political authority and political science differently. It is based on the claim that there exists an authoritative standard of right and truth above the human will which requires the mediation of human authorities—priests, philosophers, and other wise men—to interpret for the rest of society. The point of contention in such societies is not whether such an authoritative definition exists but *which* definition (Catholic or Protestant? monarchist or democratic?) should be recognized as right, true, or orthodox. The claim of the Enlightenment philosophers is that such a view leads necessarily to persecution and sectarian warfare (the self-destruction of civilization) and to the enslavement of the mind to authorities whose claim to superiority seems to rest on little more than their own self-appointment. Accordingly, the enlightenment thinkers seek to replace the whole notion of 'higher authority mediated by human authority' and to found civil society on the self-reliant mind, the individual mind freed from all trust in authority, or the constructs of autonomous reason. Enlightenment thereby transforms the fundamental political question from 'Which authority should rule?' to 'Why should there be authority at all?' The task of political science (which we shall later consider) is to found the state on the newly emancipated, self-reliant mind.

In seeking to revolutionize the way people think about authority, the philosophers of the Enlightenment faced a paradox. They recognized that the refounding of civilization required a complete obliteration of the old way of thinking; they had to wipe the slate clean and begin anew. But they acknowledged that enlightenment could take place only at an advanced stage of civilization, when the notion of science itself was already established and could become the means of emancipating the human mind, especially the minds of the common people, from the influence of the clergy and other traditional authorities. The precise mechanism for such emancipation would be the bastions of traditional learning themselves, the universities. The first priority would be the development of a new concept of science or philosophy that would replace the traditional sciences (Aristotelianism, Scholastic theology, the jurisprudence of the common law) and the reeducation of the intellectual authorities themselves. Once the intellectual elites were converted to the new way of thinking, they would diffuse such learning to the public at large.

The project for enlightenment thus turns on a paradoxical need to develop a new set of intellectual authorities whose message will be to question and challenge authority, indeed to reject authority as such in favor of independent, self-reliant thinking. This paradox produces the familiar but strange phenomenon of anti-authority authorities that pervade the modern world: teachers who teach their students to distrust all teachers and to think for themselves (the prototype of the modern university professor); leaders who warn the people to distrust all leaders and to decide for themselves (the Jeffersonian model of leadership); modern societies that originate in rebellion against tradition and then inculcate a "revolutionary tradition" in future generations (the American and French as well as the Russian, Chinese, and Third World revolutionary traditions); and even the state itself in liberal societies which uses public education to indoctrinate its citizens in self-reliant thinking.

Despite these paradoxes, the proponents of enlightenment claim that their doctrine is not simply another form of dogmatism, requiring blind trust and imposing a new orthodoxy on the masses, but a new kind of nondoctrinal doctrine: a notion of science or philosophy that somehow is not really a doctrine in the traditional sense but a means for liberating the mind from all doctrinairism. The ultimate claim, of course, is that an intellectual equivalent of the Archimedean point (a point outside the world which can be used as a leverage point to move the world) can be discovered or created. This point will be one that relies on no external authority and has the power truly to emancipate the human mind for the first time in human history.

The Two Casts of Mind: Trust in Authority vs. Self-Reliance

The science of enlightenment which produces so many strange paradoxes in the modern world is not an easy phenomenon to grasp. It claims to make a historic break with all previous thinking but in fact does not constitute a wholesale rejection of the rationalism of classical antiquity. According to Socrates, Plato, and Aristotle, the essence of philosophy is to question the conventional opinions and authoritative wisdom of society in the name of a higher kind of intellectual enlightenment. For this reason, Hobbes's metaphor for enlightenment science—bringing light to the kingdom of darkness—may very well have been inspired by Plato's image of the philosopher ascending from the darkness of the cave to see the light of the sun. And Kant's motto, "Dare to know," as well as his call for critical thinking about authority, would hardly seem objectionable to the classical philosophers. If one looks only on the surface, one may be tempted to see the Enlightenment as a revival of Greek rationalism, a struggle against the religious superstition of the Dark Ages and an awakening of the old philosophical spirit in the newly educated masses.

Although the attack on superstition and the popular diffusion of rational knowledge are dominant themes of the Enlightenment, it would be misleading to see this movement simply as a kind of democratization of classical philosophy. For the Enlightenment involves a radical redefinition of philosophy or science which is directed not only against religious superstition and medieval Scholasticism but also against the classical tradition of philosophy—against "the kingdom of darkness *and vain philosophy*," as Hobbes emphatically states. The Enlightenment philosophers as a whole, and Hobbes perhaps more than any other, aim at a historic change that eradicates the fundamental attitude or general cast of mind underlying all traditional modes of reasoning.[3]

3. The importance of the Enlightenment for Hobbes's political science has received renewed attention in a recent noteworthy study by David Johnston, *The Rhetoric of "Leviathan": Thomas Hobbes and the Politics of Cultural Transformation* (Princeton: Princeton University Press, 1986). Johnston demonstrates with admirable clarity that

As we have seen, the traditional form of philosophy or science—developed by the classical, Scholastic, and common law traditions—is dialectical. It is an intellectual movement that begins by "trusting" in opinion, by recognizing that there is no way to begin thinking other than by reflecting on conventional or commonly received opinions. The claim of dialectics is that one cannot begin thinking without already knowing something, and that even the most ordinary opinions are helpful because they contain some intuition or divination of the way things really are. More precisely, dialectical science begins by assuming that ordinary speech and common-sense perceptions in some way reflect the "essences" and "attributes" of things as they truly are in the natural or divinely created order. Dialectical science then seeks to ascend from such opinions, by questioning and testing and continual revision of original premises, to final and genuine knowledge of things as they really are. Traditional philosophy or science rests, therefore, on a distinction between opinion and knowledge, which ultimately establishes a metaphysical distinction between seeming and being or appearance and reality.

In distinguishing opinion from knowledge, however, dialectical reasoning does not view these categories as poles of a strict dualism or antithesis. Opinion and knowledge are not absolutely opposed to each other but exist on a continuum. Opinion contains within it, by virtue of intuition or a kind of divination that seems like dim recollection, elements of truth. Likewise, the final product, true knowledge, bears some of the patterns of opinion. Hence Plato's ultimate grounds of reality, the invisible and intangible forms, mirror the patterns of speech and common sense. And the cosmology of Aristotle accords with the common-sense view of the earth at rest at the center of the universe, just as his whole teleological way of thinking draws ideas of natural perfection from ordinary notions of what is healthy and normal.

The revolutionary aim of enlightenment science, by contrast, is to build a theory of knowledge *without beginning from opinion.* Enlightenment science rejects the need and the desirability of trusting in the speech and common-sense perceptions that make up opinion. It

---

Hobbes's project of scientific enlightenment is "linked to a specific historical moment" and undertakes a historic "cultural transformation" (pp. 120–133). But he treats this transformation too narrowly as the struggle of reason against rhetoric and superstition without looking more deeply into the radical redefinition of reason or science which is involved (pp. 61, 92–113). Hobbes's theory of enlightenment is directed not only against the irrationality of rhetoric and superstition but also against every form of reasoning that has prevailed hitherto, including the philosophical tradition of Socrates, Plato, and Aristotle.

therefore attempts to replace the traditional distinction between opinion and knowledge, which is a continuum, with a new dualism of trusting in authority versus thinking for oneself, which is understood to be an absolute antithesis. Indeed, the absolute nature of this antithesis constitutes the claim of enlightenment science to be qualitatively different from traditional scientific doctrines.

According to Strauss, the new antithesis is best captured by the words "prejudice" and "freedom":

> The word 'prejudice' is the most appropriate expression for the dominant theme of the Enlightenment movement, for the will to free, open-minded investigation. . . . [Indeed,] the struggle of the Enlightenment against prejudice has an absolute meaning. For this reason, the age of prejudice and the age of freedom can stand in opposition to one another. For the age of freedom, it is essential that it be preceded by the age of prejudice. *'Prejudice' is an historical category. This precisely constitutes the difference between the struggle of the Enlightenment against prejudices and the struggle against appearance and opinion with which philosophy began its secular journey.*[4]

As this passage reveals, the difference between traditional philosophy or science and modern enlightenment science is subtle but profound. Both believe in the possibility of discovering true or scientific knowledge through rational analysis. Both are rationalist in this sense. But enlightenment science seeks an absolute beginning point outside of opinion (and kindred phenomena, such as belief, trust, faith, prejudice, tradition, custom, habit, common sense, convention, reasoning from authority) and views the traditional attempt to reason from opinion as insufficiently radical. It does so by treating both opinion and traditional science as a *historical category*—as a thing of the past which can be and must be transcended, once and for all times. In other words, enlightenment science seeks to bring about the emancipation of the mind from authoritative opinion by a historical leap rather than by a dialectical ascent. In so doing it introduces an implicit utopian claim: that opinion or prejudice will eventually disappear and be relegated to the past ('the Dark Ages') rather than persist and coexist alongside true knowledge, as the classical philosophers believed.

To support such a utopian claim, enlightenment science must begin with a kind of grand conspiracy theory which shows that the

4. Leo Strauss, *Spinoza's Critique of Religion*, trans. E. M. Sinclair (New York: Schocken, 1965), pp. 178, 181; emphasis added.

human mind hitherto has been kept in the dark. It must argue, in effect, that the mind has been deceived about reality since the beginning of human history. This demonstration usually takes the form of a typology of two types of mind which are absolutely opposed to each other: the unenlightened mind of the past and the enlightened mind of the future. These two casts of mind, of course, are known prior to or independently of enlightenment science itself. They are grasped by reflection on experience, both historical and personal, and constitute the prescientific psychological teaching upon which the science proper is built.

For the founders of the Enlightenment—thinkers such as Bacon, Hobbes, Descartes, Spinoza, and Locke—their dissatisfaction with Scholastic training in the universities and the challenges posed by the Copernican-Galilean revolution in natural philosophy led them to reflect on the question of the progress of the arts and sciences since classical antiquity, and more generally on the question of the historical development of the human mind. They wondered: Did the failure of the Aristotelian-Scholastic tradition to produce certain knowledge, as well as the contemporary experience of doctrinal politics and sectarian wars, and the stunning successes of Galileo in showing that the order of the universe is contrary to its appearance in common sense, suggest that the whole way of thinking hitherto was untrustworthy? These thinkers faced a radical possibility. Perhaps someone or something has deceived the mind since the beginning of human history, keeping it in the dark. Perhaps it is given to a few men at this historic moment (the sixteenth and seventeenth centuries in the Western world) to see the light for the first time.

These momentous thoughts explain their interest in method, in rules for correct thinking that would help them consciously, even willfully, to resist the temptations that have deceived or misled the mind throughout history. Hence we find such works as Bacon's *Advancement of Learning* (1605); Descartes's *Rules for the Direction of the Mind* (1628) and the *Discourse on Method* (1637); Spinoza's *On the Improvement of the Understanding: A Treatise on the Correction of the Understanding and on the Way in Which It May Be Directed toward a True Knowledge of Things* (1663); Hobbes's thoughts on method in *De Corpore*, chapters 1–14 (1640s); and Locke's *Essay on Human Understanding* (1680s) and *Conduct of the Understanding* (1690s). While presenting various rules of method or correct thinking, these works presuppose something prior to and more fundamental than method, namely, an analysis that contrasts two types of mind and their characteristic ways of thinking: the unenlightened mind of the past, which has been deceived by its trust in authority, conventional speech, and the testimony of the senses; and the enlightened mind, which will be freed from all such deceptions and will accept as trustworthy only deductions from evident conceptions of the mind. While all the philosophers of the Enlightenment presuppose the same fundamental dualism of mental types and all present essentially psychological explanations of the two casts of mind, not all point to the same passions as the causes of unenlightened and enlightened thinking. A comparison of Descartes and Hobbes will illustrate this point.

For Descartes, as we noted earlier, the two fundamental ways of thinking are expressed by the opposition of trust and radical doubt. The tendency to trust is the cause of the most fundamental human error or deception, the belief that Nature really exists in the way it appears to the human mind through the senses. The senses seem to suggest that things exist in Nature independently of our perception of them, that we are not simply dreaming or deluded when we think that the world of objects 'out there' is real. The senses also suggest that those objects possess as part of their 'natures' certain kinds of qualities, attributes, or accidents (color, size, weight, place, etc.) and that there is some kind of similarity or correspondence between our perception of the qualities and the qualities themselves. But, Descartes asks, is there any way we can know for certain that the senses can be trusted? His answer is no. The senses frequently deceive us in suggesting, for example, that distant objects are smaller than those that are nearby, in imagining and dreaming things that do not exist, in sensations of pleasure and pain that prove to be illusory. Thus there is no way of knowing with certainty that the teaching of the senses about the deepest question, the ultimate nature of reality, is trustworthy.

Yet trust in the teaching of the senses is the most common and ordinary assumption of human life. According to Descartes, it has two origins that are universal and inescapable, the experiences of childhood and the necessary assumptions of practical action. As young children, before we can possibly be "enlightened" about such matters, and as acting persons who must navigate the world, we necessarily presuppose the existence of objects outside the mind and a similitude between the qualities of objects and our perceptions of them.[5] These unproven beliefs arise naturally; no human authority has tricked us or fooled us into believing such things. Thus, even

5. "The Principles of Philosophy," in *The Philosophical Works of Descartes*, trans. Elizabeth S. Haldane and G. R. T. Ross, 2 vols. (Cambridge: Cambridge University Press, 1969), I, principles 1, 66, 71.

though Descartes mentions both teachers and senses as causes of our deceptions about Nature, the role of teachers, and hence the role of words, speech, and language, is secondary. Words (and the Aristotelian and Scholastic philosophies that reason from words) merely reinforce the deceptions that already are present in habits that have grown from trusting in the senses.[6] For Descartes, neither illusions of speech nor deceptions by human authority are the primary cause of our unfounded trust in common opinion. The primary reason is that "our mind [is] so immersed in the body." Thus Descartes traces the cause of our darkness and blindness not so much to a conspiracy of human authorities as to the physical limits our body imposes on the mind in childhood and in everyday action. Or, as one recent scholar elegantly states, "the human body is the cave" for Descartes.[7]

In regarding the human body as the cave, Descartes is pointing to the feeling of limitation, dependence, and vulnerability of the body as the primary experience. This experience is the origin of fear, the passion most responsible for trust in the teaching of the senses. Fear is a loss of hope and confidence, a feeling of fatalism or dependence on things that are out of our control.[8] Fear leads to trust in appearances because it creates weak minds, minds that take what is given by the world and that take for granted our dependence on things outside of our power. Such weak minds trust in appearances because they cannot conceive of mastery, either mastery of their minds or mastery of the world. By contrast, the process of enlightenment, the process of overcoming the natural fear that makes one trust, requires a strong mind.[9] The radical doubt of enlightenment—the resolve to doubt everything—requires mental courage and resoluteness. Such intellectual qualities are inspired by the passion of generosity or magnanimity, a feeling of justified pride, a feeling of confidence in the mastery of one's passions and the challenges of

6. Ibid., principles 72–74.
7. Ibid., principle 47; Richard Kennington, "The 'Teaching of Nature' in Descartes' Soul Doctrine," *Review of Metaphysics*, 26 (1972), p. 100. See also James Collins, *Descartes' Philosophy of Nature* (Oxford: Blackwell, 1971), p. 58: Descartes's "criticism falls upon abusive infancy, upon an age of childhood which is unduly prolonged for the individual and the human race. . . . But Descartes is not despairing. . . . In our very recognition of naively realist and sensist concepts of nature as being instances of arrested reflection, we can assign them to the childhood beliefs of the human race and can look forward to a growth beyond the first age of man in nature."
8. "The Passions of the Soul," pt. 3, art. 165–166, in *Philosophical Works of Descartes*, I.
9. Ibid., pt. 1, art. 48–49.

the world.[10] In short, Descartes correlates trust with weak and fearful minds, radical doubt with strong and generous minds. (Kant also seems to associate the self-incurred tutelage of the unenlightened mind with cowardice and weakness, while viewing independent thinking as the product of courage, daring, and resolution.)[11]

When we turn to Hobbes, we see a different account of the passions responsible for the two fundamental casts of mind. As Strauss has shown, Hobbes's whole system rests on the antithesis of vanity and fear: "Vanity is the force which makes men blind, while fear is the force which makes men see."[12] This view seems to be exactly the reverse of Descartes's position. The cause of darkness for Hobbes is vanity, while Descartes points to fear. The source of enlightenment for Hobbes is fear, while Descartes points to pride or magnanimity. How can one account for the different explanations of apparently similar mental phenomena?

One answer is that Hobbes's position is a bit more complicated than Strauss's quote suggests. As we noted earlier, Hobbes admits the existence of two kinds of fear. One kind of fear is "the natural seed of religion"—the anxiety about future harm or benefit, which causes one to believe in demons and ghosts and powers invisible. Such fear of death or harm, when joined with ignorance of causes, leads to "trust"—to believing that dreams and imaginations are real and to surrendering one's mind to the authority of priests, prophets, and wise men. In this respect, Hobbes's explanation of trust is close to that of Descartes.

But Hobbes argues that fear is merely the "seed" of religion. There is also the "culture" of religion, its development into doctrines and institutions by men, especially by those who cultivate the arts and sciences of speech. Because the culture is so much more powerful than the natural seeds, the fear of invisible powers which arises from imagination is secondary to the belief in inspired speech as a cause of faith and trust. Thus, Hobbes says, though we imagine and dream of ghosts and attribute to them real existence as "external substances," the "opinion that such spirits are incorporeal . . . could never enter the mind of man by nature . . . [but only by] words of contradictory signification" (*Leviathan*, ch. 12, p. 89). In short, Hobbes holds that the primary deception of mind is caused not by sensation and imagination but by speech: the belief that

10. Ibid., pt. 3, art. 156.
11. See the statement in Kant, "What Is Enlightenment?" p. 3.
12. Strauss, *The Political Philosophy of Hobbes*, p. 130.

speech corresponds to reality, that universal terms refer to abstract essences, immaterial bodies, or suprasensible universals in Nature.

To account for the trust in speech, Hobbes develops the psychology of intellectual vanity. He seems to think that the passion of fear explains certain kinds of mental deceptions (primarily those of sense and imagination), but the most important and pervasive illusions about reality arise from speech and are really forms of self-love—the longing of the mind to believe that Nature is made intelligible through language about essences and qualities, or the longing of the mind to believe that the First Cause of the universe speaks to it. These are forms of madness that go beyond a superstitious belief in ghosts to a belief in the harmony of mind and reality. This belief is an ultimate trust in the beneficence of the divine and natural order—the trust that Providence or Nature cares for the human mind and particularly for human speech. Such ultimate trust is more closely akin to vainglory than to fear.

In emphasizing the deceptions of speech over those of sense and imagination, Hobbes diverges from Descartes in his account of the passions. Another consequence of this point is that Hobbes views the darkness of the mind as a *human error* rather than as a natural error. Since speech is created by human authorities and attributed to higher authorities for the purpose of dominating others, the use of speech reflects a willful, human desire for recognition of superiority. This, too, must be attributed to vainglory rather than to superstitious fear. Indeed, vainglory is so powerful and pervasive that it actually supersedes fear as the dominant passion of the mind, not only among the intellectual elites but also among ordinary men when they are exposed to the arts and sciences of speech. Thus Hobbes departs from Descartes in his emphasis on trust in speech as the primary deception of the mind and on vainglory as the dominant passion of all unenlightened minds.

Nothing illustrates the difference between Descartes and Hobbes more clearly than their views of who or what has deceived the human mind throughout history. Each has a different conspiracy theory. Descartes suggests that the deception involved in trusting the senses may be likened to the act of an "evil genius" or an "evil demon," by which he means an evil god operating through natural forces. Descartes's idea of the deception of the senses as a natural error, not a human error, suggests a divine deceiver rather than a human one.[13] For Hobbes, however, the deception of the human

13. "Meditations on First Philosophy," in *Philosophical Works of Descartes*, I, 148.

mind is almost entirely a human error, a conspiracy of men seeking to dominate others by controlling their minds. Thus Hobbes defines the "kingdom of darkness" as a "*confederacy of deceivers,* that to obtain dominion over men in this present world, endeavor by dark and erroneous doctrines, to extinguish in them the light, both of nature and of the gospel" (*Leviathan,* ch. 44, p. 604; emphasis added). Hobbes's description of the darkness of erroneous doctrines as a conspiracy of deceivers makes the whole predicament a human responsibility in which human beings are to blame, while Descartes's hypothetical divine deceiver makes it more of an impersonal problem in which no one in particular is to blame.

These differences between Descartes and Hobbes, of course, are differences of degree rather than of kind. Both point to the illusions of speech and sensation as causes of mental darkness. But Descartes points to the senses first and speech second, while Hobbes blames speech first and sense (as well as imagination) second. Such differences between Hobbes and Descartes, we may infer, are due primarily to differences of observation. Hobbes derives his observations from civil history, from historical reflections that are essentially political in character, while Descartes derives his insight primarily from personal experience. Thus Hobbes focuses on the role of human authorities as intermediaries in knowledge, on speech as the main source of belief, and on vainglory as the main cause of erroneous thinking. Descartes, on the other hand, draws an unforgettable portrait of himself in the "Discourse on Method" sitting all alone in his stove-heated room, resolved to doubt everything; there he sees from personal introspection the dependency of the mind on the body in early childhood and the fear and weakness of mind that this dependency breeds, before the influence of education and custom.

Accordingly, Hobbes differs from Descartes on which passion is most likely to bring light to the kingdom of darkness. For Descartes, the passion that leads to enlightenment is a form of pride: magnanimity or generosity provides the strength of mind to doubt all opinions. Interestingly, Hobbes seems to be aware of magnanimity as an antidote to vainglory. As we noted in chapter 3, Hobbes makes an important distinction in his historical works between kings, patriarchs, and military conquerors, who are motivated by a desire for real coercive power or command, and the intellectual authorities, who seek illusory power by controlling opinions and doctrines. This distinction is preserved in Hobbes's scientific treatises as the difference between vainglory—a false estimate of one's power based on the recognition of others—and magnanimity or true glory—a well-grounded confidence based on certain evidence of power. Moreover, it is quite clear that Hobbes sees a significant role for such magnanimous men in the liberation of the world from the influence of vain intellectuals. In *Behemoth* he openly courts the kings and conquerors of the world, daring them to execute seditious ministers in order to prevent future civil wars. And in *Leviathan* he recognizes "commonwealth by acquisition"—the establishment of sovereign power through the natural force of patriarchs and conquerors—as one way of overcoming the traditional reliance of the state on the authoritative doctrines of intellectuals. Thus Hobbes's praise of magnanimity as an "enlightened" passion is consistent with his rejection of vainglory as an "unenlightened" passion and parallels the thought of Descartes.[14]

Yet Hobbes clearly does not think that magnanimity is sufficient to liberate the mind from intellectual vainglory and the widespread trust in authoritative speech. As Strauss convincingly argues, Hobbes ultimately contends that the passion to be relied on is fear, the fear of violent death. We may wonder, however, why this kind of fear is capable of liberating the mind from trust in authority, while the fear of invisible powers enslaves the mind to superstition and blind obedience. Why does Hobbes regard the fear of violent death as the only effective antidote to the illusions of intellectual vainglory?

Here we can only speculate, for Hobbes does not give a detailed or systematic explanation. A clue is provided by the precise meaning of the phrase "fear and danger of violent death" (*Leviathan*, ch. 13, p. 113). Such fear is not simply a general awareness of human mortality or a fear of bodily harm, whatever the cause (for example, disease or starvation). For these kinds of fear are impersonal; their object is not death by violence at the hands of other men, and their effect is most often the enslavement rather than the liberation of the mind.

To understand precisely what Hobbes means by the fear of violent death, we must refer to his historical analysis of civilization. According to that analysis, civilization arises when men have the leisure to cultivate the arts and sciences. These intellectual pursuits give rise to doctrines in speech which some men seek to impose on others, and in their zeal they persecute and destroy those who disagree. For

14. Hobbes's recognition of magnanimity as an "enlightened" passion, however, does not seem to be due to the temporary influence of Descartes, as Strauss suggests in *Political Philosophy of Hobbes*, pp. 56–57. It is a view that Hobbes held throughout his career, not a temporary aberration. (Strauss seems to retract his original suggestion and acknowledges the continuity of Hobbes's view of magnanimity in his later review of Polin's book, "On the Basis of Hobbes's Political Philosophy," p. 196).

civilized men, then, *the fear of violent death is the fear of being persecuted and killed for the disagreement of one's opinions.* Such fear is different from other kinds of fear because it arises from a specific state of historical consciousness. It requires the awareness that previous attempts to answer the question of what is right or true by appeals to higher authorities (God, Nature, or custom) have been vitiated by the need to answer the practical question 'who shall judge?' or 'which human authority shall decide?' Knowledge of right and truth, then, has never been impersonal or disinterested; it has involved the mediation of human authorities—men who are really human deceivers because they lack the superhuman support to have their wisdom prevail without persecuting and destroying others. This distrust of *mediated knowledge* as such is the precise meaning of the "fear of violent death." It is the foundation of enlightenment, according to Hobbes, because it liberates the human mind from trust in authoritative wisdom.

We must emphasize, of course, that such liberation occurs not by refuting the existence of superhuman beings but by denying their effective power in human affairs. Thus experiencing the fear of violent death is not identical to embracing atheism or to denying that superhuman beings exist. Rather, it is a recognition that, whether or not such powers exist, their intervention in human affairs has no direct effect in making men believe or obey. The fear of violent death is closer to a feeling of abandonment by superhuman powers (which may be only one step away from denying their existence) but takes place independently of any metaphysical view of the ultimate nature of reality. Its vital premise is not the radical denial of a Supreme Being or a natural order but a denial of God's providence or Nature's support for the human mind. For Hobbes, then, the fear of violent death is not the same as the anguish and terror of facing the existential abyss; and it does not even require the prior acceptance of a mechanistic view of the universe (although mechanistic materialism may be introduced subsequently as corroboration). The issue at stake is the nature of power rather than the nature of being.

Perhaps the passage that best captures the fear of violent death in this sense is the one in *Leviathan*, chapter 5, "Of Reason and Science," where Hobbes 'enlightens' the reader about the true meaning of the term "right reason":

> And therefore, as when there is a controversy in an account, the parties must by their own accord, set up, for right reason, the reason of some arbitrator, or judge, to whose sentence they will both stand, or their controversy must either come to blows, or be undecided, for want of

right reason constituted by nature; so it is also in all debates of what kind soever. [For] when men that think themselves wiser than all others, clamour and demand right reason for judge, [they] seek no more, but that things should be determined, by no other men's reason but their own. (Ch. 5, p. 31)

The contrast here is between two casts of mind in their respective understandings of right reason. On the one hand, there are those who appeal to "right reason constituted by nature," believing that reason is supported by superhuman powers; they are the vainglorious men who claim to be wiser than everyone else. The ineffectiveness of their appeals is shown by the simple fact that "their controversy must either come to blows or be undecided." On the other hand, a different sort of man recognizes that such claims are merely those of self-appointed wise men who seek to impose their own partial opinions on others. Foreseeing the conflict and destruction that inevitably ensue from the pretensions of self-appointed wise men, he experiences the fear of violent death. This experience makes him aware of the need for arbitration—a settlement of the controversy by the arbitrary decision of an impartial judge. Such a resolution is different from the mediated knowledge of self-appointed wise men because it arises from conscious awareness that the settlement is an arbitrary human decision rather than authoritative truth delivered from 'on high.' The fear of violent death is enlightening because it pierces the illusion of authoritative truth and exposes the need for an arbitrary decision of the human will.

This prototype of the new thinking shows that the task of enlightenment is reduced to a change in self-consciousness. It requires men not to learn a new doctrine but to be honest about what they already know: that appeals to higher authority merely disguise human self-appointment, that claims of orthodoxy simply hide the establishment of arbitrary opinions. Through radical honesty (or cynicism), the enlightened mind arrives at the simple but momentous insight that the arbitrary human will has been sovereign all along but has never been acknowledged as such. When this fact is finally admitted, the disguised arbitrariness of authoritative wisdom will give way to undisguised arbitrariness in politics and in language.

Popular Enlightenment and the Paradox of Autonomous Reason

Hobbes's theory of enlightenment, I have argued, is motivated by the desire to find a permanent solution to the problem of doctrinal warfare. This motive explains why he seeks to build a science that does not begin from opinion or trust in authoritative wisdom. Instead of beginning with opinion and ascending to true knowledge (the method of classical philosophy), Hobbes criticizes the whole mental attitude that leads to trust in opinion and discredits it as a vain belief in the harmony of mind and reality. By rejecting this harmony, Hobbes exposes the mind to an experience of fear that is both humbling and exhilarating. Herein lies his claim of making a historic break with the past. He uncovers the autonomous reason of the enlightened mind that relies on no external authority and stands on its own self-evident foundations. Yet herein also lies the greatest difficulty for Hobbes. How does he know that the enlightened mind can successfully and permanently triumph over the unenlightened mind of the past and fulfill its promise of establishing everlasting peace?

Hobbes's answer, it would appear, entails a fundamental paradox. On the one hand, he claims that the enlightened mind is wholly autonomous or conscious of the sovereignty of the arbitrary human will. On the other hand, Hobbes must claim that autonomous reason is somehow more "natural"—more in accord with human nature and the natural order of things—so that he may be assured of its triumph over the unenlightened mind and the erroneous thinking of the past. The two facets of the enlightened mind, its arbitrariness and its naturalness, create the central paradox of Hobbes's entire system of thought.[15] Let us explore this paradox in connection with Hobbes's theory of popular enlightenment.

Through historical analysis Hobbes can know with a high degree of probability (though not with absolute certainty) that the triumph of the enlightened mind is possible because it is in accord with man's original or primitive nature. History shows that civilization is artificial, a creation of intellectual authorities whose vanity has produced authoritative opinions and doctrines from speech. By attributing their speech to superhuman powers, they have deceived themselves about their wisdom and have deceived the naively trusting people into following them. But the course of history can be reversed,

15. John Dewey astutely observes that this is the central problem of Hobbes's political science: "There exists, indeed, a paradox in Hobbes. . . . [his] position is precisely the paradox of attempting to derive by mathematical reasoning the authority of the sovereign to settle *arbitrarily* all matters of right and wrong, justice and injury, from *rational, universal axioms regarding the nature of good and evil.* His method of dealing with the paradox takes us to the meaning given by him to natural law" ("Motivation of Hobbes's Political Philosophy," pp. 24–25; emphasis added). This problem in Hobbes's natural law teaching is analyzed in chaps. 6 and 7.

Hobbes thinks, if he can break the bond of trust between the common people and the intellectual authorities or "cut off the hands of ambition," as he says in *Behemoth*.[16] Indeed, Hobbes's most extravagant claim about the prospects for perpetual peace rest on this assumption. In the Epistle Dedicatory to *De Cive*, he boldly proclaims that if true doctrine of justice were "distinctly known ... the strength of avarice and ambition, which is sustained by the erroneous opinions of the vulgar as touching the nature of right and wrong, would presently faint and languish; and *mankind would enjoy such an immoral peace, that unless it were for habitation, on the supposition that the earth should grow too narrow for her inhabitants, there would hardly be left any pretence for war*" (emphasis added). The means for a dramatic and definitive end of history can be found in popular enlightenment, the reformation of "the erroneous opinions of the vulgar" about the doctrines of authorities.[17]

History shows that this change is possible, according to Hobbes, because the common people are actually like the primitive or barbaric people who preceded the founding of civilizations. They are naturally indifferent to opinions that are expressed in abstract and learned language and believe such things (without actually understanding them) only when they are corrupted, seduced, or bewitched: "the common people's minds, unless they be tainted with dependence on the potent, or scribbled over with the opinions of their doctors, are like clean paper" (*Leviathan*, ch. 30, p. 325). Furthermore, the common people care primarily about immediate and personal things, such as their families, their business, their private pleasures, and personal security. Their language, when not corrupted by professors, theologians, and learned men, is practical and down-to-earth. Their superstitious belief in powers invisible may be more natural (and thus harder to eradicate) but does not pose a political problem if it does not lead to blind trust in those who deceive them with strange words. To enlighten the people—that is, to free them from trust in authorities and to have them think for

16. Deborah Baumgold brings out nicely Hobbes's focus on "the victimization of common people in the power struggles of political elites" but does not explain the theory of enlightenment by which Hobbes hopes to solve this historic problem (*Hobbes's Political Theory* [Cambridge: Cambridge University Press, 1988], p. 135).

17. Hobbes's advocacy of popular enlightenment should be contrasted to the attitude of Descartes, who espouses enlightenment but pointedly rejects popular enlightenment: "My design has never extended beyond trying to reform my own opinions and to build on a foundation which is entirely my own.... The simple resolve to strip oneself of all opinions and beliefs formerly received is not to be regarded as an example that each man should follow" ("The Discourse on Method," in *Philosophical Works of Descartes*, I, 90).

themselves—means essentially to reawaken their natural indifference to authoritative speech and disputes over doctrines and to return them to their primary concern with personal security.

In crude, practical terms Hobbes presents popular enlightenment
as anticlericalism, inculcating fear and distrust of priests and prophets, and more broadly as 'antiintellectualism,' engendering suspicion
and aversion to pretensions of higher learning. The focus of such
education will be to alert the common people to the hidden motives
of profit and love of domination which lie behind all doctrines pro-
claiming "orthodoxy," "the true way to salvation," "right reason constituted by nature," or the authoritative good for men. The point is
simply to force naive and trusting people to see the man behind the
doctrine, to see the human authority behind the claim of impersonal
higher authority, and to be aware of the exploitation, persecution,
and destruction that follow from naive trust in such men. Popular
enlightenment is thus an education in cynicism about the self-
serving motives and destructive effects of all authorities who claim
to know what is good for other men.

This lesson in 'opening the eyes' is the intent of Hobbes's discussion of "belief" and "faith" in *Leviathan* and other works. Hobbes
insists emphatically that the phrases "I believe *in* . . . " and "I believe
him" are identical in meaning. The words "I believe in . . . " are used
by divines in order to give a doctrine the appearance of impersonal
truth—that Scripture, God, or the nature of things rather than a
self-appointed man is the source of words and doctrines. But in reality belief is not "from the thing itself, nor from the principles of
natural reason, but from the authority, and good opinion we have
of him that saith it, . . . of whose ability to know the truth, and
whose honesty in not deceiving, [we] doubteth not" (*Leviathan*, ch. 7,
pp. 54–55). Hobbes also proposes the test of asking *"Cui Bono?"*—
Who benefits?—from a doctrine in order to encourage cynicism
about the motives of those who propound it. The implicit premise of
such advice is that the power of authoritative doctrines is destroyed
when the base and self-serving motives of the man who propounds
the doctrine are exposed. Such exposure alone is sufficient, he
thinks, to shatter the bond of trust that gives mere human beings
the mystical glow of superhuman wisdom.

Hobbes also seeks to destroy the trust in prophets who proclaim
new doctrines by appealing directly to the fear of violent death—to
the fear of chaos and civil war. This fear, he hopes, will make
people, even ordinary people, more assertive in questioning doctrines and motives:

[For] men had need to be very circumspect and wary, in obeying the voice of a man, that pretending himself to be a prophet, requires us to obey God in that way, which he in God's name telleth us to be the way to happiness. For he that pretends to teach men the way of so great felicity, pretends to govern them; that is, to rule and reign over them; which is a thing, that all men naturally desire, and is therefore worthy of being suspected of ambition and imposture; and consequently, ought to be examined and tried by every man, before yielding obedience. . . . [Otherwise] they must suffer themselves to be led by some strange prince; or by some fellow-subjects, that can bewitch them by slander of government, into rebellion; . . . and by this means . . . reduce all order, government, and society to the first chaos and violence of civil war. (*Leviathan*, ch. 36, pp. 423, 427)

The thrust of this passage is to advance the new spirit of distrust and fear which should motivate the critical thinking of the masses. As strange as it may seem, Hobbes claims that the fear of violent death will not make the people cower but will make them more confident, more assertive, more self-reliant in their thinking—more willing to question and criticize rather than to trust and surrender their minds to authority. In all of these examples of popular enlightenment, Hobbes relies on the historical premise that independent thinking is more 'natural' than deference to authoritative wisdom because it accords with the original or uncorrupted nature of the common people.

Hobbes's optimism about popular enlightenment depends upon historical knowledge for another important assumption: the belief that the time is ripe for enlightenment. This belief can be inferred from several of Hobbes's historical observations. First, the history of barbarism and civilization points to the seventeenth century as a kind of peak or privileged historical moment. Hobbes observes that the intellectuals from the universities, particularly the educated gentlemen (the "democratical gentlemen" of *Behemoth*) and the preachers of the Protestant Reformation, have already widely diffused academic learning among the masses. Philosophy of a sort—a version of classical dialectics and theological disputation—has been popularized. A crucial precondition of enlightenment has been realized: the philosophical and academic tradition of the West has been established in the universities and is widely recognized. Thus as a historical fact Hobbes sees the common people of his day not so much as the blind followers of others but as possessors of their own philosophical and theological doctrines.

This is not yet enlightenment, however, because everyone believes his own doctrine is orthodox and that he is wiser than everyone else—a condition that Hobbes describes as a sort of democracy of vanity in which everyone is "equal" in thinking that he is the wisest.[18] This unusual situation is one step away from recognizing that no one possesses superior wisdom—a recognition of true equality by humble men who think *only* for themselves and have no pretense of imposing on others. Stated differently, Hobbes recognizes that a king of 'individualism' has already developed from the influence of the 'democratic' ideas of classical political philosophy and the private inspiration of the Protestant Reformation, producing the near-infinite sectarianism of the present doctrinal age. As Eldon Eisenach argues, a notion of historical development toward "individualism" can be discerned in Hobbes's thought, although Eisenach wrongly attributes it to a "prophetic" or "millennialist" streak in Hobbes.[19] For it is not prophetic history but civil history—the record of intellectual vanity in the growth and dissolution of civilization—that provides the crucial premises of his thought.

A case in point is Hobbes's account of the development and unraveling of authority in the Christian churches of the Western world. Hobbes uses the metaphor of tying and untying a knot to illuminate the tightening of authority from the early churches to the Roman church, and the relaxation of authority from the Reformation to the state of independence in the present age. At the end of this account he concludes:

> After [the power of the popes was dissolved in England and replaced by the bishops], the presbyterians lately in England obtained the putting down of episcopacy. . . . And almost at the same time, the power was

18. "For such is the nature of men, that howsoever they may acknowledge many others to be more witty, or more eloquent, or more learned; yet they will hardly believe there be many so wise as themselves. . . . But this proveth rather that men are in that point equal, than unequal. For there is not ordinarily a greater sign of the equal distribution of any thing, than that every man is contented with his share" (*Leviathan*, ch. 13, p. 111).

19. "There is in *Leviathan* an incredible coincidence between the possibility of the reappearance of true Christian liberty and the historical possibility of establishing a political order based on reason and justice. This moment in history anticipates the millennium in joining reason and revelation, works and faith, true philosophy and true religion. *Leviathan* is a single book whose halves are held together by hope in this prophetic moment." Eisenach, *Two Worlds of Liberalism*, p. 66. Similar sentiments about the religious impulse of Hobbes's politics can be found in Henning G. Reventlow, *The Authority of the Bible and the Rise of the Modern World*, trans. John Bowden (Philadelphia: Fortress Press, 1985), pp. 194–222. For a more sober assessment of Hobbes's arguments about prophecy and sacred history, see Johnston's remarks that Hobbes intends "the subordination of prophecy" and "the refounding of Christianity . . . to transform men into rational and predictable beings" (*Rhetoric of "Leviathan,"* pp. 134–142, 164–184, 190–204).

taken also from the presbyterians: and so we are reduced to the inde-
pendency of the primitive Christians, . . . which, if it be without contention, and without measuring the doctrine of Christ by our affections to
the person of his minister . . . is perhaps best. First, because there
ought to be no power over the consciences of men, but of the Word
itself. . . . And secondly, because it is unreasonable in them, who teach
there is such danger in every little error, *to require of a man endued with
reason of his own, to follow the reason of any other man.* (*Leviathan*, ch. 47, p.
696; emphasis added)

The lesson Hobbes draws from church history is the parallel development of individual conscience, which now resembles the independence of early Christians, and individual reason, which reflects the
self-reliant thinking of the Enlightenment. Hobbes recognizes, of
course, that the parallel does not overcome a crucial difference between individual conscience and individual reason: the former appeals to the Word itself guided only by the inspiration of the Spirit;
the latter involves the use of one's own natural faculties without direction from another. Both reject the mediated knowledge of human authorities. But the individual conscience still has lurking
within it the belief that words come from an external authority and
should be imposed on others (if only to gain recognition of Noncon-
formity). To move from the individual conscience of the Reformation to the individual reason of the Enlightenment, one must make a
quantum leap by humbly recognizing the arbitrariness of words and
by looking for truth in the mind itself.

Thus Hobbes relies on history to show that the people's self-
reliant thinking is natural in the sense of preceding the growth of
(Western) civilization and accompanying its present dissolution. This
does not mean, however, that enlightenment could occur in a primitive condition in which natural independence of mind is identical
with naive or prescientific thinking. On the contrary, it is possible
only in the most advanced stage of civilization, when science or philosophy has been established in the universities and the people can
be taught a highly intellectualized kind of fear or skeptical distrust.
Because it arises in this specific historical context, the Enlightenment must deploy a new doctrine of science that asserts both the
arbitrariness and the naturalness of autonomous reason.

The reason for this paradox is that the Enlightenment seeks to
stand on self-evident foundations; but it is born in a historical context that makes it inescapably polemical. Although the time may be
ripe for enlightenment, as indicated by the growing independence
of the people, the most powerful props for traditional authority re-

main. Metaphysical doctrines about abstract essences and theological doctrines about supernatural beings have not been expunged from historical consciousness. To be fully triumphant, enlightenment requires a doctrine of Nature to replace those that previously captivated the human mind. Hobbes, therefore, must develop a new kind of natural science that supports the self-reliant mind in its struggle against authority and adequately explains the phenomena of nature.

» 5 «

The Enlightened Mind
and the Science of Nature

From Dialectics to Introspection: The New Approach to Natural Science

We are now in a position to see the sweep of Hobbes's philosophical thought as a whole. It can be understood as taking place in three stages or steps. The first is historical critique, the analysis of authoritative opinion and doctrinal politics as the problem of preexisting civilization. The second is methodical analysis, the resolution of authoritative opinion into its constituent elements (speech, thoughts, and passions) and the identification of intellectual vainglory as the root cause of inexact and insignificant speech. The culmination of this argument is the theory of enlightenment. By recognizing that trust in superhuman support for knowledge is a dangerous illusion, the human mind frees itself from the spell of authoritative opinion and becomes self-reliant, determined to stand on its own evident foundations.

The next step in Hobbes's thought is constructive. Hobbes must, so to speak, pick up the broken pieces of authoritative opinion shattered by enlightenment and put them back together. Enlightenment subverts and destroys the trust in speech and sense experience that has been the basis of all previous opinions about the nature of things. From the vantage point of the enlightened mind, speech and the testimony of the senses have no necessary connection to the way things really are in nature or in the divinely created natural order. With this assertion of radical distrust, the Enlightenment makes its claim to surpass all previous doctrines and to provide the foundation for a new edifice of science that will be indisputable (exact and certain).

But precisely at this point—in the separation of the mind from every kind of trust that links it with the external world—the enlightened mind encounters its greatest challenge. Without trust of some kind, the operations of the human mind seem to be left in a world of free construction which is subjective or arbitrary, telling us nothing about Nature and having no grounding in reality. This objection might not be so formidable if enlightenment were simply a form of prescientific skepticism, like the teaching of the ancient Sophists, which subverted all social conventions but never claimed to be a science. Enlightenment, however, is a more 'sophisticated' kind of skepticism. Although it propounds a more radical kind of doubt than did the ancient Sophists, the enlightenment builds upon the later philosophical tradition by seeking to discover scientific knowledge of justice and the natural order; it even raises the stakes of science by the polemical claim of superseding the doctrines of the tradition. But how can the radical doubt of enlightenment be reconciled with knowledge of the natural order? How does the enlightened mind find a grounding in Nature for its own thoughts and actions and reconcile the apparently contradictory demands of arbitrariness and naturalness? To answer these questions, we shall examine Hobbes's new approach to natural science, turning first to his theory of science (logic or method) and then to his natural science proper (metaphysics and physics).

Hobbes presents his theory of science as logic or method. It is most systematically presented in the first book of *De Corpore* but also appears in abbreviated forms (with some variations) in each of the political treatises. This theory has been given a variety of descriptive labels. Sometimes it is referred to as "the resolutive-compositive method" and "the demonstrative method" (labels that Hobbes uses) and sometimes it is described more loosely by scholars as "artificial construction" or even "nominalism."[1] For reasons that will be discussed in a moment, I think the most appropriate label for Hobbes's theory of scientific method is "exact deductive science."

When scholars explain the origins of Hobbes's method, they are usually content to say that he adopted his particular view because he was impressed by the way Galileo and Harvey used resolution

1. *De Corpore*, 1.3, 1.5, 6.1, 6.8, 6.12, 25.1; Watkins, *Hobbes's System of Ideas*, secs. 8, 12; Peters, *Hobbes*, pp. 46–52; Michael Oakeshott, "Introduction to *Leviathan*," in *Hobbes on Civil Association*, (Berkeley: University of California Press, 1975), pp. 1–74; and Frithiof Brandt, *Thomas Hobbes's Mechanical Conception of Nature* (Copenhagen: Levin & Munksgaard, 1928), pp. 318–320, 372–380.

and composition and was awestruck by the certain demonstrations of Euclidean geometry. Hence Hobbes's doctrine of method is viewed as a synthesis of two methods, the Galilean and the Euclidean, combined in a general theory of deductive logic which could be applied to philosophy as a whole (body, man, and citizen). This suggestion is true as far as it goes, but it does not go very far. It fails to recognize that Hobbes's view of philosophy as deductive logic is necessarily preceded by a whole set of presuppositions that are deliberately omitted or hidden in Hobbes's presentation of the method itself.

When these presuppositions are uncovered or found tucked away in obscure places, they reveal the polemical origins of Hobbes's theory of method in his critique of authoritative opinion and the traditional dialectical or disputative sciences that rely on opinion. They reveal as well that Hobbes's method presupposes the theory of enlightenment—the process by which the mind, through fear and distrust of human authorities, overcomes the passive trust in empty speech and realizes the need for clear mental conceptions in the use of words.

Thus Hobbes begins *De Corpore* with two candid admissions that prepare the reader for the argument about method which follows:

> I am not ignorant of how hard a thing it is to weed out of men's minds such inveterate opinions as have taken root there, and been confirmed in them by the authority of the most eloquent writers; especially seeing true (that is, accurate) philosophy professedly rejects not only the paint and false colors of language, but even the very ornaments and graces of the same. (1.1)

And

> I am confident, if any confidence of a writing can proceed from a writer's fear, circumspection, and diffidence, . . . that all I have said is sufficiently demonstrated from definitions. (Epistle Dedicatory, p. xi)

In these passages Hobbes reveals that his theory of scientific method is built on the enlightened or self-reliant mind that has been freed by "fear, circumspection, and diffidence" from the spell of authoritative opinions expressed in captivating speech. From these admissions he derives the most important characteristic of science: the necessity of beginning with clear, accurate, or exact definitions of words and the need to draw all conclusions from such definitions by logical deduction. Herein lies the equation of method with exact deductive science.

With little fanfare Hobbes embarks on an intellectual revolution. He requires the reader to make a conscious effort to resist the passive acceptance of conventional usages of words and actively to assert his own individual mind against authority. He also encourages a more subtle kind of intellectual change. When asking for definitions of words, Hobbes insists, the individual should recognize that clear or exact definitions must be given in terms of mental thoughts or conceptions. The purpose of a definition is to raise a mental picture or image, an idea in the mind, rather than to add new words to one's vocabulary which call for further definition. As Hobbes says more directly in *Leviathan*, "the use of words, is to register to ourselves, and make manifest to others the thoughts and conceptions of our minds" (ch. 46, p. 484). Only by defining words with mental ideas rather than with other words can one put an end to verbal controversies.

Hobbes states in *De Corpore* that this notion of exact definition is the new alternative to the dialectical or disputative method of traditional philosophy. In his well-known "definition of a definition" in *De Corpore,* he says "definitions . . . are principles, or primary propositions; they are therefore speeches . . . [but] they are used for the raising of an *idea* of some thing in the mind of the learner" (6.14; Hobbes's emphasis). Hence, he continues, "the properties of a definition" are "that it takes away equivocations, as also all that multitude of distinctions, which are used by *such as think they may learn philosophy by disputation*" (6:15; emphasis added). This view of defining the meanings of words is new and significant because it changes the whole plane of reasoning from speech to mental ideas—from verbal discourse, which entails trusting other men, to mental discourse, which can be confirmed by examination of one's own mind.

Hobbes's argument can be described as a reconstruction of science which changes the method of discovery *from dialectics to introspection.* Like Descartes, who appeals to clear and distinct ideas in the mind, Hobbes looks for the source of truth not in speech, which points outward to Nature, but to "thoughts and passions" of the mind, which point to self-reflection on the mind itself. Thus the real revolution in method for Hobbes is not simply the adoption of the Galilean method or the Euclidean method (or some combination of the two) but the introspective method, which makes the mind itself the subject and object of understanding. Despite his great admiration for analytical and geometric reasoning, Hobbes recognizes that the application of these methods to the whole of philosophy is made possible by a more fundamental methodological revolution, the introspective method of the self-reliant mind.[2] Accordingly, Hobbes says in the introduction to *Leviathan* that the final confirmation of his doctrine requires one to follow the maxim *nosce teipsum*, "read thyself"—that is, examine in an honest and systematic fashion the thoughts and passions of one's own mind.

Hobbes's maxim, of course, is a modification of the Delphic oracle's "Know thyself." It thus reminds one of Socrates, who was inspired by the oracle to begin his dialectical investigation of the received opinions of his day in order to discover true wisdom. But the dialectical science begun by Socrates (and developed by Plato, Aristotle, and the Scholastics) is fundamentally different in method and purpose from the introspective method of Hobbes and the Enlightenment. Indeed, one could almost say that Hobbes seeks to reverse the Socratic revolution, turning philosophy away from the investigation of speech as a mirror of reality to a direct look at the impressions that Nature implants in the mind through the senses (see Plato, *Phaedo*, 99e). Thus the two apparently similar sayings—"Know thyself" and "Read thyself"—actually reflect two very different ways of doing philosophy.

The difference between the two methods—dialectics and introspection—may be described more precisely as follows. Dialectical science, as we noted earlier, is the ascent from opinion to true knowledge. It is essentially a science of speech, an analysis of the universal terms employed in common speech on the assumption that such speech contains an intuition of the essences of things, a divination of the universal patterns or forms. The goal of dialectics is to analyze speech in order to understand the natures and causes of things as they truly are—to understand the being of things in Nature. Thus Socrates's quest to "know himself," to understand the kind of wisdom he is capable of possessing, leads him to investi-

---

2. Even in geometry, Hobbes argues, the proper method avoids reasoning about words and relies on introspection: "To imagine motions with their lines and ways is a new business, and requires a steady brain, and *a man that can constantly read in his own thoughts, without being diverted by the noise of words*" (emphasis added). Hobbes therefore claims that he has advanced geometry beyond Euclid, that he is "the first that hath made the grounds of geometry firm and coherent" (*EW*, vii, 272, 242). Contrary to Peters's suggestion, it is not simply the attempt to turn geometry into a science of motion that distinguishes Hobbes but the emphasis on the *imagination* of motion—on the examination of one's mental thoughts and conceptions—that is the novelty in Hobbes's geometry (Peters, *Hobbes*, p. 82).

gate through speech and conversation the human soul and its connection to the forms and structures of the natural order. Socratic dialectics, no matter how tentative or final its wisdom may be, reflects a harmony of soul, speech, and being (or mind, language, and reality).

Introspective science, by contrast, begins with deliberate abstraction from common opinion, rejecting all trust in speech and common sense—and thus rejecting any connection they may have by intuition or divination to the nature of things. In so doing, introspective science changes the goal of science or philosophy. The goal of introspection is not knowledge of the being of things in Nature but knowledge of *the appearances of things in the mind*—knowledge of how the appearances look to the mind and how the appearances may be generated in the mind rather than knowledge of the reality behind the appearances. Nature (or Nature's God) remains mysterious; it is viewed as nothing more than an efficient cause of appearances in the mind. The beginning and end of introspective science is the self-reliant mind itself: its thoughts, conceptions, phantasms, appearances, and passions (Hobbes's terms) or its ideas and passions (Descartes's and Locke's terms) and the evident deductions from such appearances in the mind.

Thus Hobbes defines philosophy in *De Corpore* as "the knowledge we acquire, by true ratiocination, of appearances, or apparent effects, from the knowledge we have of some possible production or generation of the same; and of such production, as has been or may be, from the knowledge we have of the effects" (1.2). This definition of philosophy may seem strange or confusing until we see that its purpose is to limit the scope of philosophy in accordance with the introspective method: it limits philosophy to explaining the relation between the observed effects or appearances in the mind and the possible causes in Nature of such appearances. What is deliberately omitted from the scope of philosophy is knowledge of the way things truly are. Ultimate knowledge of being—what things truly are and why things are the way they are, the order and final purpose of Nature or Nature's God—remains mysterious or hypothetical. Science is thereby freed from theology and metaphysics (in the traditional sense) and is focused on knowledge of the human mind or understanding.

For this reason the science of the self-reliant mind known through introspection is sometimes referred to as "positive" science. This is a useful label because it means that one can be certain ("positive") about knowledge of appearances in the mind, and one can even trust that they do come from Nature, from something 'out there.'₃ But one can never know the ultimate nature of reality—its metaphysical character (whether it is material or immaterial) or its moral character (whether it is a moral order or a chaos)—except insofar as the nature of reality can be deduced from its appearances in the mind. Hence the positive mind is capable of metaphysics and theology only by inferences from ideas or conceptions in the mind, as Descartes argues about knowledge of God and as Hobbes argues about knowledge of matter in motion and mechanistic causality. In this way introspective science supports the self-reliant or positive mind while still claiming that it is in accord with Nature, because it limits knowledge of Nature to its appearances or apparent effects in the mind.

Hobbes's conception of philosophy as an exact deductive science that begins and ends with introspection (with "positive" or clear thoughts in the mind) creates a complicated relation between mental thoughts, speech, and reality. Some scholars argue that, in fact, his account is confusing and contradictory because it seems to leave unresolved several important issues. One issue is whether defining words in terms of mental thoughts achieves clarity and precision because the choice is completely arbitrary and conventional or completely nonarbitrary and self-evident. As Richard Peters says, "when Hobbes is speaking in a predominantly *political* context, he . . . usually puts forward a *conventionalist* theory of truth; whereas, when . . . [discussing] the *natural sciences,* his theory is less conventionalist and more like a *self-evidence* theory such as Descartes [propounds]."₄

The second question is whether Hobbes's view of scientific knowledge is ultimately "empiricist" or "rationalist." As Frithiof Brandt argues, Hobbes sees two kinds of knowledge, one derived from sense experience (independent of words), the other from formal logic (in which words are used as signs and symbols for logical computation). The problem here is that Hobbes seems to oppose science to experience but also requires science to incorporate experience in the definition of words.₅

3. Andrzej Rapaczynski emphasizes the importance of this label as the correct characterization of both the metaphysics and the politics of Hobbes and as a way of reconnecting the natural and political science of the liberal tradition: *Nature and Politics: Liberalism in the Philosophies of Hobbes, Locke, and Rousseau* (Ithaca: Cornell University Press, 1987), pp. 12–14, 23–24. See also Strauss, "On the Basis of Hobbes's Political Philosophy," p. 178.
4. Peters, *Hobbes,* p. 57; Watkins, *Hobbes's System of Ideas,* p. 149; and McNeilly, *Anatomy of "Leviathan,"* pp. 69, 83.
5. Brandt, *Hobbes's Mechanical Conception of Nature,* pp. 228–229; Harold Hoffding, *A History of Modern Philosophy,* trans. B. E. Meyer, 2 vols. (London: Macmillan, 1900), I, 265–266; Watkins, *Hobbes's System of Ideas,* pp. 144–147.

The third question is how Hobbes can make the claim that examination of mental conceptions ultimately leads to the conclusion that reality consists of bodies in motion.

These criticisms are serious ones, but our scholars do not even attempt to explain why Hobbes speaks in an apparently contradictory manner on these subjects; nor do they suggest how the ambiguities might be resolved. The problem with most contemporary Hobbes scholars is that they are, so to speak, post-Enlightenment students of the Enlightenment. They take for granted the destruction of authoritative opinion and its replacement by one form or another of Enlightenment science or post-Enlightenment critique of modern science. Thus certain categories—such as arbitrary and self-evident or empiricist and rationalist—appear as opposing concepts to them, whereas Hobbes apparently did not think they were opposites or did not notice a contradiction between them.

In reply to his critics, Hobbes would argue that his statements have an underlying consistency. It lies in the introspective method of the self-reliant mind. Rejecting the trust in speech that is built into traditional dialectics, the self-reliant mind seeks, first and foremost, to define words in terms of mental conceptions rather than by means of other words. Introspective science makes a qualitative leap from the realm of speech, which leads via intuition to knowledge of the being of things in Nature, to the realm of mental thoughts, which leads via deduction to the possible causes of appearances in the mind. Since the shift from verbal discourse to mental discourse is the decisive change, the difference between a definition in which a word is arbitrarily assigned to a mental thought or a definition in which a word necessarily signifies a single, self-evident mental thought is a secondary matter. Both kinds of definition consist of mental thoughts that can be known without trust in the authority of other men. And both can be explicated with the precision, accuracy, or exactness of a sensible image. Hence arbitrary or self-evident definitions serve equally well as foundations for exact deductive science.

Moreover, in accordance with the requirement of the self-reliant or positive mind, such mental thoughts must themselves be purged of trust—purged of the illusion that mental thoughts can be known to be anything more than appearances or phantasms in the brain. As Hobbes says in the *Elements* and *De Corpore*, when we think of mental appearances, we must first go through the mental exercise of "feigning the world annihilated"—imagining the whole external world, the whole world outside the mind, annihilated or destroyed so that we may consciously refer our mental thoughts to the mind alone (*De Corpore*, 7.1; *Elements*, I, 1.7). Words, therefore, are defined by mental thoughts that tell us nothing about the actual structure of the world outside the mind, but only about how the mind conceives of the external world.

Accordingly, it does not matter in principle if words signify mental thoughts that are chosen arbitrarily or that are chosen through a mental process of careful abstraction which leads to self-evident mental thoughts. In both cases the truth of definitions and of deductions from definitions is measured solely by the consistent application of words to mental thoughts, comprised of sense impressions or of images derived from sense impressions. For this reason scientific or philosophical truth, according to Hobbes, transcends the distinction between empiricism and rationalism by requiring an exact fit between words (logical symbols) and mental thoughts (conceptions derived from sense experience). The words merely serve as "counters" or numerical devices for adding and subtracting mental pictures.

This unusual combination, which might be described as 'logical empiricism' or 'mathematical empiricism,' does not appear contradictory to Hobbes because it involves a reconstruction of the elements of opinion: when words and sensations are purged of the vain illusion that they refer to natural essences and attributes, they may be refitted together by mental manipulation, as long as men humbly acknowledge that words refer only to appearances in the mind. Without seeing the polemical origin of Hobbes's theory of scientific method—its development as an alternative to the traditional method of reasoning from received opinion—its consistency is difficult to see. Having said this much, however, we must acknowledge that the link between such appearances and the natural world becomes even more tenuous and creates unusual problems for Hobbes's metaphysics.

Metaphysics

We have seen that Hobbes conceives of method or logic as exact deductive science whose foundation is the introspective knowledge of the self-reliant mind. This foundation provides the link between exact science and the knowledge of nature—metaphysics, physics, and human psychology. Metaphysics, or First Philosophy, is the definition of words that are most universal—space, time, cause, effect, body, accident, matter, form, and so on. According to Hobbes, we know these definitions not by reasoning about the conventional usages of words, as Aristotle does in the twenty books of his *Metaphysics*, but by thinking about how they must necessarily be conceived in our minds. This process of explicating self-evident mental thoughts, Hobbes claims, enables him to treat completely the subject of metaphysics in a few brief chapters of *De Corpore*. Like Descartes, who argues for the existence of God as a necessary idea of the mind (inferring that only God could be the cause of ideas of infinity and perfection in a finite mind), Hobbes erects his whole metaphysical theory on inferences from ideas in the human mind. Its central claim—that all change is due to mechanical causes or that bodies in motion are the only reality—is inferred from the way the mind necessarily conceives of change and causality.

Hobbes's metaphysics, in other words, is introspective rather than dialectical. He claims that he does not dispute, argue, or even prove his theory, but settles the significance of words by explicating necessary mental ideas. Such explication is possible because metaphysics deals with the most universal words, whose meaning one can uncover by "limiting" or "paring" a mental image—eliminating contingent particulars until a clear "universal picture" exists in the mind (*De Corpore*, 6.12, 6.15), a process that resembles what Locke calls "abstracting" (*An Essay Concerning Human Understanding*, III, 3.6). These definitions, Hobbes asserts, are "manifest of themselves," which means they are evident to any man whose "natural discourse is [not] corrupted with former opinions received from [his] masters" (*De Corpore*, 6.5).

In the second part of *De Corpore* (after treating method in the first part), Hobbes shows how this new kind of introspective metaphysics is done. He begins by feigning the world annihilated, imagining that nothing exists but our thoughts of the previously existing world. These are the "phantasms" of the mind from which metaphysical knowledge will be built. The first self-evident metaphysical definition is "space"—"the phantasm of a thing existing without the mind simply" or the strange sensation that mental thoughts seem to refer to a real "space" outside the mind (7.2). Next he defines "time"—"the phantasm of before and after in motion" and "infinite"—the imagination of no beginning and no end (7.3, 7.11). All of these initial definitions convey the eerie sense that knowledge of reality is a phantasm or imagination, an illusion of the mind. Yet it is an illusion whose most powerful sensation is that of something really existing outside the mind. In reading Hobbes's definitions, one is struck by the extraordinary tension that enlightenment creates in the mind—compelling the mind to reject the trust in appearances and humbly to admit that its most cherished opinions are phantasms.

Only when we get to the definition of "body" does Hobbes leave the realm of phantasms and assert that something can be known to exist independently of our thoughts. Only here is the enlightened mind permitted to trust. This indeed is the very definition of body—"that which having no dependence upon our thought, is coincident or coextended with some part of space" (8.1) This, of course, tells us nothing about body except that it is the only thing that truly exists outside the mind and thus must occupy some real space or have extension. All other knowledge of bodies occurs only through their "accidents," the faculties by which a body "works in us a conception of itself" (8.2). The aggregate of these accidents when perceived by the mind is what we mean by a "cause" of observed effects (9.3). And such causes can be conceived as occurring only by some change—that is, by "motion," the relinquishing of one place by a body and the acquisition of another place (8.10) or some mutation within a body itself (9.6). Causality, therefore, can be conceived only mechanically, as bodies moving and touching other bodies in a full medium or space (9.7).

At this point we are compelled to stop and ask how Hobbes could be certain that bodies and their motions alone are real, while all other observed properties of things are mere phantasms. This seems to be a dogmatic assertion; Hobbes's enlightened mind seems to halt its process of radical doubt and come to rest on a solid foundation of trust. Most scholars are dumbfounded by this fact, for it suggests that one of Hobbes's most important doctrines—metaphysical materialism or mechanistic causality—is utterly groundless, a dogmatic assertion, a leap of faith, an unsupported assumption, or, at best, a methodological and conceptual necessity but not a proven metaphysical truth.[6] How can this strange fact be explained?

To answer this important question, we must delve into the unstated premises of Hobbes's position and try to uncover the whole logic of intention, so to speak, behind the unusual presentation of his metaphysical doctrine. One point we shall consider is the general character of Hobbes's enlightenment science, its paradoxical combination of arbitrariness and naturalness, and the significance of this paradox for claims of metaphysical truth. A second concerns the polemical way that Hobbes uses his mechanical conception of nature, in physics, in human psychology, and in political science. These considerations will enable us to suggest plausible reasons for the ambi-

6. As Stephen succinctly states, "Hobbes takes for granted, for he scarcely argues the question, that the material world is the only world." Sir Leslie Stephen, *Hobbes* (London: Macmillan, 1904), p. 82. See also Peters, *Hobbes*, pp. 88–95; Brandt, *Hobbes's Mechanical Conception of Nature*, p. 381; Strauss, *Natural Right and History*, p. 174.

guity surrounding Hobbes's doctrine which most scholars recognize but rarely attempt to explain.

The first and fundamental point to understand is the way enlightenment science affects the search for metaphysical truth. As I have frequently remarked, Hobbes conceives of enlightenment as a new kind of science that will bring about a historic change: an end to doctrinal warfare by the emancipation of the mind from trust in received opinion and the establishment of the mind's self-reliance. In working for this historic change, Hobbes expects that once the spell of authoritative opinion and of Aristotelian-Scholastic thought is completely broken, the enlightened mind will stand self-evidently on its own foundations. It will not need to struggle against the "kingdom of darkness" that preceded its discovery because the metaphysical illusions of the past will have been banished once and for all times. The enlightened mind will have triumphed completely and will be free to reflect on its own thoughts and passions without reference to the external world of reality. At this point, one may surmise, the enlightened mind will not need a grounding in Nature. Indeed, the clearest sign of the triumph of enlightenment will be the claim that metaphysics and theology are obsolete (a claim later made, of course, by positivists and analytical philosophers).

Like all modern 'liberation' movements that have sought final emancipation for the human mind, however, Hobbes's project faces the greatest difficulty in the transition period. The old order may be weakened by fear, distrust, and systematic doubt. But it is far from being irrevocably defeated because it has on its side the powerful human tendency (which almost seems natural and ineradicable) to trust—in authority, in speech, in common-sense experience, in the whole Aristotelian and Scholastic elaboration of these tendencies into scientific and theological doctrines of immaterial Being. The Enlightenment philosophers hope that once these tendencies and doctrines are exposed as creations of human authority or ridiculed as speech without sense (as "nonsense"), they will simply go away—vanish into thin air, wither away, be forgotten, or be treated as relics of an earlier 'dark age' that will never return.

But the kingdom of darkness does not vanish of its own accord; it must be willfully (and sometimes even violently) destroyed. As a result, enlightenment, at least at its inception, must engage the enemy on its own terms. It must fight fire with fire. In other words, it needs a rival doctrine to use polemically against the erroneous doctrines of the past. The necessity of replacing previous doctrines with a new doctrine forces the Enlightenment thinkers to provide a grounding for their new idea of the self-reliant mind in Nature. As a

matter of principle, however, they cannot argue, prove, or demonstrate the case for their rival view of Nature. Resort to argument
or to refutation would be a relapse into the old dialectical or disputative method that produced all the doctrinal disputes of the past.
Hence the new doctrine of Nature must be presented as a *self-evident*
idea of the enlightened mind—as an idea that produces assent
without argument, as soon as it is stated. But a doctrine of Nature
that is no more than a necessary idea of the mind can be at most
conceptually or methodologically certain (hypothetically true). For
its criterion of truth is clarity to the mind, not correspondence
to reality.

Despite this admission, a competing pressure exists, which is the
crucial interpretive point for understanding Hobbes. There is a necessity to assert dogmatically that what is certain conceptually or
methodologically is also true metaphysically, an explanation of the
way things really are. This might be called the 'dogmatism of the
Enlightenment'—the polemical necessity of providing an absolute or
dogmatic foundation in Nature for the newly emancipated, self-
reliant mind if the kingdom of darkness is to be repelled. Such dogmatism is not merely the claim of exact or certain knowledge—the
dogmatism built on skepticism of which the Enlightenment thinkers
proudly boast. It is the assertion of conceptual certainty as metaphysical truth, deliberately undertaken to advance the cause of enlightenment against its enemies. Although such a move may seem
unwarranted, it can be justified on the grounds that, by helping to
defeat the unenlightened thinking of the past, it will bring about the
successful transformation of human nature. At that point the distinction between conceptual and metaphysical truth will disappear
(indeed, the very question of metaphysical truth will no longer seem
intelligible, or it will seem like such a divisive and dangerous question that men will be afraid to discuss it seriously). The enlightened
mind will then stand on its own as the unchallenged victor in the
final struggle of civilization.

If this account of the dogmatism of the Enlightenment is correct,
we can understand why it arises most vividly in the metaphysical
doctrine of Thomas Hobbes. He, more than any of his contemporaries and successors, felt the power of "the kingdom of darkness"
(even coining this immortal phrase) and understood it to be "a confederacy of deceivers"—a willful imposition of human authorities.
As a result, providing a radical alternative to the old metaphysical
doctrines of incorporeal bodies and abstract essences was the strongest polemical necessity for him. Moreover, he asserted metaphysical
materialism in the most uncompromising fashion and felt no incon-

sistency in claiming, on the one hand, that it was merely a conceptual certainty, and on the other that it was a metaphysical truth.

It is no accident, therefore, that Hobbes moves back and forth between the two senses in which his mechanistic materialism—his doctrine of bodies in motion—can be said to be "true." Sometimes he claims it is merely a necessary mental conception and therefore hypothetically true. At other times he claims that it is a description of the way things really are and therefore is metaphysically true. An example of the first view is his statement that metaphysics, or First Philosophy, is the definition of those names that are "of all others the most universal . . . and *necessary to the explaining of a man's conceptions . . . of bodies*" (*Leviathan*, ch. 46, p. 671; emphasis added). Hence all knowledge is either of "internal accidents of our mind . . . , or as species of external things, not as really existing, but only appearing to exist, and to have a being without us" (*De Corpore*, 7.1). On the other hand, we find statements such as the definition of "body" quoted above, as the only thing that exists of itself, independently of our thoughts of it. Or we find the simple assertion, so characteristic of Hobbes's dogmatic side, that "Nature worketh by motion" or that "every part of the universe is body, and that which is not body, is no part of the universe" (*Leviathan*, ch. 46, p. 672). That Hobbes could make such statements without proof and without feeling the need to reconcile his claims can be explained only by the unusual demands of his enlightenment science.

Physics and Psychology

The inherent difficulties of building a science of nature on the principles of enlightenment also appear in the second half of *De Corpore*. Here Hobbes argues that the purpose of outlining the theory of exact deductive science and metaphysical materialism at the beginning of *De Corpore* is to build a mechanical model of the universe which can be applied to the explanation of natural phenomena (physics) and human nature (psychology). Throughout this argument we see further use of the introspective method and more wrestling with the distinction between hypothetical explanations and metaphysical truths. The important point is to see that Hobbes's efforts do not lead to a better understanding of natural phenomena, especially in comparison with the more experimental and empirical work of his contemporaries. Hobbes's real achievement is to provide a scientific doctrine that explains the mental processes of the newly emancipated enlightened mind.

The purpose of physics is to explain the causes of natural phenomena. But in Hobbes's presentation, physics does not begin this task with observations or experiments; it begins with postulates about the mechanistic universe. Hence Hobbes's physics is preceded not only by metaphysics but also by a priori principles that govern knowledge of the mechanistic universe—a kind of geometric mechanics that demonstrates deductively the principles of cosmology. This logical sequence determines the structure of *De Corpore:* Part i treats logic or method (exact deductive science); part ii, metaphysics or first philosophy (universal mental conceptions of bodies in motion); part iii, geometric mechanics (postulates of the mechanistic universe or cosmology); part iv, physics (causes of natural phenomena, including mental phenomena).

The basis of the third part, Hobbes's mechanics, is a postulate about the cause of motion in the whole universe: all the observed effects of motion are caused by some kind of simple circular motion, whose effects are transferred in a medium of full space (chs. 21–22, "Of Circular Motion" and "Other Variety of Motion"). Hobbes uses this model as both a cosmological thesis—to explain the motion of the solar system in a vortex around the sun—and as the basic mechanical explanation of the observed effects of natural phenomena.[7] Physics for Hobbes is simply the use of these postulates from geometric mechanics to explain the observed effects of Nature.

Accordingly, the process of physics can be divided into two steps. The first is to isolate or determine the identity of a natural phenomenon by noting its observed effects or appearances in the mind. This step is called establishing the *oti* (in Greek), or the "what it is," from some kind of prescientific knowledge of things. Hobbes's formulation of this step is unusual not only for its indifference to careful observation and measurement but also for the ambiguity about whether the definition of the phenomenon in question—the "what

7. In an unpublished work attributed to the 'early' Hobbes, the so-called *Little Treatise,* mechanical causality is explained by the emission theory—particles or waves emitted by dilation and contraction. In *De Corpore* Hobbes uses the simpler postulate of circular motion in a full space. One scholar has recently cast doubt on Hobbes's authorship of the *Little Treatise* by pointing out that it lacks Hobbes's most characteristic teaching about sense perception, that visible properties inhere not in the objects but only in the brain of the observer; the treatise, therefore, was probably composed by another member of the Cavendish circle in the late 1630s. Richard Tuck, "Hobbes and Descartes," in *Perspectives on Thomas Hobbes,* ed. G. A. J. Rogers and Alan Ryan (Oxford: Clarendon Press, 1988), pp. 16–18. This argument seems plausible (although impossible to confirm) because Hobbes's radical doubt about the senses logically precedes his mechanical postulates. As Tuck nicely shows, the claim that "one could have true knowledge of an internal world, of one's perceptions themselves" is the crucial issue in "the invention of modern philosophy" (pp. 28–29).

it is" or "whatness"—is merely an arbitrary collection of properties or involves some notion of essential properties grasped in the "whole idea" of the thing.

In the earlier chapters of *De Corpore* on method, Hobbes tends to equate "whatness" with the "whole idea" of a thing (in a quasi-Aristotelian manner) and even admits that we usually intuit this whole idea when we call things by universal names (1, 6.2). However, in part IV of *De Corpore*, on physics proper, Hobbes equates "whatness" with any loosely chosen collection of properties or observed effects. When he investigates the phenomenon of fire, for example, he defines fire as simply "shining and heating," and says that physics requires only a possible explanation of the generation of these two properties which is "agreeable to the rest of the phenomena of [fire]" (p. 451). So long as the properties are not asserted to be the *essential* attributes, Hobbes is willing to trust in the intuitions of common speech and common sense for the initial identification of phenomena.[8]

The second step in physical science, as this example suggests, is to construct a *dioti* (in Greek), or cause—that is, to develop a possible explanation from the postulates of geometric mechanics for the cause of these observed effects or appearances in the mind. Hobbes emphasizes in his discussion of physics that this cause can never be known to be the true cause; it will always be hypothetical. Even if we had the power to generate the phenomenon ourselves, only God could know if this was Nature's actual way of generating the apparent effects. To assert that a merely possible cause is the true cause would be "a revolt from philosophy to divination" (ch. 29, pp. 507, 531). Hobbes's physics, in short, is radically positivistic because it insists that the precise causal nexus that produces an effect such as fire is necessarily hypothetical; but it is absolutely dogmatic in the metaphysical claim that the chain of events is mechanically induced.[9]

Many scholars have observed that this version of mechanistic physics is peculiar to Hobbes and is even idiosyncratic in comparison with other mechanistic theories advanced by the illustrious

8. But this willingness to rely on common speech would not necessarily imply, as Jerry Weinberger suggests, that Hobbes's arguments against the naturalness of speech (nominalism) are mere rhetoric to disguise and achieve the Baconian project of conquering nature: "Hobbes's Doctrine of Method," *American Political Science Review*, 69 (1975), 1350–1353. It implies only that ordinary opinion can be as useful as arbitrary choice in deciding what natural phenomena to investigate.

9. Hoffding, *History of Modern Philosophy*, 1, 269–274.

founders of modern natural science—such as Galileo, Descartes, Gilbert, Boyle, and Newton. In the first place, as Brandt points out, Hobbes's theory of geometric mechanics is a "disaster" because it equates geometric demonstrability with mechanical possibility, ignoring reality. Hobbes never tested empirically the postulate of simple circular motion in a full space to see if it actually occurs in Nature, or how it is mechanically possible.[10] And his emphasis on the priority of simple circular motion to inertial motion in a straight line puts him outside the mainstream of modern mechanics.[11]

In the second place, as we noted, Hobbes was indifferent to observation for establishing the *oti*, or "what it is," of a phenomenon, resting satisfied with any partial or subjective definition. Nor did he develop an experimental method for testing the *dioti*, or possible mechanical cause, as did the more successful modern scientists. Hobbes was indifferent to empirical observation of phenomena because he rejected the idea of a complete or exhaustive definition of the "essence" of a substance. And he was indifferent to empirical verification of causes because he was content to show that a mechanical explanation of all phenomena of nature, however perfunctory, is possible. The result, as Peters remarks, is that Hobbes often "produced a redescription of what we already know in rather bizarre terminology or descriptions which seem absurd because of the inapplicability of mechanical concepts."[12]

A third peculiarity of Hobbes's physics is that it does not focus on the cause of a natural phenomenon as such but on the cause of our *sensations* of the natural phenomenon. Physics, therefore, ultimately reduces to the study of man—to conjectural human psychology and finally to human physiology. To take another example, when Hobbes examines the cause of heat in the sun, he does not give an account of physical or chemical reactions in the sun but a conjectural account of heat, perspiration, and swelling in the sentient man (*De Corpore*, 27.3). It is undoubtedly because his physics involves an a priori cosmological hypothesis applied to human physiology that Hobbes makes this surprising statement in the Epistle Dedicatory of *De Corpore:* Not Galileo, who founded "natural philosophy universal" as the knowledge of motion, but such physicians as Harvey are "the

10. Hobbes even boasts that "when we calculate the magnitude and motions of heaven and earth, we do not ascend into heaven that we may divide it into parts, or measure the motions thereof, but we do it sitting in our closets or in the dark" (*De Corpore*, 7.1).

11. Brandt, *Hobbes's Mechanical Conception of Nature*, pp. 323–325.

12. Peters, *Hobbes*, p. 94; Brandt, *Hobbes's Mechanical Conception of Nature*, p. 81.

only true natural philosophers."[13] In short, Hobbes regards the science of man—psychology and physiology—as the ultimate foundation of the science of Nature.[14]

Finally, the most distinctive trait of Hobbes's physics is the way Hobbes applies mechanistic causality to all natural and human phenomena, insisting that everything has a mechanical cause, even if he has not yet discovered it. Hobbes therefore seeks mechanical explanations for phenomena such as gravity and magnetism—phenomena that seem to defy notions of bodies touching other bodies in a full space, and that more "experimental" scientists of the day, such as Gilbert and Boyle, felt compelled to explain in terms of nonmaterial causes.[15] Moreover, Hobbes applied mechanistic causality to all mental phenomena, which even Descartes, who otherwise defended an a priori mechanistic science, was unwilling to do. Unlike Hobbes, Descartes left room for an incorporeal mind or a nonbodily substance to explain thinking.

In sum, most scholars readily agree that Hobbes's mechanistic physics is somewhat quirky and rather pathetic in comparison with the work of other seventeenth-century founders of modern natural science who thought in predominantly mechanistic terms. Yet such scholars are at a loss to explain why this is so. Even a scholar such as Frithiof Brandt, who has written a thorough and laborious treatment of Hobbes's mechanical conception of nature, is content to conclude that, despite its failures in method and application, Hobbes's system is distinguished by being the strictest, most consistent mechanistic philosophy ever written. This, of course, is a dubious distinction! The only remark that Brandt adds to his judgment is that Hobbes uses his mechanistic science for two special purposes: to provide a mechanistic account of sensation, thought, and the "subjectivity" of the qualities of sense; and to prove that immaterial causes or incorporeal substances are unnecessary assumptions for

13. Epistle Dedicatory, pp. viii–ix. Brandt discusses the dedication to *De Corpore* in detail but omits this crucial statement about the true foundation of the science of nature: *Hobbes's Mechanical Conception of Nature*, pp. 372–378.

14. This view is later echoed by David Hume in his Introduction to *A Treatise of Human Nature*: "It is evident, that all the sciences have a relation, greater or less, to human nature. . . . Even *Mathematics, Natural Philosophy, and Natural Religion*, are in some measure dependent on the science of MAN. . . . [for] the science of man is the only solid foundation for the other sciences": *A Treatise on Human Nature*, ed. A. D. Lindsay, 2 vols. (London: Everyman's, 1911), I, 4–5 (Hume's emphasis and capitalization).

15. *De Corpore*, 30.2, 30.15. See Edwin A. Burtt, *The Metaphysical Foundations of Modern Physical Science* (Garden City, N.Y.: Doubleday, 1954), pp. 166–167.

explaining the phenomena of nature.[16] But Brandt never asks the simple question: Why was Hobbes so dogmatic and uncompromising in maintaining that all natural and human phenomena could be explained mechanistically? Why was Hobbes so interested in proving that there are no abstract essences in nature and that the mind is corporeal?

The Construction of Mechanical Man

That Hobbes himself was aware of his restrictive purposes can be inferred from the conclusion of *De Corpore*. In the last paragraph of the book (ch. 30, p. 531), he says that his argument is sufficient to show that all nonmechanical explanations of nature—substantial forms, abstract essences, self-motion, occult qualities, intelligible species—are unnecessary. Moreover, he declares that the phenomena of nature which he finds most fascinating or "admirable" are mental phenomena, the thoughts and passions of the human mind. These remarks point to the primary purpose of natural science, to construct a model of mechanical man that will replace historical man.

As is well known, Hobbes explains all mental phenomena by a stimulus-response model. Thoughts are reduced to motions of the brain caused by reactions of the sense organs to external objects; and actions are shown to proceed from thoughts as they stimulate motions of the heart, producing desire and aversion, hope and fear. This is mechanical man, whose behavior can be explained in terms of "voluntary action"—action that is voluntary not in the sense of being freely chosen but in the sense of proceeding from the will and aimed at some apparent good, which is the necessary result of appetites and aversions. Thus, to understand man, we have no reason to presuppose any immaterial causes in the soul or suprasensible ideas in the mind, and no need to assume spiritual qualities such as freedom of the will (ch. 25.1–13).

When we look at this science of nature as a whole and see its applications, it is impossible to avoid the conclusion that Hobbes's science of nature is designed not primarily to understand nature but to explain the mind—to show that a fully satisfactory account of all operations of the human mind can be given without recourse to the doctrines of immaterial causes and immaterial minds or souls. By

16. Brandt, *Hobbes's Mechanical Conception of Nature*, pp. 7, 150, 370. Similarly, Burtt cites Hobbes's doctrine of the corporeal mind as his most important achievement among the early mechanists: *Metaphysical Foundations*, p. 129.

showing that the mind itself is body and hence a continuum of the natural necessity that governs the external world, Hobbes deflates the last pretensions of intellectual vanity and provides doctrinal support for the self-reliant mind.

In the process, however, something else occurs, which almost seems like an act of magic. Because Hobbes once again equates hypothetical truth with metaphysical truth, he not only describes mechanical man; he actually creates mechanical man. Almost magically, out of phantasms, so to speak, Hobbes brings into being a new kind of man who replaces historical man.

The doctrine of mechanical man is built entirely from introspective knowledge, from mental thoughts purged of trust in authority and trust in appearances of sense. Such introspective knowledge separates the mind from the external world of nature and thus makes it impossible to know the true causes of any given natural phenomenon. But when the phenomenon in question is the mind itself, the distinction between what is inside the mind and what is outside the mind breaks down; the subject and the object are the same. Thus it is possible for a philosophical description of the mind to become a practical act of making or creating the mind—the description becomes the reality. For this reason the model of mechanical man seems to fulfill the need of Hobbes's enlightenment science to perfection: it enables the self-reliant mind to be self-grounding (to stand on its own foundation without reliance on external authority) and to be in conformity with the necessary order of nature.

The only problem with this claim is that the leap from historical man to self-grounding mechanical man cannot be assured when the concept of mechanical man is introduced into the political world.[17] Historical man is the product of civilization, a creature motivated by intellectual vanity and attached to all kinds of opinions, prejudices, beliefs, and doctrines about immaterial causes and incorporeal minds. He can be lead by scientific enlightenment to see these things as dangerous illusions, but will not automatically accept the mechanical model of man as a self-evident truth. Hobbes's political treatises wrestle with the dilemma of combining historical knowledge of man and self-evident scientific knowledge of man. The result is Hobbes's strange and original teaching about the state of nature or the natural condition of mankind.

17. Johnston's account of the "two models of man" in Hobbes clearly draws the contrast between the historical, irrational model and the scientific, rational model but does not address the perplexing metaphysical question of how the latter comes into being: Rhetoric of "Leviathan," pp. 106–113.

»6«

The Enlightened Mind
and the Science of Politics

Redefining the 'Natural' Basis of Politics

Students of politics are usually surprised and puzzled when they open Hobbes's political treatises. Instead of finding an analysis of politics in the conventional sense—studies of institutions and laws, political parties, forms of government, guidelines for the conduct of statesmen—they encounter an elaborate series of definitions, stated as if they were self-evident, that present a mechanistic theory of knowledge and human motivation. The culmination of this theory is Hobbes's account of the state of nature, a description of individuals in a prepolitical condition of anarchy and brutish warfare, and a teaching about the natural right of self-preservation. When confronted with this theory, many readers do not ask why Hobbes proceeds in this unusual fashion. They tend to assume that Hobbes had a personal obsession with the breakdown of civilization as a result of the English Civil War but was so impressed by geometric reasoning and mechanistic science that he abandoned the insights of historical experience and constructed a self-contained, deductive science of politics.[1]

Although this view contains important elements of truth, it fails to uncover the reasons for Hobbes's pattern of thought. Hobbes, I have argued, made a deliberate choice to abandon the common-sense or conventional perspective on politics. As his writings on civil

1. See, for example, Maurice M. Goldsmith, *Hobbes's Science of Politics* (New York: Columbia University Press, 1966); Richard Peters, *Hobbes* (Baltimore: Penguin, 1967); and, more recently, Tom Sorrell, *Hobbes* (London: Routledge & Kegan Paul, 1986).

139

history reveal, he is perfectly capable of discussing political phenomena in such terms—analyzing institutions, the behavior of parties and factions, the folly and courage of kings and generals, the strengths and weaknesses of various forms of government. But he claims that all such phenomena exist only by virtue of the opinions and beliefs that men hold about right and wrong, justice and injustice, and the ultimate nature of reality. Politics, therefore, is reducible to one primary fact: the struggle over opinions, refined and developed by intellectual authorities into 'doctrinal politics.'

Hobbes's boldness lies not only in this enormous simplification of political history; it also consists in thinking that political science can make a radical break with the past, that the whole world of opinion in which politics historically has operated can be changed. This goal requires a new kind of political treatise, one that does not accept as naturally given or divinely ordained the world of received opinions and authoritative wisdom. Such a treatise must accomplish nothing less than the reconstruction of the human mind and the redefinition of reality, starting from self-evident thoughts of the enlightened mind and deducing a system of political science.

To be successful, however, the treatises must deliberately omit or obscure their real beginning point in prescientific historical reflection. If they are to avoid creating another doctrinal dispute by a polemical confrontation with the past, they must appear to stand on a point outside of history that is timeless and universal.[2] Historical knowledge is thereby transcended and replaced by an ahistorical political science. That science in turn will be paradoxical because it is, on the one hand, an arbitrary construct of the enlightened mind (a science freed from trust in the harmony of mind and reality) and, on the other hand, a theory in accordance with nature (a "science of natural justice").

All of these strange and complicated layers of self-consciousness go into the doctrine that is the foundation of Hobbes's political science: the state-of-nature teaching. As we shall see in a moment, this doctrine has three dimensions: a historical teaching about the warfare of primitive man and preexisting civilized man; a psychological teaching about natural appetite and vainglory; and a logical construction of mechanical man in an isolated condition. Although these three dimensions can be distinguished, they are deliberately mingled together by Hobbes in his portrait of natural man or "the natural condition of mankind." For Hobbes's purpose is to make a

2. Following Eisenach's formulation: "The new political order will be timeless and will represent a victory over . . . history" (*Two Worlds of Liberalism*, p. 32).

transition from historical man to scientific or mechanical man without forcing a direct confrontation between the two. In so doing he seeks to redefine the 'natural' basis of politics without causing a doctrinal dispute that would defeat the very purpose of his political science.

The State of Nature

To understand the sources and significance of Hobbes's state-of-nature teaching, one must first clarify some of the confusion created by contemporary scholarship. The prevailing scholarly view is that Hobbes's account of the state of nature is not a statement of historical fact but a logical fiction—a hypothetical construction from self-evident premises. As Gordon Schochet remarks, the older critics of Hobbes held that "the Hobbesian state of nature was intended as an actual historical account of man's prepolitical condition. It is generally argued today, however, that Hobbes designed his state of nature as a logical and reductionist device to demonstrate the necessity of absolute government."[3] For the most part, this approach reflects the influence of Anglo-American analytical philosophy, which inclines students of the history of philosophy (as well as such contemporary philosophers as John Rawls) to treat state-of-nature doctrines and social contract theories as purely logical devices for generating theories of justice and obligation.

Surprisingly, this view of the state of nature is also held by such scholars as Macpherson, who presents a Marxist reading of Hobbes, and Strauss, who attempts to explain Hobbes's transformation of the natural law tradition. This view is particularly striking in Macpherson's case because he emphasizes the historical assumptions of Hobbes's abstract postulates. Nevertheless, he asserts that "Hobbes's state of nature is a logical hypothesis." Similarly, Strauss devotes a great deal of attention to Hobbes's ideas about the historical origins of the state but concludes that "the state of nature is for Hobbes not a historical fact, but a necessary construction."[4]

---

3. Schochet, "Hobbes on the Family," p. 429. For examples of scholars who view Hobbes's state of nature as a logical fiction, see Howard Warrender, *The Political Philosophy of Hobbes: His Theory of Obligation* (Oxford: Clarendon, 1957), pp. 30, 237–242; Watkins, *Hobbes's System of Ideas*, p. 72; F. C. Hood, *The Divine Politics of Thomas Hobbes* (Oxford: Clarendon, 1964), p. 74; Gregory Kavka, *Hobbesian Moral and Political Theory* (Princeton: Princeton University Press, 1986), p. 84.

4. Macpherson, *The Political Theory of Possessive Individualism*, p. 21; Strauss, *The Political Philosophy of Hobbes*, p. 104.

One of the few dissenters from the prevailing view is Schochet, who calls for a systematic integration of Hobbes's historical works and scientific treatises. His interpretation, however, is limited to Hobbes's views on the patriarchal family in the state of nature and thus is not comprehensive. Despite these limitations, he points the way toward a more complex interpretation of Hobbes's state-of-nature teaching by showing that Hobbes does not "maintain a consistent distinction between the historical and logical aspects of his political theories."[5] The full significance of this insightful remark needs elaboration.

Hobbes's state-of-nature doctrine actually has three aspects—the historical, the psychological, and the logical—and these three aspects reflect the complicated process by which Hobbes's political science frees the enlightened mind from authoritative opinion and finds a new grounding in nature. My interpretation draws upon all of Hobbes's political treatises without attempting to distinguish them; for the chapters devoted to the state of nature—in *The Elements of Law,* part 1, chapter 14, "The Estate of Nature"; in *De Cive,* chapter 1, "Of the State of Men without Civil Society" (called the "state of nature" in section 4); and in *Leviathan,* chapter 13, "Of the Natural Condition of Mankind, concerning their Felicity and Misery"—are sufficiently similar to permit common treatment.[6]

The State of Nature as a Historical Teaching

On the simplest level, the state of nature is a historical account of barbarism or savagery. It is described as a condition in which no "common power" exists to keep men in awe and hence is a state of general warfare. Because life in this state is a continuous struggle for survival, men lack the leisure and the incentive to cultivate the arts and sciences: "there is no place for industry, . . . no arts; no letters; no society; and which is worst of all, continuous fear and danger of violent death" (*Leviathan,* ch. 13, p. 113). Such conditions, as

5. Schochet, "Hobbes on the Family," pp. 429, 445. Eisenach's study is also very insightful on this point but draws the distinction too sharply in stating that Hobbes's account of "man in 'mere Nature' . . . considers the manners, passions, and powers of men in a nonhistorical context" (*Two Worlds of Liberalism,* p. 33).

6. François Tricaud attempts to show that the accounts of the state of nature in Hobbes's three treatises differ, reflecting an evolution of thought over an eleven-year period. But the differences he cites are minor ones of emphasis and wording, as he admits in concluding that Hobbes "held fast to some basic intuitions, . . . [although] we have no proof that he was ever satisfied with the wording he gave them": "Hobbes's Conception of the State of Nature from 1640 to 1651: Evolution and Ambiguities," in *Perspectives on Thomas Hobbes,* ed. Rogers and Ryan, pp. 107–123.

I argued in chapter 1, are precisely what Hobbes attributes to the historical condition of barbarism or savagery—the absence of centralized political power, the absence of leisure to cultivate the intellect or the arts and sciences (except for a primitive kind of speech and the arts useful for survival), and the continuous struggle for existence.[7]

Moreover, Hobbes states explicitly in all three political treatises that this is an actual description of life among savage people. In the *Elements* he calls upon the reader to confirm his description by comparing it to "the experience of savage nations that live in this day, and by the histories of our ancestors, the old inhabitants of Germany" (1, 14.12). In *De Cive* and in *Leviathan*, he cites the case of "savage people in many places of America" who have no government at all "except the government of small families, the concord whereof depends on natural lust" (1.13; ch. 13, p. 114). In making these references Hobbes clearly indicates that "the natural condition of mankind" is one that once really existed in primitive times and still exists in his day in some parts of the world where life is prepolitical (confined to families and tribes without great cities or great nations) and prescientific (without the luxury of cultivating the arts and sciences).

In addition to describing the condition of barbarism, Hobbes's teaching about the state of nature refers to the imperfectly constituted civilized societies of the past and present. Explicit references

---

7. As I also argued in ch. 1, Hobbes may have been influenced by the ancient Roman historian Diodorus Siculus in his understanding of the earliest human condition. One passage in particular from Diodorus is worth quoting at length for its similarity to Hobbes's account of precivil life:

But the first men to be born, they say, led an undisciplined and bestial life, setting out one by one to secure their sustenance. . . . Then, since they were attacked by the wild beasts, they came to each other's aid, being instructed in expediency, and when gathered together in this way by reason of their fear, they gradually came to recognize their mutual characteristics. And though the sounds which they made were at first unintelligible and indistinct, yet gradually they came to give articulation to their speech, and by agreeing with one another upon symbols for each thing, . . . made known among themselves the significance which was to be attached to each term. . . . Now the first men, since none of the things useful for life had yet been discovered, led a wretched existence. . . . Little by little, however, experience taught them both to take to the caves in winter and to store such fruits as could be preserved. And when they had become acquainted with fire and other useful things, the arts and whatever else is capable of furthering man's social life were gradually discovered. (*Diodorus of Sicily*, trans. C. H. Oldfather, Loeb ed. in 10 vols. [London: William Heinemann, 1933], 1.8).

Hobbes, of course, departs from Diodorus in emphasizing the family and fear of other men rather than fear of wild animals by isolated individuals as the origins of sociality.

to such societies can be found in all three political treatises. In the *Elements,* for example, he says that the state of "hostility and war" which exists "by nature" refers not only to "savage nations . . . [and] the old inhabitants of Germany . . . [but also to] *other now civil countries,* where we find people few, and short-lived, and without ornaments and comforts of life, which by peace and society are usually invented and procured" (i, 14.12; emphasis added). In the *Leviathan* Hobbes cites as examples of this brutish condition of warfare "the manner of life, which men that have formerly lived under a peaceful government, use to degenerate into, in a civil war" (ch. 13, pp. 114–115). This remark clearly indicates that the imperfectly constituted governments of past and present civilizations which tend to dissolve into civil war are not fundamentally different from savagery.

In *De Cive* Hobbes provides a more detailed explanation of why these two conditions may be equated. The defect of so-called civilized societies, he says, is "the discord arising from the comparison of wits," which produce wars "between sects of the same religion, and factions of the same commonweal, where contestation is either concerning doctrines or political prudence" (1.5). In other words, the state of nature is a description of both savagery, in which no common power exists and wars of conquest and plunder occur, and preexisting civilization, in which the common power is so weak that discords over opinions and doctrines make life as miserable as savagery.

Obviously, one purpose of such a comparison is to deflate the pretensions of civilized men and to refute their traditional claims of superiority over savages. Hobbes even suggests, though he does not emphasize the point, that government, religion, and science as traditionally conceived are largely responsible for the degradation of civilization; they generate the disputes over doctrines which lead to general warfare. Like Rousseau in his *First and Second Discourses,* Hobbes believes that civilization itself is a cause of human misery. And although he certainly does not romanticize savage life, Hobbes does suggest in a Rousseauian way that savages are more humane (more innocent, less vengeful) than civilized men in their conduct of war.

Savage wars are caused by natural appetite, which, Hobbes says in the first chapter of *De Cive,* is "the most frequent reason why men desire to hurt each other" because they must compete for scarce goods. But wars caused by "the combat of wits" cause the "fiercest and greatest discords" because they are motivated by "mutual scorn and contempt" (1.5–6).[8] As a historical teaching, then, the state-of-nature doctrine punctures the illusions of stability and self-sufficiency held by civilized men and destroys the claim of moral superiority of civilization to savagery.

This moral critique is also implied in Hobbes's account of justice and right in the state of nature. In one formulation he says that the state of continuous warfare and struggle for survival in the natural condition means that "the notions of right and wrong, justice and injustice, have there no place" (*Leviathan*, ch. 13, p. 115). According to a more succinct formulation, "might is right" in the state of nature (*Elements*, 1, 14.13). In the light of the historical conditions to which these statements refer, they should be interpreted as follows.

In the primitive state of savagery, the statement that justice and right "have no place" is literally true. For not only did authority rest on physical coercion or natural force, but the very notions of "right" and "justice" and "law" did not exist. They were not yet invented. They were not even thought of or conceived because general rules require abstraction from particular sensations, which can be achieved only with the cultivation of speech in civilized conditions of relative ease. For civilized societies of the past and present, however, Hobbes's statement about the absence of justice is not literally true. There such notions abound. Opinions of justice, as well as philosophical doctrines of right, prudence, and other moral terms, exist and are known to all. But none is effective in securing agreement and obedience, so force and physical coercion actually determine who rules. Hobbes therefore uses the ambiguous phrase—justice and right "have no place"—to equate the literal nonexistence of notions of right in the savage state with the ineffectiveness of notions of right in civilized societies. In so doing he takes the readers of his books, readers living in a civilized age of doctrinal politics, as closely as possible to the perspective of barbarism where moral notions of right and wrong do not exist at all. Thus savagery and preexisting civilization are virtually (but not exactly) identical in their lack of felicity, sociality, and morality.

The State of Nature as a Psychological Teaching

Although Hobbes's teaching about the state of nature refers to actual historical conditions, the historical references are kept in the

8. This observation is similar to the one in *De Homine*, where Hobbes claims that revenge and cruelty are peculiar to man because they arise from the human capacity for language or speech(x.3).

background. They are unmistakable, corresponding precisely to the descriptions found in Hobbes's histories. But they are made almost parenthetically and can be easily overlooked or ignored. Scholars are therefore correct in arguing that the state of nature is in some sense an abstraction from historical conditions. But the reasons for this abstraction are generally misunderstood. Hobbes abstracts from history not by omitting it altogether and presenting general postulates that are either arbitrarily invented or self-evidently asserted. He abstracts in accordance with his method of reducing, resolving, or distilling the given phenomenon into its constituent elements. As we saw in chapter 3, those elements are essentially psychological. Hobbes's state-of-nature teaching is an abstraction in the sense of being a reduction of historical views of barbarism and civilization to psychology.

Consider the psychological postulates that Hobbes presents in his descriptions of the natural condition of mankind. They are designed to explain why authority is nonexistent or ineffective in preexisting societies, and hence why men are "apt to invade and destroy one another." In the *Elements* and *De Cive,* Hobbes cites two passions as the cause of such conflict: vainglory and natural appetite (I, 14.3–5; 1.4–7). In the *Leviathan* he cites three: the desires for security, gain, and glory or reputation (ch. 13, p. 112). Although Hobbes presents these psychological postulates without showing their derivation, it is evident that they are reductions of historical observations, for his descriptions of the passions include significant details that reveal their historical contexts.

In describing the passion of vainglory or the desire for reputation, for example, Hobbes alludes briefly to the social phenomena that historically have been the causes or stimuli of this passion, namely, words and opinions. In the *Elements* he says that vainglory is a desire for "precedency and superiority over others," which makes men "apt to provoke [each] other by comparisons . . . [that is,] by words and other signs of contempt and hatred, which are incident to all comparison" (I, 14.3–4). In *De Cive* he also cites vainglory as the reason some men who "suppose themselves above others . . . [from] a false estimate of their strength" are led to challenge and hurt other people. Here, as we noted above, Hobbes explicitly links vainglory with the "combat of wits" over opinions and doctrines (1.4–5). And in *Leviathan* he presents the most detailed description of vainglory, indicating that it is primarily *intellectual* vainglory. At the beginning of his chapter 13, on the natural condition of mankind, Hobbes argues that men are essentially equal by nature with respect to mental abilities because wisdom is artificially acquired. But, he adds, "that which may perhaps make such an equality incredible is but a vain conceit of one's own wisdom, which almost all men think they have in greater degree than the vulgar; that is, than all men but themselves, and a few others, whom by fame, or for concurring with themselves, they approve."

This statement is a reduction of the entire problem of civilization to a succinct psychological observation. It indicates that the belief in inequality or in the right of one man to claim superiority over another is essentially a feeling of intellectual superiority, which men seek to confirm through approval and recognition. It is a passion that has the effect of turning all men into intellectual snobs, believing that they and a few colleagues are the only possessors of wisdom, the only ones who are justified in looking down on the vulgar. The universality of this passion is consistent with Hobbes's observation that one can usually distinguish between the many who are "content to live within modest bounds" and the few who seek honor and precedence above the rest. For it is a latent tendency in everyone who speaks and seeks recognition for his speech, and it is particularly prevalent in the present age of learned opinions, when even common people have acquired the arts of rhetoric and disputation. Thus Hobbes's description of vainglory in his account of the state of nature is a succinct summary of the general tendency of human beings throughout the history of civilization.

His descriptions of the other dominant passions—natural appetite or the desires for security and gain—also reflect historical experience. In *De Cive* Hobbes says that natural appetite is the reason why "men at the same time have an appetite for the same thing; which yet very often they can neither enjoy in common, nor divide." In the *Leviathan* he adds the observation that "if one plant, sow, build, or possess a convenient seat, others may probably be expected to come prepared with forces united, to dispossess and deprive him, not only of the fruit of his labour, but also of his life and liberty." From the appetites for security and gain Hobbes deduces the principles of "competition and diffidence," which are the most frequent causes of human conflict (*Leviathan*, ch. 13, p. 112). This psychology of natural appetite is obviously derived from historical sources, either from accounts of savage life or from ordinary observations of the competition for scarce goods which continues in various degrees in civilized societies.

In the following passage from chapter 13 of *Leviathan*, Hobbes succinctly summarizes his psychological teaching with brief allusions to historical contexts:

So that in the nature of man, we find three principal causes of quarrel. First, competition; secondly, diffidence; thirdly, glory.

The first maketh men invade for gain; the second, for safety; the third, for reputation. The first use violence to make themselves *masters of other men's persons, wives, children and cattle;* the second, to defend them; the third, for *trifles, as a word, a smile, a different opinion,* and any other sign of undervalue. (P. 112; emphasis added)

This passage is striking because it actually enumerates the objects that stimulate the passions for security, gain, and glory. They are the objects of contention in the two most typical historical conditions. In the primitive or savage stage, the heads of families and tribes contend for necessary or natural things, such as women, servants, animals, and instruments of production; hence their motivation may be reduced to "natural appetite." In the more civilized societies of the past, men struggled primarily for recognition of superior wisdom, reflected in words and opinions; hence their motivation may be reduced to vainglory.

Thus, while preserving a few historical details to indicate his sources, Hobbes for the most part dispenses with history and presents his state-of-nature teaching in a simple but powerful statement about the most prevalent human passions.

The State of Nature as a Logical Construction

By beginning with historical observations and reducing them to a few psychological maxims, Hobbes presents a teaching about human nature or man's natural condition that is neither hypothetical nor fictional but factual and real. There is, however, another dimension to this teaching which is not derived from historical observation of real men. This dimension, when properly understood, is one that scholars correctly regard as a logical construction or invention. It is a dimension of the state of nature which Hobbes himself admits lies outside the bounds of historical experience. He calls it "the natural liberty of particular men."

In a well-known passage of the *Leviathan,* Hobbes says that the condition of general warfare which has prevailed throughout human history is a "war of every man against everyman." He immediately adds that, literally and precisely speaking, there never has been a condition of every man fighting against every other man, or a complete liberty of isolated individuals: "It may peradventure be thought, there never was such a time, nor condition of war as this; and I believe it was never generally so, over all the world; . . . [for] there never ha[s] been any time, wherein particular men were in a condition of war one against another; . . . [or] that misery which accompanies the liberty of particular men" (ch. 13, p. 112). Hobbes acknowledges, in other words, that there never has been a condition of pure individualism, that is, a condition of individuals detached from social groups who are mutually hostile to each other. Historically, Hobbes knows, men always have been found in groups—either in natural groups, such as the families, clans, and tribes of savages or in artificial groups, such as the communities of shared opinions and common speech among civilized peoples. Hence wars have always been waged between groups rather than among individuals.[9] Nor has there ever been a condition of natural liberty in which isolated individuals have a right to all things necessary for their preservation. Rather, men have been in the savage condition *without* a notion of right, following mere instinct and obeying the natural force of conquerors and patriarchs. Or they have lived in civilized conditions, in which their liberty has been limited by the opinions and doctrines of authorities which bind them to higher laws and obligate them to obey right reason. Thus the liberty of isolated individuals or the liberty of particular men with a right to all things has never existed at any time or anywhere in the world.

Where does Hobbes get this revolutionary idea? On what grounds can he claim that this condition is natural or real? A clue is provided in the following remark about the absence of justice in the natural condition: "[in] this war of every man against every man, . . . nothing can be unjust. The notions of right and wrong, justice and injustice have there no place. . . . Justice, and injustice are none of the faculties, neither of the body, nor mind. *If they were, they might be in a man that were alone in the world, as well as his senses, and passions.* They are qualities that relate to men in society, not in solitude" *Leviathan*, ch. 13, p. 115; emphasis added). As this passage reveals, Hobbes arrives at his view of the isolated individual by a mental exercise that abstracts from or removes the social context in which men always have been found. In other words, he abstracts from the opinions formed from speech which men have created to express their notions of right and wrong. These opinions have created the social bonds (as well as the conflicts and divisions) in preexisting civilized societies.

Hobbes's justification for abstracting from such opinions and social bonds is twofold. One reason is the historical fact that they have proved to be ineffective or impotent: they lack the power to com-

9. See Preston King, *The Ideology of Order: A Comparative Analysis of Jean Bodin and Thomas Hobbes* (London: Allen & Unwin, 1974), pp. 187–191.

mand assent or obedience and hence can be ignored. The other reason is the scientific argument that such opinions are metaphysically nonexistent: they have no metaphysical reality because they are nothing more than empty words or verbal sounds or motions of the tongue. These arguments are the two pillars of enlightenment science, the historical and scientific proofs that the human mind can be freed from trust in authoritative speech. When such speech disappears into thin air by the 'magic' of enlightenment, the self-reliant mind remains. The self-awareness or self-consciousness of this mind is the foundation of the radically free or isolated individual: the individual who possesses only his senses and passions and is aware of nothing more than a necessary impulsion to satisfy his own selfish desires or to seek his own apparent good.

Yet how can Hobbes claim that such an individual, stripped of the language that creates social bonds and possessing only sense experiences and passions, is natural? Obviously, he is not natural in the sense of being primitive, naive, or prescientific. He is a product of scientific construction in an advanced stage of civilization and therefore possesses reason and a capacity for science. Accordingly, he can think of himself as an example of Hobbes's mechanical man. Moreover, such a man actually comes into being when the reader of Hobbes's treatises throws off the illusions of intellectual vanity and conceives of himself as a product of natural necessity. This process is possible because man, unlike other phenomena of nature whose generation can be explained only hypothetically, is what he appears to be in his own mind. Indeed, Man is Mind, which means that the hypothetical explanation of his being and the real explanation of his being are indistinguishable. When the reader becomes aware of himself as a product of natural necessity, his mechanical conception of himself is, so to speak, an ontological event: it abolishes the previously existing civilized man, whose being is simply a vain illusion, and brings into being the only right and true nature of man. Human nature is thereby reconstituted by the self-evidence of introspective science, and mechanical man becomes natural man.

In this way Hobbes invents the individual, an altogether new phenomenon in human history, and then brings him into being as natural man. But a crucial ambiguity remains. Hobbes cannot redefine human nature without leaving reminders of what man once was, a creature of vanity and metaphysical illusion. Hobbes may have stripped away the opinions and speech of historical man in his account of the natural condition, but he still includes a description of the destructive and irrational passions that have reigned hitherto.

Hobbes, in other words, tries to expunge history as much as possible from his state-of-nature teaching, creating the impression (largely successful, judging by the reaction of modern scholars) that the state of nature is a timeless and universal condition that 'wipes the slate clean.' But Hobbes cannot expunge history completely. He needs the contrast between the old view of the 'natural' and his new view of the 'natural' to show the superiority of the new view (the old leads to war, whereas the new leads to peace). Moreover, he needs to borrow some of the characteristics of existing civilized man—chiefly the concern with right reason and natural right—to make his own doctrine succeed. As much as Hobbes would like to do without history, he cannot do so because his own political science rests on historical premises that can be hidden but never wholly eliminated.

The Denial of Superhuman Support for Justice and the Collapse of Natural Right into Natural Necessity

A good example of Hobbes's unacknowledged use of historical premises is the assertion that the isolated individuals of the state of nature are rational actors—individuals endowed with "reason" who can emerge from the condition of mutual hostility by grasping the rational precepts of natural law. Such individuals, according to Hobbes, are capable of obeying the command of reason to desire what is good and to avoid what is evil. Above all, they are capable of avoiding "the chiefest of natural evils, which is death. . . . It is therefore neither absurd nor reprehensible, neither against right reason, for [such] a man to use all his endeavors to preserve and defend his body and the members thereof from death and sorrows" (*De Cive*, I.7)

Hobbes never explains or justifies the attribution of this crucial characteristic to "natural man." As the philosopher Rousseau and many scholars have asked, how can such men—who are by nature isolated, asocial, and without the faculty of speech—be endowed with the capacity to obey right reason? Is not the capacity to obey right reason found only among civilized men who have discovered and developed rational science? Clearly, to answer these questions and to uphold the view that natural man is an individual rational actor, Hobbes must rely on some premise about man's nature that is not derived from mechanistic science. A stimulus-response model of human behavior guarantees that the actor will pursue some apparent good; but it does not guarantee the rational pursuit of what is really good. The assertion that isolated individuals are not only natural but rational actors must rely on a premise derived from historical knowledge about how the enlightenment transforms the existing world.

Hobbes's position presupposes the following logical steps. When the reader of Hobbes's political treatises encounters the state of nature in which "notions of right and wrong, justice and injustice have no place," in which there is "no law" and "force and fraud are . . . the two cardinal virtues," he recognizes that *there is no natural sanction or superhuman support for justice.* He feels abandoned by nature and nature's God and becomes distrustful of all men who claim to speak for higher authorities. He experiences, in short, the fear of violent death. But in his isolation he also discovers the need to think for himself. Although his condition resembles that of primitive or prescientific man in its freedom from authoritative opinions, it involves a sophisticated form of doubt—enlightenment—that is possible only in the advanced stages of Western civilization. Such a person is a strange combination of barbarism and civilization: a kind of civilized barbarian. For he has rejected every preexisting doctrine without rejecting rational science itself, the activity that makes the whole process of enlightenment possible.

Because the isolated individual created by Hobbes resembles primitive man while accepting the progress of science in civilization, he remains a rational actor, an individual capable of right reason. But reason stripped of illusions about superhuman support for justice now means *enlightened* reason, not the reason that trusts in authority. For the awareness of being abandoned by superhuman powers engenders the fear of persecution and death at the hands of men who trust in such powers. Hence enlightened reason commands the individual to act on such fears, to do what is necessary to preserve himself and rationally pursue his own good. This command of reason—to do what is right—is easy to obey. Indeed, it is indisputable. For it requires the enlightened individual to do what he already wants to do or what he necessarily must do as a result of his nature. Natural right thereby coincides exactly with natural necessity, with the imperatives of fear and utilitarian satisfaction. All that remains for Hobbes to show is the best means for attaining these ends, either submitting to superior physical force or establishing a common power to overawe every individual.

When looking at the state-of-nature doctrine, we could not be more unfair or mistaken than to accuse Hobbes of committing the so-called naturalistic fallacy—of attempting to derive an 'ought' from an 'is' or a moral obligation from a natural necessity. Such criticisms, the focus of so much scholarly debate, misconstrue the problem Hobbes is trying to solve. Hobbes is attempting not to create moral obligations but to weaken or destroy obligation—to 'de-obligate' men, as it were. He seeks to overcome the problem of doctrinal politics, wherein justice is derived from superhuman authorities (God, Nature, and custom) but never coincides with what men actually do or actually think. Living in a doctrinal age, however, Hobbes cannot abolish doctrines of right or make them disappear. Nor does he want to. He realizes that the doctrinal age provides the opportunity to do something better. He can devise a doctrine of right which in simple terms equates right with might or in more complex terms makes right coincide with what men do as a necessary impulsion of their (newly discovered) nature. Thus Hobbes seeks not to derive an 'ought' from an 'is' but to collapse 'ought' into 'is'—to make right coincide with what exists by natural necessity.[10]

He can do so because mechanical man is a necessary conception of the mind who actually comes into being when existing civilized man dispels the illusions of intellectual vainglory and rediscovers his natural indifference to doctrines. Mechanical man thereby provides a normative standard (a standard of right) simply by being what he is, an individual motivated by the necessity of avoiding death and satisfying his selfish desires. With this claim Hobbes believes he has solved the problem of doctrinal politics: he has created a doctrine that cannot be disputed because what is right coincides with what already is in the mind of every individual.

Strictly speaking, of course, Hobbes has created a new doctrine that is paradoxical. Natural right is equated with the *absence* of right—with natural liberty or freedom from obligation to higher authority. Although natural right is equated with absence of right, it is

---

10. Thus the debate about 'political obligation' in Hobbes, engendered by the Taylor-Warrender thesis, seems unresolvable because the nature of the problem has been imperfectly understood. See Peters, *Hobbes*, pp. 158–165; the articles in Keith C. Brown, *Hobbes Studies* (Cambridge: Harvard University Press, 1965); and a more recent summary in D. D. Raphael, *Hobbes: Morals and Politics* (London: Allen & Unwin, 1977). Macpherson's remarks on this problem are more insightful; he claims that Hobbes commits no logical fallacy because an obligation can sometimes be derived from factual observations, such as "the postulate of equality": *Theory of Possessive Individualism*, pp. 74–87. But Macpherson's position is also misleading because it too is based on an inadequate understanding of the problem. Hobbes's goal is to destroy the sense of obligation to higher authorities and to collapse right into necessity so that existing men will overcome their addiction to doctrinal politics.

not abolished. The reason Hobbes does not simply dispense with natural right altogether is that he cannot do without a notion of 'the natural.' Just as he needs to ground the self-reliant mind in a doctrine of nature which expels the kingdom of darkness, so he needs to ground the selfish behavior of the enlightened individual in a notion of natural right which expels the obligations of higher authorities. In other words, the polemical character of Hobbes's enterprise requires a paradoxical formulation that seems confusing to later generations who have forgotten the problem, while being perfectly acceptable and even necessary for Hobbes.

The Rhetorical Strategies of the Three Political Treatises

The fact that Hobbes's new doctrine of right remains paradoxical—equating right with necessity—means that there is no guarantee that it will be realized. The new doctrine that is designed to end all doctrinal disputes is still a doctrine open to dispute. It is not simply self-evident but rests on a *free choice*—a choice between two mutually exclusive alternatives. On the one hand, men can perpetuate the "kingdom of darkness" that has existed since the beginning of civilization (in the West, and even before that time in Africa and Asia). Or, on the other hand, they can make a radical break with the past and follow the path of enlightenment: they can free the human mind from authoritative wisdom and promote autonomous or self-reliant thinking, which rejects every form of trust in authority, speech, and sense experience. The whole choice depends on simple honesty: admitting that superhuman powers (whether they exist or not) do not provide for men by giving the human mind clear guidance and support.

But that honesty is neither automatic nor guaranteed; it can occur only through a kind of rational persuasion. The kind of rational persuasion that is required for the realization of Hobbes's political science is most unusual. It is not simply the use of a new scientific method, which gives his doctrine the appearance of being derived deductively from evident premises. Nor is it simply a form of rhetoric, the use of vivid metaphors such as "Leviathan" and "the kingdom of darkness" and "Behemoth" and "the kingdom of fairies," which convey the ideas of a complicated scientific doctrine in simple images accessible to popular understanding. Recent studies of Hobbes which seek to explain his special form of persuasion as either a new method or adaptations of traditional rhetoric fail to see the profound problem of persuasion created by Hobbes's project for enlightenment.[11]

Stated succinctly, the problem for Hobbes is to write political treatises that enable the reader to make an intellectual leap from the realm of history to the timeless realm of science without engaging in disputation, polemics, and intellectual controversy. To do so would defeat the purpose of presenting an indisputable doctrine. But not to do so would mean omitting the real reasons for the superiority of his doctrine (its derivation without trust in authority). The way Hobbes handles this dilemma is the most subtle and elusive feature of his strategy for 'persuasion' in the political treatises. Instead of presenting the exclusive choice that lies at the heart of his doctrine as a free choice (to be debated and voted up or down), he presents it as a fait accompli, as a leap from history to science which has already occurred.

Hobbes realizes that in order to make his doctrine succeed—to be received without disputation—he must present the exclusive choice between the kingdom of darkness and the world of enlightenment as already accomplished in the writing of his political treatises. His doctrine must appear as a series of self-evident propositions that cannot be denied or disputed, even though they have been previously derived from the intellectual process of enlightenment. Thus the resolution of authoritative opinion into its constituent elements, the expulsion of the metaphysical illusions of opinion by radical distrust and fear of death, the discovery of the self-reliant mind through introspection—all these steps have taken place backstage, as it were, and remain hidden from the reader. To uncover these steps through an elaborate process of reconstruction is to subvert

11. David Johnston recognizes that Hobbes's rhetoric is different from older forms of rhetoric by being an action as well as a kind of speech—an act of cultural transformation. But ultimately he treats Hobbes's rhetoric in fairly conventional terms. He points to the use of metaphors or "speaking pictures" and claims that this art is perfected only in the *Leviathan*, apparently forgetting that the "dry discourse" of the earlier *Elements* also includes the powerful metaphor of life as "a race" (I, 9.21): *Rhetoric of "Leviathan,"* pp. 66–91. Others describe Hobbes's rhetorical strategy as the art of persuading influential audiences, such as rebellious Puritans or gentlemen with royalist sympathies, by subtly co-opting their language. See Mark Gavre, "Hobbes and His Audience: The Dynamics of Theorizing," *American Political Science Review,* 68 (1974), 1542–1556; and Richard Ashcraft, "Political Theory and Practical Action: A Reconsideration of Hobbes's State of Nature Doctrine," *Hobbes Studies,* 1 (1988), 63–88. Perhaps the best treatment of the subject is Jeffrey Barnouw's, where Hobbes's rhetoric is distinguished from mere metaphor or manipulation and viewed as "persuasive argumentation . . . that [opens] an inner space in which secular enlightenment can take root": "Persuasion in Hobbes's *Leviathan,*" *Hobbes Studies,* 1 (1988), 3–25.

the whole process of Hobbes's persuasion. I have uncovered Hobbes's doctrine as a choice—a choice that can be disputed like any other choice—whereas Hobbes seeks to deliver it as if no choice were involved. The reader then has no alternative but to accept Hobbes's premises as self-evident.

Hobbes would deny, of course, that the presentation of his doctrine as a series of self-evident propositions that constitute a new beginning (even though they have been previously derived through a process that is kept out of our sight) makes his doctrine either dishonest or dogmatic. If this were so, his doctrine would be virtually indistinguishable from traditional Aristotelian or Scholastic doctrines, which reason from the authority of received opinions. Rather, Hobbes would claim, there is a qualitative difference between the authoritative 'truths' of traditional doctrines and the self-evident truths of his own enlightenment science. The former are built on opinion—on blind faith or trust in authority—and contain all kinds of hidden as well as dishonest metaphysical assumptions. The latter are the opposite of dogmatic assertions. In Hobbes's words, they "take [no] principle upon *trust,* but only . . . put men in mind of what they *know already,* or *may know* by their own experience" (*Elements,* 1, 1.2; Hobbes's emphasis). Hence Hobbes would say that his principles are not really dogmatic but self-evident, like the axioms of geometry. Or they are an altogether new kind of dogmatism—dogmatism built on radical skepticism. They are thought to be beyond doubt or to be absolutely certain, not because they rest on authority or on trust of any kind but because they are the only thing that is indubitable after everything else has been doubted or subjected to skeptical critique. They are the indisputable axioms of the self-reliant mind.

Nevertheless, one can readily understand why naive readers of Hobbes's political treatises (even serious scholars who have puzzled over the boldly asserted but unproved definitions) could easily regard the works not as models of enlightenment but as new authoritative dictionaries of political and philosophical terms—dictionaries in which Hobbes makes himself the new authority and says, in effect, 'trust me.'

Hobbes's awareness of this very danger is probably what led him to compose three versions of his political treatises, without ever saying which one is the preferred or perfect version, *The Elements of Law* (1640), *De Cive* (1642), or *The Leviathan* (1651). Although most scholars interpret the existence of three similar but not identical treatises as evidence of intellectual development on Hobbes's part, it is more plausible (precisely because Hobbes never ranked them) to see the treatises as three different but equally valid strategies for dealing with the same fundamental dilemma. That dilemma, which appears as a literary question—How to compose a political treatise?—is nothing less than the dilemma of the enlightenment project as such: How can one end the wars over authoritative opinions and doctrines without engaging in disputes, controversies, or polemics with those very doctrines, thereby perpetuating rather than solving the problem of doctrinal controversy? How can one build a political science that does not begin from opinion, except by wiping the slate clean of all previous opinions and then hiding this fact from the reader or hinting at it indirectly here and there?

I think that Hobbes was aware of this fundamental dilemma when he composed his political treatises. Clearly he had to decide how much time he should spend engaging in scriptural polemics or in attacking Aristotle. He also had to determine how much of the process of enlightenment to show the reader: Should be present the first step, the historical view of political opinion as a whole, or only bits and pieces of history? Should he show the whole process of resolving previous opinion into its constituent elements of speech, mental thoughts, and passions or only the conclusions? Should he show the emergence of the self-reliant mind, purged of vanity by fear of death, or merely assert that self-preservation is the strongest and primary desire? Should he show or merely assert the reconstruction of the abstract individual from self-evident mechanistic premises (stripped of 'vain' metaphysical opinions about immaterial minds, immaterial causes, and the naturalness of speech)?

Although important, the differences in presenting these matters are strategic or tactical, differences of degree rather than of principle. To present different strategies in different treatises, then, would not indicate fundamental changes in thought. For Hobbes the basic problem (the unreliability of authoritative opinion) and the basic solution (absolute sovereignty created by self-reliant individuals who are fearful but rational) remained the same, and he apparently did not really care in the last analysis which version became the standard one.

Reflecting on this point, one can see that three equally valid strategies were possible for Hobbes, depending on how much he wanted to engage polemically the opinions of the past. Obviously, the cleanest and purest strategy is the minimalist one followed in *De Cive*. In part I of *De Cive*, "Of Liberty," Hobbes begins immediately with the state-of-nature teaching; previous opinions are simply ignored, and the reader begins with the slate wiped clean. Only minimal hints appear in the first chapter about what actually is the problem

Hobbes seeks to solve. Brief statements about vainglory and the contest over political and religious doctrines are intended to suffice (although an extended Epistle Dedicatory and a very revealing Preface to the Reader compensate for the stinginess of the first chapter of the treatise). The whole mechanistic account of man is omitted (although it is presupposed in the theory of voluntary action). The grand principle of self-preservation is simply asserted as a necessity of man's nature, with no other proof than an analogy to gravity (1.7). In part II of *De Cive*, "Of Dominion," Hobbes presents the doctrine of sovereignty, with a focus on the practical differences between government by public assemblies (the problem of orators) and the advantages of a monarchy. The third and last part, "Of Religion," engages in brief scriptural polemics to show that Scripture properly understood supports Hobbes's doctrine of sovereignty.

The minimalist version in *De Cive* has the advantage of being the least disputative (Aristotle is hardly mentioned); but for precisely the same reason it has the disadvantage of being the most dogmatic (it actually reads like a reconstructed version of Aristotle's *Politics*— the newly revised and 'authoritative' version by Hobbes—with the doctrine of man's natural sociality stood on its head by the dogmatic assertion that man is vain and selfish).[12] This is the dilemma of what might be called the minimalist strategy of enlightenment literature: to ignore the polemical context of received opinions is to begin with a clean break (a blank slate), which is most consistent with the intent of enlightenment; but this approach appears most dogmatic and is probably least convincing.

The second general strategy is to engage polemically the opinions and doctrines of the past. This approach is more convincing than the first; but it is also more disputative and tends to undercut the objective of developing an indisputable science that does not begin from opinion. Hobbes can mitigate the potential damage, however, by treating "opinion" as such rather than specific opinions (Aristotelianism, Scholasticism, Reformation theology, common law doctrines) and by beginning with opinion already resolved into its constituent elements. The whole argument begins anew from these elements (speech and sense) purged of trust. This general strategy is followed in both *The Elements of Law* and *The Leviathan*, with a variation on the primary theme found in each one.

---

12. Thomas A. Spragens, Jr., describes the various ways in which Hobbes 'stood Aristotle on his head,' but fails to come to grips with Hobbes's unusual way of doing so and merely asserts that a Kuhnian "paradigm transformation" has occurred: *The Politics of Motion: The World of Thomas Hobbes* (Lexington: University Press of Kentucky, 1973), pp. 41–47, 97–124.

On the simplest level, the difference between *The Elements* and *Leviathan* is one of length and thoroughness in treating the polemical context. The *Elements* consists of only two parts, "Human Nature" and "The Body Politic," whereas *Leviathan* consists of four parts, "Of Man," "Of Commonwealth," "Of a Christian Commonwealth," and "Of the Kingdom of Darkness." In its latter parts the *Leviathan* treats more extensively than any of the treatises the biblical and ecclesiastical doctrines that underlie Christian politics, as well as the philosophical and moral doctrines that underlie Aristotelian-Scholastic thought. But this difference in thoroughness between the treatises is not an essential difference, nor does it reveal the real difference in strategies.

On a more subtle level, the difference between the *Elements* and the *Leviathan* is often described in terms of divergent views of scientific knowledge. As McNeilly has ably shown, the *Elements* is more "empiricist" (it almost equates science with "evidence" or sense "experience" to the neglect of formal logic), while the *Leviathan* is more "formalist" (emphasizing formal logic over experience in the definition of science). Although McNeilly documents his case very well, he offers nothing to explain why Hobbes advocated both views of science at different times without stating a preference. McNeilly simply states that his own preference is for the formalism of the *Leviathan* (he even suggests that we dismiss the mechanistic psychology of the work as being insufficiently formal).[13] Without disagreeing with this characterization of the two treatises, I see the two views as equally valid strategies for building an enlightenment science. The two strategies can be explained in the following way. The immediate polemical context of Hobbes's political treatises is the philosophical and academic tradition of Western civilization. The treatises are designed specifically to reeducate readers who have been trained in this tradition—that is, those who equate rational science with dialectics or disputing the definitions of words. To reeducate these learned intellectuals, Hobbes attacks their characteristic defect: reasoning from opinion or, in precise terms, borrowing words on trust from other men without clear and evident thoughts in the mind. In developing an alternative view of rational science, Hobbes takes the elements of opinion apart and puts them back together in a new form. Hence the new definition of science in all of Hobbes's treatises is exact deductive science: words accompanied by clear mental thoughts that can be used for reckoning and computation. The im-

13. McNeilly, *Anatomy of Leviathan*, pp. 35–45, 83–84, 106; also Brandt, *Hobbes's Mechanical Conception of Nature*, pp. 125, 161, 272.

portant point is that scientific knowledge requires both elements, words and mental thoughts, to be present (making it a curious kind of 'logical empiricism,' as I called it in chapter 5). In addition, both elements must be purged of trust and then fitted together by conscious choice. Within this new formula for science, however, one can emphasize either (1) the need for clear mental conceptions, achieved by 'empiricism,' or (2) the need for conscious arbitrariness in the use of words, achieved by 'logical formalism.' This difference in emphasis within a commonly accepted formula for enlightenment science accounts, I believe, for the differences between the *Elements* and the *Leviathan.*

For example, the argument of the *Elements* focuses on the opposition between two types of thinking and two types of learned men. On the one hand, there are the "dogmatici" or dogmatic thinkers, such as Aristotle, who create nothing but controversy because they take as their starting point "those opinions which are already vulgarly received" from "their education, and from the authority of men, or of custom, and take the habitual discourse of the tongue for ratiocination." On the other, the "mathematici" or mathematical thinkers produce certain knowledge because they "proceed from most low and humble principles, evident to the meanest capacity," beginning with the imposition of names and moving slowly by careful deductions to certain conclusions; they are "absolved of the crime of breeding controversy" (*Elements,* Epistle Dedicatory; 1, 13.3–4).

With this opposition in the forefront of the work, the *Elements* focuses on the need to recover in a systematic way the original or natural experience of words which has been lost in the artificial civilization created by the dogmatici. In civilized life "custom hath so great a power, that the mind suggesteth only the first word and the rest follow habitually." As a result, words are taken on trust and merely parroted without experience or evidence consisting of mental conceptions that are "the life of truth . . . as the sap to the tree" (1, 6.3). The *Elements* seems to reflect an optimism about some kind of original understanding or agreement about the definitions of words. For it presents the primary task of science as simply *recovering the original conceptions* of words. The method of science, therefore, is almost historical: a return to the natural sense that has been lost in artificial civilization.

Accordingly, the *Elements* suggests the new method of "reading thyself," or introspection, which enables one to recover the original, natural sensations that once accompanied words (1, 5.14). Exact science is achieved through a kind of methodical empiricism that places more emphasis on having evidence or clear mental pictures than on logical formalism in the use of words. Thus in this work Hobbes defines science as "evidence of truth" and right reason as reasoning from principles "found indubitable by experience"; and he defines understanding as "recovering those conceptions for which the name was ordained ... but since have been obscured by custom and common speech" (I, 6.4; 5.12; 5.8).

Because of the emphasis on 'empiricism,' the *Elements* tends to downplay the arbitrariness of language, so long as words are accompanied by a clear mental conception, even if the definitions follow common experience. In a most surprising admission, Hobbes says that even though experiential knowledge may not be universally valid, it is extremely useful in defining words: "[Although] we cannot from experience conclude, that any thing is to be called just or unjust, true or false, or any proposition universal whatsoever, except it be from remembrance of the use of names imposed arbitrarily by men ... [nevertheless] it is necessary for the drawing of such conclusions, to trace and find out, by many experiences, what men do mean by calling things just and unjust" (I, 4.10). The correct use of words and science itself, then, are not far from common experience; but those who practice them must treat experience skeptically and cynically, without being misled by intellectual vanity into accepting any of the naive (metaphysical) illusions of experience. In the *Elements* Hobbes seems to be satisfied with a notion of science that is a halfway house between trust in authority and complete arbitrariness—following convention for the sake of convenience in achieving clarity and consensus. His goal is to achieve indisputable knowledge primarily by the modest strategy of "understanding" the meaning of words—making sure that two people have the same thing in mind (the same mental image) when they speak. The alternative to the empty verbalisms of authoritative opinion, then, is true science; but true science is essentially mental evidence or empirical knowledge or common experience purged of trust.

The *Leviathan,* by contrast, emphasizes formal logic over sense experience in the theory of science. Table 1 brings out the differences clearly. The differences between the two treatises with regard to science, understanding, and right reason are apparent. In the *Elements,* science is primarily recovering, by a historical-introspective search, the original conceptions of words, which are indubitable when purged of trust (all the deceptions of language and sense). In the *Leviathan* the case is quite different. There Hobbes does not move backward, as it were, to recover an original common experience; he moves forward to advance artificiality. Science becomes mere conse-

Table 1. Definitions of three terms in *Elements of Law* and *Leviathan*

Term	*The Elements of Law*	*Leviathan*
Science	"*Evidence* of truth" (I, 6.4)	"Consequences of *names*" (ch. 5, p. 35)
Understanding	"*Recovering* those conceptions for which the name was ordained" (I, 5.8)	"*Nothing else but conception caused by speech*" (ch. 4, p. 28)
Right reason	Reasoning from principles "found *indubitable by experience*, all deceptions of sense and equivocation of words avoided" (I, 5.12)	"The reason of some *arbitrator*, or judge . . . for want of right reason constituted by nature" (ch. 5, p. 31)

Note: Emphasis added in all instances.

quences of names or affirmations based on logical formalism—contingent truths of a formal kind. This definition reflects a different attitude toward words. In the *Elements* words are supposed to derive their meanings from a kind of common experience purged of trust, which is actually a middle ground between trust and arbitrariness. In the *Leviathan,* however, definitions of words are either wholly arbitrary, as in politics, or simply self-evident, as in metaphysics; ordinary common sense loses all value (Hobbes calls it "natural sense" and equates it with ignorance in the *Leviathan*).

This dichotomy between original experience in one treatise and formal logic in the other should not be exaggerated, however. Each work includes the views of the other; the question is simply one of emphasis. In the *Elements* empiricism predominates; but arbitrariness, formal logic, nominalism, and mechanism are also defended as part of the theory of science. Similarly, in the *Leviathan* formal logic predominates; but a certain method of historical recovery is often used to define words. For example, Hobbes treats three very important words—"conscience," "tyranny," and "heresy" (the words most frequently used to foment rebellion)—in a historical or etymological fashion that contrasts the earliest definitions with the contemporary usage of civilization.

In all cases he shows that there is a distinct pattern of evolution. Originally words were used as mere signs referring to facts or experiences; then words were corrupted somewhat by metaphorical usage that still refers to experience but stretches the connection for the sake of display; finally, words are completely separated from experience for the sole purpose of expressing disgrace, dishonor, and superiority. The pattern in the evolution of language is the familiar one of progressive development of intellectual vanity. Thus "conscience," Hobbes says, originally meant witnessing facts together with other men, so that it was difficult to "speak against one's conscience" (presumably because one could be easily found out, not because conscience was considered sacred). Afterward "men made use of the same word metaphorically, for the knowledge of their own secret facts, and secret thoughts; and therefore it is said rhetorically that conscience is a thousand witnesses"—an expression that exaggerates the probable truth of private experience. Finally, "conscience" has come to be used by men "in love with their own new opinions" in order to make it seem "unlawful to change or speak against them" (*Leviathan,* ch. 7, p. 53). Using this etymology, Hobbes defines "conscience" according to the conventional usage, but does so with the cynicism of historical awareness: conscience is the love of one's own novel opinions, asserted with a claim of inviolable higher law.

The same pattern can be seen in the etymologies of the words "tyranny" and "heresy" as well as in the history of titles among the European gentry (*Leviathan,* ch. 46, pp. 682–683; ch. 10, pp. 83–84). All evolved from signs originally used to designate real facts or experience to metaphors that exaggerate to expressions of vanity. Hobbes's suggestion is that the original definitions of words, the ones closest to natural or primitive experience, are best. The *Leviathan,* then, is not without a historical dimension that parallels the *Elements.* But the *Leviathan* ultimately sides with conscious arbitrariness rather than recovery of natural experience as the foremost property of science.

In sum, we may state the similarities and differences among Hobbes's political treatises as follows. The common goal of all three is to end the historic controversy over the opinions and doctrines of civilized society, particularly those of contemporary Western civilization, by building a political science on the principles of enlightenment. Instead of beginning with the opinions of the past and disputing them, Hobbes begins with the conceptions of the self-reliant mind—the mind freed from every form of trust in authority, speech, and sense experience and refocused solely on introspective knowledge of its own mental thoughts and passions. To achieve this goal, however, three strategies are possible. One strategy is to ignore opinion altogether and begin with the state-of-nature teaching: the strategy of *De Cive.* A second possibility is to show opinion already resolved into its constituent elements (speech, sense conceptions, and passions) and to present simultaneously an alternative view of science which emphasizes the sense conceptions or empirical evidence that must accompany words: the strategy of *The Elements*. A third possibility is to show opinion resolved into its elements and to emphasize as an alternative view of rational science the arbitrary or formal use of words: the strategy of *Leviathan*. Understood in this light, no one treatise is in principle superior to any of the others, even if the *Leviathan* spends many more pages disputing the opinions of the past and redefining key ecclesiastical and philosophical terms. The relative merit of each treatise lies in strategic treatment of the polemical context of Hobbes's doctrine.[14]

The debate about strategy in the presentation of Hobbes's political science goes to the heart of the question about its prospects for success. That question is simple: Can one really develop a political science that does not begin from received opinion? Is it possible to reason without proceeding in 'dialectical' fashion? Hobbes may have wished to answer these questions with a resounding and unequivocal yes. Instead, as the forms of his various treatises suggest, he gives a more ambiguous response. He waivers between making a complete and absolute break with the past (beginning with the 'blank slate' of the state of nature or the abstract individual devoid of all opinions) and developing a more complicated relationship with the past (engaging it polemically in bits and pieces with historical observations and disputations). As a reflection of this fundamental ambivalence, Hobbes seeks to conceal as well as to reveal the very problem he must solve. He realizes, in other words, that the complete break with the past required by enlightenment science does not happen all at once and cannot be portrayed as a fait accompli. Rather, it is an ongoing struggle in which controversy is unavoidable. Such an admission does not necessarily mean that the enlightenment project will fail; but it does make the outcome more problematic. And it illustrates once again Hobbes's dilemma: that he can neither live with history nor live without it.

14. One might generalize from this observation and say that Hobbes's whole career involves much less change of view or maturation than the articulation of three equally valid strategies. See Strauss, *Political Philosophy of Hobbes;* Reik, *Golden Lands of Thomas Hobbes;* and Johnston, *Rhetoric of "Leviathan."*

» 7 «

Absolute Sovereignty and
the End of Doctrinal Warfare

From the Natural to the Artificial State

In Hobbes's state-of-nature teaching a complicated and subtle view of natural man emerges, reflecting the strange relationship of the enlightened mind to nature. On the one hand, the enlightened mind feels abandoned by superhuman powers that ought to care for human association and to provide sanctions for just authority. Instead of receiving clear guidance and support from above, men are left with the contest of opinions and the deadly conflicts of self-appointed authorities. Feeling a cosmic sense of betrayed trust and a more immediate fear of persecution or death by other men, the enlightened mind sees nature and nature's God as indifferent to human association and human authority. Accordingly, Hobbes argues that men have no natural inclination to society; they are by nature isolated, mutually hostile, and without notions of justice or right.

Since nature and nature's God have abandoned men, the human mind must stand on its own and assert that truth lies within itself. Yet even when freed from trust in external authorities, the enlightened mind feels the need for a grounding in nature, not only for the sake of scientific objectivity but also for the polemical purpose of expelling the doctrines of the kingdom of darkness. Hence Hobbes's firm belief that, by uncovering the natural condition of mankind and discovering the workings of nature as a whole, the self-reliant mind finds that its operations are in accordance with nature: the fear of violent death which emancipates the mind is ultimately the strongest and most universal human tendency. This tendency provides a standard of natural right which can serve as a guide to lead men out of the chaos of nature to a new order of civilization. Fear of death, then, is both natural and unnatural, a kind of halfway house between the natural and the artificial.

At the precise moment when this passion is experienced, the creation of modern civilization begins. The scientific account of mechanical man—the abstract individual isolated from social groups—comes into being as natural man. At the same time the abstract individual is more than a natural man when he comes into being. For he is a mental creation of enlightenment science, not a primitive man of the past. The abstract individual is created at a historic moment in modern civilization through a change in self-consciousness, a change in which the mind has been purged of all received opinions while maintaining a belief in the science of natural justice.

As a product of autonomous reason, the abstract individual is endowed by Hobbes with the power of rationality. Possessing a new sense of right reason (skeptical and calculating, rather than trusting and intuitive), he acts like a rational egoist and sees the need to construct and to obey an artificial sovereign. This means that the abstract individual is not only a product of natural necessity but a creature with the power of free creation—a creature who can make the state, as well as language, by his arbitrary will. Because of this capacity, mechanical man—the civilized barbarian, the rational egoist of the modern age—bridges the gap between the natural and artificial worlds.

In so doing, the fully enlightened individual steps outside of the historical realm of doctrinal politics and makes an absolutely new beginning in a timeless realm of natural necessity and artificial construction. In this realm right is identical to what all men necessarily desire (self-preservation and their own selfish good) and truth is identical to what all men necessarily perceive as self-evident (the mental concepts accompanying words, especially the concept of mechanical causality). When these notions of right and scientific truth are fully recognized, the historic problem of doctrinal politics—the ineffectiveness of all previous doctrines of right, the disparity between right and might, the gap between 'ought' and 'is'—will be overcome and a new political order will begin.

The central feature of the new political order is the doctrine of absolute sovereignty. This doctrine is the institutional embodiment of Hobbes's enlightenment science. It is designed to abolish doctrinal disagreement as a pretext for rebellion and to end the changes of government by civil war that have plagued civilization throughout history. Thus the new doctrine of sovereignty will be the basis of an "everlasting" commonwealth and will advance civilization to its highest and final stage.

In practical terms, the doctrine of absolute sovereignty is extraordinarily simple: it gives the head of the state the final authority to settle all disputes according to his arbitrary will and grants him absolute power to impose his settlement on the people. Although the practical aspects of this doctrine are easy to state and to understand, its theoretical grounding is complicated. For it involves the same fundamental paradox as Hobbes's enlightenment science as a whole—the combination of arbitrariness and naturalness. The arbitrary will of the sovereign is recognized as supreme, but its supremacy is justified by the (nonarbitrary) natural right to self-preservation. Stated differently, the doctrine of sovereignty combines positive law and natural law. This paradox will now be explored in detail as we examine Hobbes's account of the origins and foundations of sovereign power.

The Argument for Sovereign Power

According to Hobbes, the difference between the defective states of the past and the properly constituted state or commonwealth of the future lies in conscious recognition of sovereign power. At first glance this claim does not sound remarkable. Sovereign power, Hobbes observes, has always existed and always can be found in every past or present state, even though most men deny its existence. To be sovereign simply means to be the final arbiter or supreme power—to have the last word without further appeal and thus to be without limitation on what one can do or decide. As a matter of fact, Hobbes argues, such a supreme power must exist somewhere in every state, even in those states that claim to place limitations on the exercise of power. For the power that sets the limits must itself be the supreme power and hence must be sovereign (*De Cive*, VI.18).[1]

---

1. Jean Hampton calls this the "regress argument" for sovereignty and vigorously defends its cogency against critics (Goldsmith and Hart) who accuse Hobbes of confusing "the need for finality in a political regime with the need for a final human authority." In reply to the critics Hampton stresses Hobbes's central insight: that the resolution of controversies always leads back to the question 'Who shall judge?' or 'Which human authority shall decide?' which can never be answered by an appeal to impersonal rules. Her brief reference to the "historical context of the regress argument" helps to explain Hobbes's insistence on this point but does not uncover the whole critique of authoritative wisdom that underlies Hobbes's position: *Hobbes and the Social Contract Tradition* (Cambridge: Cambridge University Press, 1986), pp. 97–113.

Sovereignty, then, is nothing new. What is new is Hobbes's effort to make his readers consciously aware of sovereignty, as well as his views on the proper location of sovereignty.

Hobbes's contention is that men hitherto (throughout the whole of civil history) have deceived themselves about sovereignty—about the fact of its existence and about its value. Their intellectual vanity has led them to believe that final authority lay in a power outside the human will. Hence they always assumed that superhuman authorities would prevail or would rule (more or less) independently of human agency. They assumed, in other words, that a sovereign in the strict and precise sense—a human agent who acts as a final arbiter and imposes his will by force—would be unnecessary.

Instead of recognizing sovereignty, men traditionally believed in 'providence' in one form or another. They believed that God would provide, that his will would be acknowledged or would prevail of its own accord, that acts of Providence (either divine intervention or divinely inspired speech and deeds) would determine the outcome of events. Or they believed that nature would provide, that teleology or the rightful order of beings and human types has a power of its own, which only needs to be discovered and helped to grow (through art and education). Men even believed that custom or tradition would provide, although it seems to have more of a human hand in its development than acts of God or nature. For custom's beginnings have been lost in time and cannot be traced to human authors; hence its perpetuity seemed guaranteed by the fact that it existed from time immemorial or that 'it has always been so.'

Assuming the existence of superhuman Providence, human beings in the past merely sought to discover the right order of things (the true way or orthodoxy) by observing certain "signs"—the signs in events, in human hierarchies, and especially in speech about the superhuman order—and to proclaim the order revealed in these signs to be "right reason." Once they had proclaimed them as such, they trusted that the rightful order would prevail. Occasionally a little force might have been necessary, but the signs or words were expected to prevail of their own power. Accordingly, one did not say that a man or a human authority ruled; he was merely an agent, a mediator, a spokesman for impersonal higher powers. No man as a man was sovereign, because his own will was not sovereign; even if he possessed the greatest coercive power, his will was subservient to a higher will. Thus in a sense the independence of the state or of politics was never acknowledged, because the political rulers and coercive powers were always regarded as subservient to higher authorities.

Hobbes exposes these beliefs as myths, not by refuting the existence of higher powers but by denying their effective power, especially their power to impose a common language or discourse about fundamental moral truths on people. This is why Hobbes studies history: to see if there is evidence for the effective power of God's providence, nature's teleology, or custom's prescriptions. For Hobbes the evidence proves that Providence has been absent from history (and natural science strengthens this conclusion by showing that one need not assume final causes in explaining natural and human phenomena).[2] The lesson of history is that the human authorities who mediate for Providence (in whatever form) have never prevailed or secured agreement by persuasion or rational argument. They have always turned to those who wield the swords—kings and generals—to achieve victory by superior force of arms. Men have given their obedience, in reality, to those with the most coercive power. The coercive powers have been the de facto sovereigns, but their supremacy has gone unrecognized by opinion leaders and the people. The historical deception about sovereignty must now be ended by a new awareness of the primacy of human will and force.

Thus Hobbes's doctrine of sovereignty arises from the simple recognition of what has always been so but never openly acknowledged because of vain hopes about superhuman Providence. Accordingly, the same process of enlightenment that emancipates the human mind from authoritative wisdom and the delusions of intellectual vanity in scientific thought also leads to the new doctrine of the state. That process, we have seen, is nothing more than honesty: skepticism or cynicism about authority.

Honesty is the means to sovereign power because it dispels the illusions that prevent one from seeing what has always been so. Right opinion, true doctrine, and orthodox speech have not been handed down from on high to guide the state. They have been arbitrary human assertions that have prevailed only by violence, usually by the head of state himself. Arbitrary will and force have always been the real basis of political authority. As Hobbes says:

For these words of good, evil, and contemptible, are ever used in relation to the person that useth them: there being nothing simply and

---

2. Even in natural science, however, the existence of superhuman powers is not finally or definitively refuted. But this does not matter to Hobbes. The crucial point for Hobbes is not the existence or nonexistence of superhuman powers but the fact that such powers have no apparent effect on human affairs or human understanding. The implications of this position for Hobbes's belief in God are discussed in ch. 8, under "How the Enlightenment Becomes a Dogma."

absolutely so; nor any common rule of good and evil, to be taken from the nature of the objects themselves; but from the person of the man, where there is no commonwealth; or in commonwealth, from the person that representeth it; or from an arbitrator or judge, whom men disagreeing shall be consent to set up, and make his sentence the rule thereof. (*Leviathan*, ch. 6, pp. 48–49)

The political implication of this statement is obvious. Since all men use moral language subjectively to express their own opinions, no agreement is possible until everyone admits that this is so and designates someone to settle the matter arbitrarily. The settlement, then, must be upheld by force because no other effective power exists:

And that which offendeth people, is no other thing, but that they are governed, not as everyone of them would himself, but as the public representative . . . thinks fit; that is, *by an arbitrary government:* for which they give evil names to their superiors; never knowing, till perhaps a little after a civil war, that *without such arbitrary government, such war must be perpetual; and that it is men and arms, not words and promises that make the force and power of the laws.* (*Leviathan*, ch. 46, p. 490; emphasis added)

The essence of sovereign power, in sum, is the arbitrary settlement of disputes, which everyone honestly and openly acknowledges to be arbitrary, upheld by men and arms rather than by words and appeals to higher powers. Hobbes's doctrine or political sovereignty, one might say, is identical to human sovereignty or 'humanism': the belief that man must rely on himself alone, on his own will and arms, to determine his fate.

From this account we can see why Hobbes could think of his doctrine as the final doctrine, the one that will end doctrinal warfare. For it establishes the state as the supreme authority over all other authorities and gives the head of state the right and the power to settle all disputes arbitrarily. Hence the state can no longer be challenged by rival powers because it claims supremacy over the church, the universities, the judicial and legal system, inherited property, and corporations, as well as the militia and armed forces.[3] In addition, the state will be immune to the most devastating kinds of doctrinal disputes—such as the accusations of priests, prophets, and theologians that it promotes heresy or false religion; or the

3. Otto Gierke, *Natural Law and the Theory of Society: 1500 to 1800*, trans. Ernest Barker (1934; Boston: Beacon, 1957), pp. 40–44, 79–81, 164.

accusations of political demagogues and gentlemen educated in classical literature that it is unjust or tyrannical, or that it perpetuates the wrong form of government (e.g., that it is monarchical rather than democratic); or the accusations of lawyers and judges that it exercises arbitrary power or violates the time-honored 'laws of the realm.' Hobbes's contention is that such disputes will disappear once the supremacy of the sovereign's arbitrary will is recognized in all matters.

At that point the justification for obeying the sovereign rests solely on the fact that he is sovereign. Although this sounds like an awesome or even an absurd claim, it is in reality a denial of pretense and accords perfectly with the views of an enlightened people. For a fully enlightened people would insist that the sovereign be recognized as nothing more than an arbiter—a man (or body) who arbitrates disputes arbitrarily or resolves controversies according to what is expedient and likely to produce agreement.[4] He cannot appeal to divine right or claim to speak for higher powers; he cannot claim that his settlements define orthodoxy or distributive justice or legal equity. Thus he cannot be criticized or disobeyed for failing to do so. Hobbes's sovereign seeks the end of doctrinal warfare by disavowing all interest in the rightness or truth of doctrines (except sovereignty itself) and by imposing arbitrary settlements for the sake of civil peace.

This notion may sound confusing to people living in liberal societies, because they see little difference between theocratic rulers who impose religious orthodoxy and Hobbes's supposedly "enlightened" sovereign who imposes an arbitrarily chosen doctrine on the people. Are not all forms of imposition equally oppressive, intolerant, and divisive? Hobbes would answer no. Although the sovereign establishes and imposes doctrines, he is supposed to be indifferent to their content and to treat them pragmatically; his arbitrary commands become the civil laws of the nation for no other purpose than to ensure lasting civil peace. As Hobbes says in *De Cive:* "[since] all controversies are bred from hence, *that the opinions of men differ concerning meum and tuum, just and unjust,* . . . and the like; which every man esteems according to his own judgment: it belongs to the same chief power to make some common rules for all men, and to declare them publicly. . . . Those rules and measures are usually called the civil laws, as being the commands of him who hath the supreme power in the city" (vi.9).

4. Dewey describes this view elegantly in "Motivation of Hobbes's Political Philosophy," pp. 23–25.

This pronouncement sounds both strange and familiar. It means that the Hobbesian sovereign imposes uniformity on his subjects particularly in the definition of words, a procedure that would seem to require legislating from a dictionary of moral terms. But the imposed uniformity is merely a 'positive' law: it is binding and must be obeyed simply because it is laid down by the sovereign, not because it claims to be right, true, or orthodox. The strangeness of Hobbes's doctrine is that it requires *uniformity but not orthodoxy*. Thus, for example, Hobbes says that the city should impose "uniformity of public worship" while acknowledging that "the city may appoint what worship of God it pleaseth" (*De Cive*, xv.15–16). This means that the city or political sovereign requires subjects to follow practices and to profess opinions that they do not necessarily believe in but conform to out of fear of the sovereign, or fear of anarchy from a multiplicity of opinions.

Hobbes's teaching is strange because it requires suspension of judgment or radical disbelief about the most important matters. It involves a kind of enlightened cynicism that inclines one to live with a given decision because the alternative—a chaos of opinions with no decision at all—is so much worse. At the same time Hobbes's doctrine sounds familiar, like a kind of political pragmatism that avoids all doctrinairism and even allows tolerance of private beliefs that do not disturb the public peace (*Leviathan*, ch. 46, p. 684). It is familiar, of course, because it reminds us of modern liberalism. Hobbes's argument for sovereign power, although it leads to an imposed uniformity of speech and action, is an argument for the 'neutral state'—the notion that the state should not judge the rightness or truth of moral and religious opinions but treat them all with suspicion, as sectarian pretexts for domination and persecution. This argument underlies the liberal principles of disestablishment and toleration, which require the state to be neutral toward religious and moral opinions and to permit the free exercise of conscience and speech. Hobbes prepares the way for such liberal principles by arguing that no human being has a monopoly on authoritative wisdom and that only the creation of a neutral sovereign can prevent doctrines from becoming pretexts for persecution and sectarian warfare.

Sovereignty by Acquisition and by Institution

Hobbes's argument for sovereign power is slippery because he says, on the one hand, that it has always existed and, on the other, that it is something entirely new. How does a phenomenon that is both old and new, that is already present but not yet created, come into being in the real world of politics? To this question Hobbes gives two answers. One is historical: sovereign power is already there in the natural origin of the state; it needs only to be recognized to come into being. The other is scientific: sovereign power must be created from the wills of abstract individuals; it comes into being when they authorize a sovereign by their voluntary consent.

In his political treatises Hobbes presents both accounts in explaining the origins of sovereignty. As he says in *Leviathan:*

> The attaining of this sovereign power, is by two ways: One by natural force: as when a man maketh his children, to submit themselves, and their children to his government, as being able to destroy them if they refuse; or by war subdueth his enemies to his will, giving them their lives on that condition. The other, is when men agree amongst themselves, to submit to some man or assembly of men, voluntarily, on confidence to be protected by him against all others. (Ch. 17, p. 159)

The first way of creating the sovereign power—by natural force—is the natural origin of the state and is known by historical experience. Hobbes calls this way "commonwealth by acquisition" and subdivides it into "dominion paternal," fathers ruling over wives and children by superior physical strength, and "dominion despotical," masters ruling over servants who have been subdued by physical force (*Leviathan,* ch. 20). In either case, commonwealth by acquisition, as the term suggests, means acquiring dominion over others by brute strength or violent conquest.

The second way, "commonwealth by institution," is not known from historical experience; it is derived from Hobbes's scientific conception of abstract individuals or isolated men who are mechanistically driven and rationally directed. They create a government by voluntary consent—by an agreement to submit to a common power, who is designated to be the sovereign and authorized to represent their wills, for the sake of peace and security. The obvious problem is to explain why Hobbes presents two accounts of the origins of sovereignty—by natural force and by voluntary consent—and to understand how they can be reconciled.

Turning first to commonwealth by acquisition, one can see that it is a 'natural' or primitive kind of authority because it rests on force without opinion. It is also present in most civil societies, although it has been hidden or submerged by the artificial world of opinion and doctrines. The rule of natural force reemerges, however, whenever civilized men see the emptiness of opinions, something that often occurs during civil wars or may be made to occur through the mental process of enlightenment. To illustrate this point, we might begin by reflecting on the most important historical challenge that Hobbes confronted: to find a justification for the Restoration of King Charles II in 1660, ending the English Civil War.

As I pointed out in chapter 2, Hobbes analyzes the contest over opinions and doctrines which led to the Civil War and to the defeat of Charles I; he then shows how Charles II was restored and speculates on how his throne might be more firmly established than that of his father. According to my interpretation, Hobbes implicitly rejects the Stuart claim, the divine right of kings, by silence or omission. In its place he suggests two bases on which the restoration of the Stuart monarchy should be grounded—the right of conquest and the safety of the people (which Hobbes claims is best determined by the king as the authentic representative of the people).

In discussing the right of conquest as a foundation for the state, Hobbes speaks favorably of this idea while recognizing its limits, particularly its possible use by usurpers such as Cromwell, whom Hobbes denounces in *Behemoth*. Yet the appeal to the right of conquest in *Behemoth* serves an important purpose; and it enables us to see the motive behind the defense of commonwealth by acquisition in the political treatises. For both arguments are attempts to collapse right into might or to equate legitimacy with de facto power.

Hobbes appeals to conquest or natural force as the foundation of properly constituted commonwealths because it comes as close as possible to establishing dominion on power that is already there— independent of opinions of justice, doctrines of right, and notions of legality. By accepting the factual existence of superior coercive power or by not protesting it, Hobbes discredits the whole realm of opinion. He does so, however, in a way that is easily missed: he simply ignores the claims of opinion and doctrine. He thereby disarms the intellectual authorities who foment rebellion by teaching the people that dominion lies with the possessors of correct doctrine (the upholders of orthodoxy). By contrast, Hobbes's equation of right with superior force means that correct doctrine or orthodoxy is irrelevant; all that matters is power. This is natural rule—domination by force without the need for opinion.

The historical model that most closely approximates this type of rule is the military conqueror who establishes a hereditary succession—in other words, an absolute monarch who combines conquest and patriarchy. This type of rule is sometimes referred to as patrimonial monarchy because the subjects are viewed as the 'patrimony' or personal possession and inheritance of the king. According to Hobbes, this kind of government is the factual origin of most states in the ancient and modern world (*Dialogue on the Common Laws*, p. 161). It is also the best kind of government measured in practical terms, rather than by theoretical arguments about right (*De Cive*, x.3).

As Hobbes says, the best practical government is an absolute monarchy in the form of a military dictatorship or rule by the general of an army. For all cities alike (kingships, aristocracies, and democracies) "give the whole command of war to one only" (*De Cive*, x.17); and "necessity teacheth both sides [in a dispute], that *an absolute monarch, to wit, a general,* is necessary for their defense against one another, and also for the peace of each faction within itself" (*Elements*, II, 2.5.8; emphasis added). Another practical argument suggests that absolute monarchy, in which the subjects are the patrimony or inheritance of the king (his personal possessions), is best. In Hobbes's words, "we cannot on better condition be subject to any, than one whose interest depends upon our safety and welfare; and this comes to pass, when we are the inheritance of the ruler, for every man of his own accord endeavors the preservation of his inheritance" (*De Cive*, x.18).

Hobbes's appeal to the force of military conquerors and to the possessive dominion of patriarchs conjures up the image of a kind of barbarian prince who rules by fear and personal loyalty: a warlord. For such princes bravery and magnanimity suffice to rule effectively. Their motive for ruling is usually love of true glory—a well-grounded confidence in their own power which leads them to command openly and directly—or desire for fame—a love of immortal glory which Hobbes says "is not vain" because it leads rulers to seek prudently the protection and prosperity of their nations (*Leviathan*, ch. 19, p. 174; ch. 11, p. 87). Such barbarian princes are admirable because they despise vainglory and abstain from cruelty out of a sense of honor and utility. Instead of using doctrines and 'ideology,' they rule by fear and interest, the direct application of rewards and punishments for loyalty or disobedience.

The type of perfect prince Hobbes seems to have in mind in *Behemoth* is William the Conqueror rather than Cromwell. For William, according to Hobbes, conquered by force of arms and secured his rule by distributing land to his generals in exchange for oaths of obedience and promises of military service. He established a hereditary succession that Hobbes believes is the rightful title for all the kings of England and ought to be the basis for King Charles II (despite his Scottish descent). Hobbes also suggests that Charles II follows in the footsteps of William the Conqueror in having his power restored by military conquest (he was able to appear as the victor in the civil war, thanks to the shrewd strategy of General Monk). Finally, Hobbes suggests, Charles II ought to rely on William's old recruiting system, the "commission of arrays," for assembling a militia rather than on the approval of Parliament (*Behemoth*, p. 312).

In contrast to the achievements of William the Conqueror, Cromwell's feats are diminished by Hobbes. The conquests of Cromwell, as well as his protectorate and succession, relied on 'ideology'—on the Puritan doctrine of saints—and a righteous zeal that made him not only cruel but also unsuccessful in establishing lasting rule. Cromwell's antimonarchical religious indoctrination made it impossible for his generals and followers to accept the hereditary succession of his son, so the dynasty was doomed to failure (even if his son, Richard, had lived longer). This circumstance explains why Hobbes believes that William the Conqueror rather than Cromwell is a better model for Charles II to follow. It also explains why in the *Dialogue on the Common Laws* Hobbes always seeks to trace English customs and laws back to the prerogatives of William the Conqueror (pp. 160–168); and why in *Leviathan* Hobbes criticizes William for giving up the prerogatives of conquest in pledging not to infringe on the liberty of the church (ch. 29, p. 309).

Other 'natural rulers' that Hobbes might favor are authoritarian leaders whose primary interests are glory and stability rather than doctrinal orthodoxy or ideological purity. A list of historical examples, both ancient and modern, might include the following:

1. The ancient heroic kings, such as Agamemnon, who is described in Hobbes's translation of Thucydides as coming from a dynasty that was founded on wealth (his ancestors practically bought their subjects) and as the king who assembled the greatest forces for the Trojan War "not so much upon favor as by fear"—fear of his wealth and power (*EW*, VIII, 10–11; *The Peloponnesian War*, bk. I, sec. 9).

2. Military dictators and generals who seize power to restore law and order in chaotic situations created by sectarian violence (e.g., the Turkish generals from 1980 to 1983).

3. Hereditary monarchs who oppose the politics of theocrats (e.g., the Shah of Iran versus the Ayatollah Khomeini).

4. Autocrats and machine politicians who rule by personal loyalty, exchange of favors, patronage, bribery, and corruption (e.g., Robert Walpole, American political bosses from William Tweed to Richard Daley).

5. Authoritarian versus totalitarian rulers, as described by Jeane Kirkpatrick, such as Anastasio Somoza, Ferdinand Marcos, the Shah of Iran, and the military rulers of South Korea (Park, Chun), whose chief

aims are stability and self-aggrandizement rather than ideological utopianism.⁵

6. In general, Hobbes's model of the natural ruler resembles none other than Machiavelli's prince—the prudent seeker of power and glory who rules by manipulating the prudent selfishness of the people.

All of these examples clarify what Hobbes means by "commonwealth by acquisition" because they are essentially nonideological or nondoctrinal rulers whose power rests on natural force. They are bold men of action who assert their instinctive or barbaric confidence against religious zealots, moral reformers, ideological crusaders, intellectual utopians, and all those who believe that politics should be based on abstract principles rather than direct manipulation of raw passions (chiefly fear, interest, and loyalty). Hobbes's defense of commonwealth by acquisition therefore serves as a reminder to all the "unarmed" prophets and effete intellectuals of the world that power, force, and might should take precedence over opinions and doctrines of right. His implicit claim is that rule by such 'primitive' or 'barbaric' types is actually more humane—more stable because less ideologically contentious, more benign because less fanatical and self-righteous—than the rule of more 'civilized' types of leaders.

Barbarian princes, however, cannot solve the problem of doctrinal politics. They prefer direct action to theoretical doctrines; they have no respect for empty words that are not backed by the power of the sword; they temper utopianism and sectarianism with pragmatism. But an appeal to natural force or direct action will not suffice in the doctrinal age; it does not abolish doctrines or make them vanish into thin air. Even to assert the right of conquest as a 'right' as opposed to a historical fact is to speak the language of doctrinal politics. One can no longer turn back the clock and return to a more naive "golden age," as Hobbes describes the pre-Socratic age in the Preface to *De Cive*, "when" princes did not sue for, but already exercised the supreme power . . . [and] kept their empire entire, *not by arguments, but by punishing the wicked and protecting the good*" (emphasis added). Nor can one hope for an 'end of ideology' in a literal sense (even though historic forces such as the Protestant Reformation and the popularization of disputative philosophy seem to be weakening the notion of doctrinal orthodoxy). For the establishment of rational science by the philosophical and academic tradition in the West is an

5. Jeane Kirkpatrick, *Dictatorships and Double Standards* (New York: American Enterprise Institute and Simon & Schuster, 1982), pp. 25, 44, 70, 96–125.

irreversible fact of history, according to Hobbes. Living in the doctrinal age of Western civilization requires one to develop a rival doctrine; and it must be a doctrine that goes beyond appeals to natural force or equations of right and might.

Hobbes's dilemma is that his new doctrine must speak the language of natural law or higher law and thus, in a sense, be a theory of the public good or common good, as the Aristotelians have always maintained. Yet it somehow must be qualitatively different from all previous higher-law doctrines so that it cannot be exploited by human ambition as a pretext for disobedience and rebellion. It must be a higher-law doctrine that teaches and actually produces perfect obedience.

The doctrine of "commonwealth by institution" is this new doctrine. Hobbes believes that it will not only defeat the doctrines of the past but actually stabilize authority in a way that the mere acceptance of brute force could never do. The essence of this doctrine is the social contract (as it later came to be called) and a new definition of natural law. The social contract is the voluntary consent of the people to obey a common power, designated as the sovereign and authorized by the people as their representative. The foundation of the social contract is natural law—the duties deduced from the natural right to self-preservation, which bind all rational actors to seek peace and to maximize their selfish advantage. Combining popular consent and natural law, this doctrine is formulated by Hobbes as "the safety of the people" or "salus populi, suprema lex" (the good of the people is the supreme law).

But how is this doctrine superior to a direct appeal to natural force, especially when it provides a standard to judge the legitimacy of regimes and could stimulate a new round of doctrinal warfare? Hobbes's answer to this question is twofold. First, he believes that all previous doctrines are simply opinions, in the precise sense of words taken on trust from a higher authority, while the doctrine of "consent" is qualitatively different because it presupposes freedom from trust and reliance on individual judgment. Consent, in other words, rests on popular enlightenment. Second, Hobbes believes that the people, understood as autonomous individuals, will actually strengthen the power of existing states by their consent. For consent does not mean establishment of a new government or destruction of an old one, but a mutual pledge of nonresistance to an already existing power. And Hobbes's natural law doctrine adds to this pledge by teaching individuals a new 'duty' to pursue their self-interest rationally, through obedience to the sovereign and enjoyment of innocent pleasures.

On the simplest level, then, Hobbes's view of popular consent is an extension of his theory of enlightenment to politics. Enlightenment frees the mind from authoritative opinion; popular enlightenment, in particular, frees the people from trust in those who claim to be holier, wiser, or more learned than themselves. Instead of surrendering their minds to such authorities, the people learn to think for themselves. Each person recognizes his own individual will as the source of right and truth: everything that binds his will must originate in himself and cannot be imposed on him from without—from the dictates of self-appointed spokesmen for God, nature, and custom. He recognizes, as well, that there is no single authoritative truth or orthodoxy that he must defer to and impose on others. He is aware, for the first time in history, that he is absolutely free from obligations to higher authorities and that all obligation is self-obligation.[6]

But he is also radically insecure, distrustful of other men and afraid for his life. So he recognizes the need to create a common power. Such a common power, however, must be acceptable to the newly emancipated individual and be a conscious choice of his autonomous will. The consent of the people is simply the collective expression (or majority) of those individuals whose wills have been emancipated by enlightenment from trust in authority. The difference between previous doctrines of right and the Hobbesian doctrine of voluntary consent is therefore significant: instead of deriving the authority of the state from above, from superhuman powers, it derives the authority of the state from below, from the individual wills of the people.

Hobbes's more technical formulation of popular consent, the juridical doctrine of "authorization," drives the same point home with greater force. He defines the state or sovereign power as a "person"—in the ancient Latin or Roman sense of a man who "represents the words or actions of another man." The one who directs this person to act or speak is the "author" (*Leviathan*, ch. 16, pp. 147–148). The author is a real person, the representative an artificial person; but every action of the representative binds the author as if it were done by the author himself. By describing the state or

6. Thus Hegel says in commenting on the significance of Hobbes's political philosophy: "Previously 'ideals,' whether it was the Holy Scripture or positive right cited as authority, were laid down; against this Hobbes sought to derive the bond of the state and the nature of its power from the principles that lie within us, that we recognize as our own": *Lectures on the History of Philosophy*, ed. G. J. P. Bolland (Leiden, 1908), p. 915.

sovereign power as the representative of the people, Hobbes conveys the thought that in obeying the sovereign, the people obey themselves.

This notion can be seen as deliberately reversing the traditional source of authority: instead of surrendering their minds to a prophet or wise man who claims to be a "representative" of superhuman powers, the people use their own judgment to choose someone (a mere human being) to be their own "representative." This device is clearly designed to protect the people from seduction by ambitious men who claim privileged knowledge from above and insist on adherence to doctrinal orthodoxy. Authorization requires the people to see themselves as the only legitimate source of obligation and grounds obedience to the sovereign in their own will (self-obligation).

Hobbes's theory of representation, therefore, does not make the sovereign any less absolute. Although sovereignty originates in the popular will, power is not really given to the people, and the sovereign is *not made accountable* to the people (if he were, he would not be sovereign). Something more subtle and strange occurs. Seeing the government as their representative, the people no longer expect it to be subject to higher authorities: the sovereign is thereby freed from accountability to everyone except himself.[7] The result is an actual transfer of power by the people from opinion leaders to whatever coercive power already exists, which is usually a patrimonial or despotic monarch. Authorization, then, serves as a reaffirmation of natural force because it removes the independent appeal of intellectual authorities and legitimizes natural rulers.

The two accounts of sovereignty presented by Hobbes—sovereignty by acquisition and sovereignty by institution—are thus complementary. Natural force receives a doctrine of right which it needs to be persuasive, and voluntary consent receives the force it needs to be effective.

To illustrate the process whereby the people disavow the claims of authoritative wisdom and institute a government of their own, only to reinforce the power of an existing monarch or conqueror, it is useful to refer to a passage in Max Weber's *Theory of Social and Economic Organization*. In his analysis of "charismatic authority," Weber

7. See Clifford Orwin, "On Sovereign Authorization," *Political Theory*, 3 (1975), 26–44. Orwin develops the subtleties of this argument and ably defends it against those who see later notions of accountability in Hobbes's doctrine. In a similar vein, Baumgold shows how the theory of authorization in *Leviathan* strengthens the pledge of nonresistance in the *Elements* and undercuts the parliamentary argument of accountability to the people, in *Hobbes's Political Theory*, pp. 36–55.

describes the process by which charismatic authority is transformed into popular sovereignty (technically called "the transformation of charisma in an anti-authoritarian direction"). This account is nearly identical to Hobbes's understanding of the proposed change from the rule of self-appointed prophets and wise men to sovereignty based on popular consent and authorization.

According to Weber, the charismatic figure claims legitimacy for himself and his decrees by demanding "recognition" as a duty, subject to "proof" of his appointment, such as miracles, prosperity, successful enterprises, or recognition itself. But by "progressive rationalization" (enlightenment, in Hobbes's terms) legitimacy becomes democratic, and "the charismatic chief becomes the freely elected leader." Consequently,

> the recognition of charismatic decrees . . . shifts to the doctrine that the group has a right to enact laws according to its own free will. . . . Under genuinely charismatic authority . . . conflicts over the correct law may [sometimes] be decided by a vote of the group. But this takes place under the pressure of the feeling there can be only *one* correct decision and it is a matter of duty to arrive at this. The most important transitional type is legitimization of authority by plebiscite . . . in spite of the fact that . . . [it takes] place only after the seizure of power by force . . . [and is] only formal or possibly a fiction.[8]

Weber's argument is that the change from charismatic authority to popular election, brought about by progressive rationalization or enlightenment, is actually a change from belief in orthodoxy to a kind of fictional consent to an already existing power who rules by force. Weber continues the analysis, however, by observing that "force" is an ambiguous phenomenon because it usually does not mean actual physical constraint. It too rests on some kind of recognition or opinion, and in fact often means "charismatic authority in which the authoritarian element is concealed [by consent]," as exemplified by the popular dictators of the ancient world (the demagogues) and by Cromwell and Napoleon in the modern world. Under such rulers, the charisma of saints becomes the charisma of military dictators under the fiction of consent.[9]

Weber, like Hobbes, is wrestling with the enigma of power and rule. Both are acutely aware that, except for direct physical control

8. Max Weber, *The Theory of Social and Economic Organization*, trans. A. M. Henderson and Talcott Parsons (New York: Free Press, 1947), pt. III, sec. vi, ch. 14, p. 387; Weber's emphasis.
9. Ibid, p. 388.

of bodies, power usually rests on what Hobbes calls "opinion" or what Weber calls "recognition"—a belief in justice, legitimacy, or rightful authority. This legitimacy may appear to reside above the ruler, requiring his decrees to conform to a notion of orthodoxy (one right answer, which requires recognition as a duty), or it may appear to reside below him, in the people, requiring the appearance of popular approval. In both cases, Weber and Hobbes argue, an elite group of self-appointed men do the ruling, and the people are kept out of power. But the two notions of legitimacy—orthodoxy or popular consent—produce different kinds of elites: prophets and wise men versus popular dictators.

From Weber's point of view there is no moral difference and very little behavioral difference between the two: the open charisma of prophets, such as Mohammed, and the concealed charisma of popular dictators, such as Cromwell and Napoleon, are virtually indistinguishable. Weber is ethically neutral, defining legitimacy as whatever is subjectively believed by anyone to be legitimate. He attempts to be a thoroughgoing positivist, recognizing the legitimacy of any society or faction within a society without judging among them as to which is objectively better or worse. He merely describes what others believe to be right—their subjective belief or understanding *(verstehen)* of justice and legitimacy. This may also explain why Weber does not see a sharp behavioral distinction between prophets and popular dictators, between charisma ascribed to higher powers and charisma derived from consent combined with force.

Hobbes, by contrast, regards the difference between charismatic authority and popular consent as decisive, in both behavioral and moral terms. In behavioral terms, the charisma of prophets rests on recognition without force and thus is insecure. The consent to obey a sovereign, although it may be a historical fiction and may never be formally given, eliminates orthodoxy as a title to rule and must be secured by force—real force, not just concealed charisma. Moreover, in contrast to Weber, Hobbes makes moral judgments because he believes in natural right and natural law. Hobbes holds that civil societies that reject charismatic authority and recognize the will of the sovereign or popular representative are legitimate or just; they alone provide real security in accordance with natural right.

But precisely because Hobbes believes in moral and behavioral differences between charisma and popular consent, his position is actually less consistent and harder to understand than Weber's position. Weber attempts, however unsuccessfully, to be ethically neutral and to avoid value judgments. Hobbes seeks to defend a certain kind of ethical neutralism or positivism, which holds that whatever the people command through their sovereign representative is just; but his equation of legality and justice is grounded in natural law.

In defending this position, Hobbes foreshadows the spirit of positivism and Weber's ethical neutralism. Hobbes's positivism tempers the deeply rooted tendency of human nature to hold one's own opinions as the single authoritative truth and to impose them self-righteously on others. Hobbes also opposes the attempts of the state to legislate the true religion and to care for the souls of its citizens. But his opposition to moral orthodoxy is not based on ethical relativism. For he, too, believes in an objective standard of right and affirms the power of reason to discover such standards. He thus opposes traditional moral orthodoxy with a brand of his own: the natural right to self-preservation and the duties of natural law to seek peace. Hobbes's position is hard to grasp because it combines positive law and natural law, relativism and absolutism: the arbitrary will of the sovereign people must be obeyed because the natural law (which is not arbitrary) requires such obedience.[10]

Because of this unusual combination, Hobbes argues that popular consent is perfectly compatible with submission to the force of a conqueror: consent is not an end in itself but a means to preservation, which can be secured only when the decrees of the people's representative are backed by unconditional force. The only difference, then, between commonwealth by acquisition (natural force) and commonwealth by institution (voluntary consent) is that, in the latter case, the people are not subdued by a conqueror. Instead, they turn to a conqueror or someone with extraordinary power out of fear and distrust of each other (*Leviathan*, ch. 20, p. 185). They transfer their natural liberty, their right to all things by nature, to a commonly acknowledged power.

The creation of a commonwealth by institution, of course, is not a recorded event that takes place in the political arena. It occurs in the quiet of one's study, in the mind of the reader of Hobbes's political treatises. For the essence of the social contract is the transferral of a right or a liberty, which is a negative action: renunciation of the right to resist. Indeed, Hobbes says, the sufficient condition of absolute power is to have everyone renounce the right to resist: for "the essence of [a body politic] is the not-resistance of the members" (*Elements*, II, 2.1.18). The implication is that for Hobbes the social con-

10. Ignoring the natural law basis of the social contract and treating Hobbes as a mere "legal positivist" are the chief defects of Hampton's otherwise insightful study. *Hobbes and the Social Contract Tradition*, p. 107.

tract or the consent of the people is not a historical event. But it is supposed to be a genuine mental event—an intellectual change, a change of opinion about the whole nature of authority in which the claims of orthodoxy by self-appointed prophets are rejected and consent is given to existing powers by acceptance of the sovereign's right to punish disobedience. Through consent, then, the people do not gain political freedom; they gain protection.

Hobbes also argues that the individual who consents to a sovereign acquires obligations, specifically the obligations of right reason to avoid contradicting oneself and to follow consistently one's self-interest. In this precise and limited sense, Hobbes believes in moral obligation—the obligation to follow one's interest in a prudent, consistent, and long-term fashion. Hobbes scholars who seek to find in this notion a proto-Kantian notion of moral duty or a residue of Christian moral duty are confused because they fail to see the strangeness of Hobbes's formulation and the polemical context from which it arises.[11]

When Hobbes formulates the law of nature, he says men have a duty or obligation: a duty to seek peace at all times and to renounce the right of self-defense whenever it is prudent to do so (*Leviathan*, ch. 14, p.117). Furthermore, he says that voluntary consent creates an obligation to obey the sovereign because by disobedience one would break one's promise or reverse one's rational will—a type of logical contradiction or absurdity (*Leviathan*, ch. 14, pp. 119–120). What is strange about these formulations is the assertion that duty does not entail self-denial or suppression of self-interest, as a Kantian or a Christian would assert, but the reverse: it entails pursuit of one's interest in a rational and consistent fashion. In other words, the duty Hobbes asserts is the duty to be selfish in a fully enlightened way.

We must emphasize here that Hobbes's notion of duty or obligation is not another case of the so-called naturalistic fallacy. Hobbes is not deriving an 'ought' from an 'is' or extracting a duty from an inclination but asserting that men have a duty to be selfish or that right is equivalent to utility. The simple explanation for this paradoxical formulation is that *men are not yet selfish enough*. Thus when Hobbes infers from his mechanistic model that "by a necessity of nature, every man doth in all his actions intend some good unto himself" (*Elements*, I, 16.6), he knows that this is not a description of

11. Kantian moral duty: A. E. Taylor, "The Ethical Doctrine of Hobbes," in *Hobbes Studies*, ed. Keith C. Brown (Cambridge: Harvard University Press, 1965), pp. 35–56. Christian moral duty: F. C. Hood, *The Divine Politics of Thomas Hobbes* (Oxford: Clarendon, 1964).

human behavior at the present time. He believes that our original or primitive nature was selfish; but civilization has made us too moralistic, too concerned with abstract doctrines of right, too zealous about orthodoxy. His goal is to temper these destructive obsessions. But because a return to naive selfishness is impossible, he must posit selfishness as a psychological necessity and then make it a duty through the conscious effort of science. What emerges is a peculiar combination, formulated in a polemical fashion, that counters previous doctrines of right with a new definition of duty—the rational pursuit of self-preservation. The hope is that in a few centuries or millennia, when human nature has been transformed and the utilitarian 'nature' of man is taken for granted, the polemical context will drop out of sight; the autonomous individual of enlightened self-interest will then reign supreme, and sovereignty will be established on indisputable grounds.

We cannot avoid wondering if Hobbes is naive in thinking that his doctrine of sovereignty can solve the historic problem of civil war and bring an era of perpetual peace. One way of answering this question is to reflect on Hobbes's own statements about his prospects for success. In a well-known passage in *Leviathan,* Hobbes betrays doubts about the influence of his teaching, fearing that the disparity between his doctrine and the received wisdom or "moral learning from Rome and Athens" will make it "as useless as the commonwealth of Plato." In addition, Hobbes worries that political sovereigns may find his book too intellectually intimidating, requiring too much mathematical or scientific ability to comprehend and apply (ch. 31, pp. 357–358). Although this passage expresses some reservations about the radicalness and difficulty of his doctrine, it does not suggest that Hobbes had fundamental doubts about the soundness of his principles. The main point is to acknowledge an element of chance: Hobbes 'prays' for the good fortune of having his book fall into the hands of an intelligent king who will read it and then act on it—that is, purge the universities and make the *Leviathan* required reading in the education of gentlemen, clergymen, and scholars, who in turn will disseminate its doctrine to the people. Thus Hobbes may not think, like Machiavelli, that chance can be conquered in every respect. But he does think that once his doctrine is publicly known, it, unlike previous doctrines, will not be disputed or will not produce another round of doctrinal warfare.

Hobbes's claim may not seem so extravagant in comparison with later theories of progress, such as Kant's prediction that history impels the nations of the world toward perpetual peace and Hegel's view that history works inevitably toward the realization of the rational state and Marx's prediction that history will bring an end to conflict in the universal classless society. Hobbes envisions a transformation of civilization of historic proportions but does not develop a theory of historical progress in the strict sense—a theory of inevitability which demonstrates by laws of historical change the necessary realization of the perfect society on a universal scale.[12]

Nevertheless, Hobbes is not lacking in boldness. With the dissemination of his political science, he says, "mankind should enjoy . . . an immortal peace" (*De Cive,* Preface). In another passage he asserts that a "long time after men have begun to constitute commonwealths, imperfect, and apt to relapse into disorder, there may principles of reason be found out, . . . to make their constitution, excepting by external violence, *everlasting*. And such are those which I have in this discourse set forth" (*Leviathan,* ch. 30, pp. 324–325; emphasis added). Hobbes's optimism, in other words, is bold but qualified. He envisions everlasting commonwealths within particular nations (the end of regime changes by civil war, the end of religious sectarian warfare, the end of factionalism and dissension) and perhaps even immortal peace among nations, if his doctrine has the good fortune to be publicly taught. But no theory of inevitable progress guarantees this outcome (even if some favorable trends can be observed). For Hobbes the opportunity is ripe for change, but the success of his enterprise does not rest on the independent working of historical forces. Instead, it requires a free choice to overcome the historical realm of authoritative wisdom and to enter the timeless realm of enlightenment science. The question that remains is whether that choice can be made without introducing a new kind of dogmatism and a new kind of doctrinal warfare.

12. Raymond Polin probably goes further than any other Hobbes scholar in viewing Hobbes as a forerunner of Hegel, particularly in his interpretation of Hobbes's idea of the rational state. But Polin goes too far in this direction, making the realization of the rational state in Hobbes seem too automatic. As if to correct his own imbalance, Polin also calls Hobbes a conservative: *Politique et philosophie chez Thomas Hobbes* (Paris: Presses Universitaires de France, 1953), pp. 150, 173–175.

» 8 «

The Dogmatism of the Enlightenment and the New Doctrinal Politics

Philosophy and Politics before and after the Enlightenment

It is often remarked that politics in the modern world is ideological in a way that ancient and medieval politics never were. Although this observation is true in some important sense, one cannot prove it merely by pointing to the many 'isms' that have shaped the modern world (liberalism, nationalism, communism, fascism, and anarchism, to mention only the most influential). For as Hobbes's historical analysis of civilization clearly demonstrates, ideological politics in one form or another has been around for a long time.

Hobbes in fact contends that theological, philosophical, and legal doctrines have been the decisive force in politics since the beginning of civilization. In the ancient kingdoms of the Near East (Egypt, Israel, India), priests and prophets shaped their nations by imposing religious doctrines. In ancient Greece, Socrates inaugurated 'philosophical politics,' demanding that every authoritatively established opinion go before the bar of reason. A standard of higher law—natural justice—was introduced to measure and criticize existing laws and customs; private men appealing to right reason and higher law became the judges of public authority. In the Middle Ages, Scholastics used Aristotle and Scripture to introduce abstract metaphysical doctrines into politics; and the Reformation brought about popular interpretation of Scripture and religious sectarian warfare over doctrines. It would seem, then, that politics in the civilized world always has been ideological in some sense of the word.

But something new begins with Hobbes and the Enlightenment which gives ideologies or theoretical doctrines even greater prominence in the modern age than in earlier periods. Faced with the seemingly interminable warfare over doctrines, Hobbes attempts to make a dramatic and historic break with the past. His strategy, however, calls not for the abolition of doctrines or the 'end of ideology' but for the development of a new doctrine, a science of enlightenment. Such a science rejects all previous claims of knowledge as forms of authoritative wisdom and builds a new edifice of science on the workings of the self-reliant mind. In accordance with this aim, Hobbes replaces the traditional method of philosophy, a dialectical analysis of speech, with an introspective science of thoughts and passions. Once that science takes hold, philosophy can be used to transform the world, beginning with the reeducation of the intellectual elites and the political leaders and proceeding to the enlightenment of the common people (eventually teaching even the humblest person to stop trusting in authority and to begin thinking for himself). With few reservations Hobbes contends that the historic battle for enlightenment eventually can be won, bringing a new age of intellectual freedom and perpetual peace to the civilized world.

This vision of the political influence of philosophy goes well beyond anything thought possible or considered desirable by previous thinkers. The classical philosophers thought that the 'cave' of the political community—its authoritative opinions and traditions fashioned by the poets, priests, and legislators—could be transcended only by a privileged few philosophers. And even the privileged few could not attain such heights without undergoing a rigorous education and making the most strenuous effort; the vast majority of men would always need authoritative beliefs, especially about the gods or God, and would react with anger and hostility to anyone who attempted to change or abolish such beliefs (*Republic*, 487a–490; 514a–517a). Moreover, the classical philosophers thought that philosophy itself would be debased if it were turned away from the lofty task of disinterested contemplation to the practical task of radically reforming the political world.[1] Hence they counseled prudence or moderation in the pursuit of justice and insisted on the

1. In Plato's *Theatetus* (180, c7–d5), Socrates refers to certain philosophers who at least entertained an idea of popular enlightenment. Such philosophers have not "concealed their meaning from the multitude . . . [but] declare their meaning openly, in order that even cobblers may hear and know their wisdom and may cease from the silly belief that some things are at rest and others in motion, and, after learning that everything is in motion, may honour their teachers." Trans. Harold N. Fowler, in *Plato*, Loeb ed., vol. 7 (Cambridge: Harvard University Press, 1976).

distinction between theory and practice as well as the need for the-oretical detachment from politics.

Hobbes departs from this course because he thinks that theory cannot be separated from practice. Since its beginnings, he argues, theory has been dragged into the practical world and is now univer-sally recognized as the source of all political opinions. Accepting these historical developments as irreversible, he opposes the pursuit of knowledge for its own sake and redirects theory to the practical goal of reforming the political world and augmenting human power.[2] With this move Hobbes introduces a new relationship be-tween philosophy and politics and sets the course for the modern enlightenment. The crucial question is whether this course will in-augurate an era of intellectual freedom and everlasting peace or ex-acerbate the very problems it is designed to solve by engendering a new kind of dogmatism and a new kind of doctrinal warfare. Ironi-cally, the latter appears to be the case.

In the first place, Hobbes introduces a new kind of dogmatism into the political world. He claims that his political science is abso-lutely certain and indisputable and implies that it is history's final doctrine (the one that will end all doctrinal disputes and bring per-petual peace). Such claims, of course, would not be dogmatic if they were adequately proved and grounded. But Hobbes is ambiguous about the ultimate status of his political science: Is it artificial or natural, a free creation or a natural necessity? Hobbes wavers on this crucial question and, as I have argued, ultimately settles for a paradoxical combination of the two.

On the one hand, his political science purports to be a purely mental exercise in which the defective elements of existing civiliza-tion are taken apart and reconstructed into a new form of civiliza-tion that is wholly artificial—a construct of the arbitrary will. On the other hand, the newly created artificial civilization is proclaimed to be in accordance with natural law and natural necessity. Hobbes never resolves this paradox in principle because he thinks it will be resolved in practice, once the kingdom of darkness is overcome and enlightenment triumphs. At that point the tension between the arti-ficial and the natural will disappear because the self-reliant mind, which produces both the artificial compacts of political society and the self-evident ideas of natural science, will stand unopposed. But in the transition period, realizing or actualizing this project requires

2. Although one still finds, in a few passages in the Epistle Dedicatory to *De Cor-pore* and the Review and Conclusion of *Leviathan*, admissions that disinterested con-templation of the "beauteous world" is Hobbes's deepest and strongest desire. These passages are discussed below.

pure mental concepts to find a metaphysical grounding that they do not possess and can acquire only by willful assertion. Thus a new and strange kind of dogmatism is born—'ideological utopianism,' it might be called—in which deliberately fashioned constructs of human nature and the perfect commonwealth prove themselves by transforming the world.

In addition to introducing a new kind of dogmatism, Hobbes gives new emphasis to the exercise of coercive power. In the past the fate of civilized nations was determined by self-appointed prophets and wise men who sought to have their pronouncements recognized as orthodoxy, or the authoritative wisdom of society. But such prophets and wise men were rarely, if ever, interested in political or military power. Indeed, they were "unarmed" prophets (to use Machiavelli's phrase). They created anarchy precisely because they were unarmed: they appealed to higher laws—divine law, natural law, common law—but refused to wield the sword themselves because they believed that higher powers, superhuman Providence, would ultimately enforce their doctrines. Or they did not care about enforcement, assuming the detached posture of distinterested contemplation or of faithful believers awaiting otherworldly salvation. Historically these intellectual authorities were responsible for creating a division of powers—between church and state, between opinion leaders and coercive powers, or, in theoretical terms, between an intangible spiritual realm and a tangible temporal realm. According to Hobbes, the defects of such intellectuals were vanity, having a "false estimate of their power," and hypocrisy, using others to do the dirty work of enforcement which they would not do themselves.

By contrast, the new doctrinal politics that emerges from Hobbes and the Enlightenment is designed to overcome the historic division of powers. It unifies right and might, opinion and force, the spiritual and the temporal realms in a single person or body. Hobbes's doctrine of sovereignty is distinguished from traditional doctrines of just authority by the claim that it does not rely on higher powers to prevail. There is to be no reliance on Providence; man must do it all by himself. Political sovereignty in its full sense means human sovereignty, the assertion that man is the master of his destiny. As a result, the doctrine of sovereignty becomes a fully "armed" doctrine. It demands more than intellectual recognition (the assent or approval of others). It demands enforcement by the sword.

When the doctrine of sovereignty is joined with the proposal for a radical change in human consciousness which redefines human nature and the nature of reality itself, a new and potentially dangerous combination of force and opinion is created. State power is brought together with the demand to recognize only abstract individuals who, as rational egoists, will create the perfect commonwealth. Sovereigns are given unlimited coercive power and charged with the responsibility of imposing a new way of thinking as well as arbitrating disputes. And it is not only or even primarily the existing political sovereigns who are empowered: a new class of intellectuals is created who, abandoning the goal of disinterested theory, are to become the agents of radical change by reshaping the minds of the people. Revolutionary forces are thus unleashed which prepare the way for a reversal of Hobbes's original intention. Instead of promoting independent thinking and lasting civil peace, Hobbes's enlightenment science inaugurates a type of doctrinal politics that leads to new kinds of mental enslavement and ideological warfare in the modern world.

How the Enlightenment Becomes a Dogma

It may seem strange to think of the Enlightenment as a 'dogma' because it defines itself, especially in the works of Hobbes, as the end of dogmatic thinking: opposition to trust or blind faith in authority, radical doubt about the ability of speech and sensation to grasp the external world, rejection of any notion of orthodoxy or authoritative wisdom. But a critical attitude toward authoritative opinion in the name of independent or self-reliant thinking does not necessarily lead to true intellectual freedom. This posture contains within it the seeds of a new kind of dogmatism that is more restrictive and potentially more dangerous than the traditional kind.

In the first place, a starting point that takes nothing on trust must appear as if it were self-evident or self-grounding, although it presupposes a polemical stance against opinion as such. Accordingly, enlightenment science needs to hide or obscure its polemical origins. It may attempt to do so in several ways (reflected in the various rhetorical strategies of Hobbes's treatises). One way is to ignore altogether the opinions of the past and begin with a blank slate. Another is to engage specific opinions outside the treatises proper, using prefaces, appendices, and separate historical works. Another is to abstract completely from the content of opinion and treat opinion as something that has already been separated into the constituent elements of speech, sense impressions, and passions.

By such procedures the whole world of common sense and conventional opinion, which is at the very center of Aristotle's ethical
and political treatises and of Plato's dialogues, is simply set aside in
the hope that eventually it will be forgotten. Or if it is not forgotten,
one can hope that it will be viewed as a relic of a more naive era that
is irrevocably gone and hardly worth serious consideration (the
usual attitude of modern readers of Hobbes who study only parts I
and II of the *Leviathan*). When conventional opinion is treated this
way, the rich and vivid world of appearances that is taken for
granted in ordinary politics (and partly captured in Hobbes's historical writings) is lost, replaced by bloodless definitions and dry logic.
The new dogmatism is to assume that epistemology and methodol-
ogy are the "first sciences," which simply stand on their own. This
assumption is common in the schools of empiricism, positivism,
symbolic logic, and linguistics, where the elements of opinion (sense
impressions, words, and passions) are analyzed and systematized.
What is usually forgotten is that formal analysis of this kind becomes important only after the world of authoritative opinion and
the traditional mode of dialectical reasoning (which takes the content of opinions most seriously) have been destroyed.

Although Hobbes may not be guilty of such blindness, he faces a
more fundamental problem. In claiming to begin from an absolute
beginning point—one that stands outside of inexact and unreliable
opinion—he expects his first principles to be accepted without disputation or challenge. He would deny, of course, that such expecta-
tions constitute dogmatism because his principles have been purged
of trust and are conceptually certain (present a clear picture to the
mind). If this were all that Hobbes claimed, his position would not
be so puzzling and could avoid the charge of dogmatic thinking. But
Hobbes is not so modest. He presents his principles not only as conceptual certainties but also as metaphysical truths—truths about nature, human nature, and the right of nature.

This kind of claim is the strangest feature of Hobbes's whole philosophy. Most scholars recognize the difficulty but ultimately assume
that Hobbes's assertions are due to a temperamental idiosyncrasy
that needs no explanation: Hobbes, by his own testimony, was a
timid man living in chaotic times who naturally thought that security, order, or preservation was the greatest good and violent death
the greatest evil. Also, his extreme hatred of abstract essences and
invisible powers led him to formulate the doctrine of materialism,
popular in his day, in the most uncompromising fashion. The implication is that one must accept the fact of Hobbes's temperamental
extremism and get on to more 'interesting' questions. For is it not

the case, as Nietzsche said, that "there is a point in every philosophy when the philosopher's 'conviction' appears on stage"—when we see his ultimate dogmatic assumption, and he appears to be no different from a stubborn ass, "beautiful and brave" but no less irrational?[3]

Aside from our chagrin at Nietzsche's unflattering comparison, there is a good reason to avoid the temptation of reducing Hobbes's thought to his personal temperament. We can learn a lesson about the dogmatic character of the Enlightenment and much of modern politics—a lesson magnified, perhaps, by Hobbes's personality but one that arises from the inherent dilemmas of his philosophical position and applies to a broad range of phenomena. Let us approach this problem by reflecting on the 'dogmatic' character of Hobbes's central doctrines—mechanistic materialism and the natural right of self-preservation.

In his presentation of these doctrines, Hobbes's characteristic pattern of behavior is to move insensibly from two kinds of claims: from conceptual certainties (statements that satisfy an exact method but remain hypothetical as claims about the world) to metaphysical truths (truths about the real world, about the nature of things, about Being). As we noted earlier in regard to Hobbes's natural science, this pattern is no accident. It grows out of the central dilemma of the Enlightenment: the need to establish a connection between the self-reliant mind and the external world.

Enlightenment begins with radical doubt about the capacity of the human mind to know the external world (so that it may attain certain knowledge and the concomitant goal of lasting civil peace). The enlightened mind thereby severs the tie between itself and the world, between the mind and nature, between subject and object, between thinking and being. After severing this tie, however, the enlightened mind ultimately seeks to reestablish a connection between its own self-knowledge and knowledge of the naturally given or divinely created order. Without such a connection or grounding, the self-reliant mind is nothing but subjective certainty; it can make no claim to scientific objectivity and has no way of standing polemically against the doctrines of the past and expelling the kingdom of darkness. Yet how can the enlightened mind reestablish a connection between itself and the world when it has surrendered that right at the outset?

In Descartes's case, it is well known that he pondered long and hard on this question and ultimately relied on the assumption that a

3. Friedrich Nietzsche, *Beyond Good and Evil*, trans. Walter Kaufmann (New York: Vintage, 1966), no. 8.

benevolent God, whose existence can be proved by reason, would not so deceive the human mind as to make all philosophical speculation futile. However unsatisfactory this move may be (because it cannot avoid a leap of faith), Descartes struggled valiantly to solve this problem in his *Meditations on First Philosophy* (especially I, III, and IV). But Hobbes never addressed this question directly, either in *De Corpore* or in the political treatises, so we may surmise that self-reflection or introspection was not sufficient for him to reestablish the connection between the enlightened mind and the world. Instead Hobbes makes the connection in the act of rebellion against the traditional order: his conceptual certainties assume the power of metaphysical truths when they are posited against the erroneous doctrines of the past. However self-evident they may claim to be, Hobbes's definitions are polemically derived; and it is only in this posture that they come alive and become real. But this derivation makes them dogmatic—assertions without proof or grounding which borrow metaphysical capital from the tradition.

Such dogmatism is new and unusual. For it turns mere definitions into imperatives to recreate reality according to mental conceptions that have no grounding of their own. While the (alleged) dogmatism of traditional philosophy and theology arises from the assumption that thinking conforms to being, the dogmatism of Hobbes's enlightenment science arises from the more radical demand that thinking become being or create being.

Recall our earlier argument about Hobbes's doctrine of metaphysical materialism. Hobbes says explicitly that he does not demonstrate its truth, nor is it demonstrable. Metaphysics is an introspective science that claims to be self-evident; it involves settling or limiting the mental conceptions necessarily associated with the most universal names; its conclusions are as undeniable as clear mental pictures are to the enlightened mind (to the mind that is freed from trust in language, whose snares misled Aristotle). Thus Hobbes claims that the only way to conceive of change or causality in the natural world is by envisioning the touching of two bodies or the touching of parts within a body. Admittedly, once truth is defined in this way—as introspection, as reflection on ideas—then mechanistic materialism has a certain kind of self-evidence. Action at a distance, without any touching, is impossible to conceive mentally; even when some change seems to have invisible causes, one needs only to imagine very tiny or thin particles at work. As a hypothetical or conceptual truth—a truth that satisfies the method of introspection and exact deduction—Hobbes's materialism has self-evidence of a sort that makes his case plausible.

Yet Hobbes insists, with no further proof, that his doctrine also describes reality, that "matter in motion" or body alone is real. In his physics he admits that the causes of all natural phenomena can never be known with certainty, although one may be assured of finding a mechanical hypothesis. This assurance is made, however, only because Hobbes has decided for some prior reason that reality is and must be material. His prior reason is the need to expel every form of immaterial cause from nature so the mind will not be tempted by intellectual vanity and slip back into the intellectual controversies of traditional metaphysics. In other words, the real "self-evidence" of mechanistic science for Hobbes arises from the necessities of his polemical stance: establishing a ground for the self-reliant mind in a doctrine of nature which destroys the props of intellectual vanity.

Mechanistic materialism is transformed from a hypothesis to a metaphysical dogma because the enlightened mind needs a grounding in something more than its own self-knowledge; it needs a home in nature. The need for a home in nature, one could say, is the 'second nature' of the enlightened mind. By contrast, the first impulse of the enlightened mind is to separate itself from nature and nature's God—to reject assumptions about a superhuman Providence (natural teleology, final causes, divine inspiration, miracles, infused wisdom, right reason constituted by nature) which cares for the human mind by providing clear guidance and support. Feeling betrayed by the absence of providential support, the enlightened mind suspends judgment about the ultimate nature of reality and becomes metaphysically neutral or agnostic. It puts metaphysics and theology on the back burner, so to speak, and focuses first on epistemology—on the mind separated from nature, on the knowing subject separated from its object, on thinking separated from being. The first questions it asks are: Why has certain knowledge eluded man throughout history? What has led the mind astray? Have nature and God abandoned the human mind or even deceived the human mind?

To these questions the philosophers of the Enlightenment give an answer that is essentially psychological (or perhaps, one might say today, phenomenological). That is, they give an account of states of mind or states of consciousness, independent of any metaphysical commitment, which explains the two basic types of mind—the unenlightened versus the enlightened. Once the initial psychological types are cast, then a grounding for the enlightened mind is sought in nature or God through metaphysics or theology. The type of metaphysics or theology that results can vary a great deal, but it must meet two requirements: it must be derived introspectively rather than dialectically, and it must deny the providential role of superhuman powers in caring for the human mind.

Although it denies support from God or nature, the enlightened mind never goes so far as to reject the existence of a moral order that is accessible to reason. The enlightened mind, in other words, never carries doubt to such an extent that it becomes the 'existential mind,' losing all faith in an objective moral order and confronting chaos or the meaningless abyss. The enlightened mind is still protected by the philosophical and academic tradition of the West and holds that a science of nature and natural justice is possible. What it seeks are metaphysical doctrines that preserve the notion of a moral order intelligible to human reason while denying the notion of providential intervention in human affairs; man alone must provide the sanctions by his own efforts and arms.

Indeed, it is the implicit faith in a moral order discoverable by reason, inherited from the Western philosophical and theological tradition, that saves enlightenment science from mere subjectivity and impotence. The tradition provides the reserve of 'metaphysical and moral capital,' so to speak, which the Enlightenment needs as the dogmatic foundation for its radical skepticism. But that metaphysical and moral capital is borrowed from the tradition without acknowledgment of the debt. Indeed, it is borrowed in the most ungrateful fashion: in the act of rebelling against or subverting the tradition. By engaging the tradition polemically in order to destroy it, the Enlightenment acquires metaphysical and moral capital that it needs but cannot generate on its own. The Enlightenment, then, may claim to be self-generating; but it is really the ungrateful child of the tradition.

Reflecting this attitude, enlightenment thought combines the denial of superhuman Providence (divine intervention and natural teleology) with the affirmation of a moral order accessible to reason for which man himself must provide the sanctions. Although materialism and deism were the most popular metaphysical and theological doctrines among seventeenth- and eighteenth-century enlightenment thinkers, they are not absolutely required by the Enlightenment. A variety of metaphysical postures is possible— Hobbes's monistic materialism, Descartes's dualism of material bodies and immaterial minds, Locke's more skeptical materialism or ultimate agnosticism, Hume's agnosticism, Kant's dualism of physical nature and metaphysical freedom. Likewise, a variety of theological postures is possible—atheism, agnosticism, deism. The crucial point about Hobbes and the enlightenment thinkers is that their meta-

physical and theological doctrines are not mere postulates or pro-
jections of their political doctrines; they are considered to be true
statements of the way the world is ordered. But the whole notion
of 'truth' has been changed by the enlightened mind: it distinguishes methodological certainty from metaphysical truth and creates the latter by willful assertion in the practical transformation of
the world.4 This is the Enlightenment's peculiar brand of 'magic,'
the use of thinking to transform being.

In moral philosophy Hobbes's teaching about the natural right to
self-preservation is a more complicated and important case of the
same tendency to move from hypothetical to metaphysical truth.
Nothing is more perplexing, as Strauss has shown, than the fact that
Hobbes's whole political science rests on a prescientific moral attitude: the proposition that vain, aggressive, domineering attitudes
are unjust; while fearful, peaceful, humble attitudes are just. Hence
Hobbes teaches that the first moral fact is not an obligation but a
right, the right of self-preservation, rooted in the strongest passion,
the fear of violent death.

What amazes commentators on Hobbes is that the most important
question of his political philosophy—the question of the moral purpose of the state, indeed the question of the moral purpose or end
of human life—is unproved or taken for granted. One can find no
systematic discussion in Hobbes's works where he weighs the various

---

4. This argument may help to clear up some confusion about Hobbes's belief or
disbelief in God. Hobbes's stance as an enlightenment thinker is compatible with several possibilities. One is the denial of God's existence (atheism). A second is the suspension of judgment about God's existence (agnosticism). A third is the affirmation
of his existence in new and strange ways, for example, believing in God as a first
cause who exists in corporeal form, as very thin particles, but who does not intervene
in the universe or interact with men (a kind of materialist deism). The latter opinion
seems to be the one adopted by Hobbes, permitting him to deny the charge of atheism while rejecting the orthodoxies of his day. The point is that Hobbes could afford
to be ambiguous on this crucial question because *it is not the existence of God but the
providence of God that he denies.*
In the latest attempt to resolve the scholarly controversy about this question, Arrigo Pacchi tries to find a middle ground between those who argue that Hobbes is an
atheist (Polin, Strauss) and those who contend that Hobbes is a Christian believer
(Hood, Warrender, Johnson, Reventlow). Pacchi argues that Hobbes's subjectivist
epistemology requires him to believe in God as "a kind of transcendent warrant [for
his] conception of reality as a material world of moving bodies, causally connected in
a necessary determined sequence of events" (Pacchi, "Hobbes and the Problem of
God," in *Perspectives on Thomas Hobbes*, ed. Rogers and Ryan, p. 183). But unlike
Descartes, Hobbes never says that it is God who provides such guarantees. God may
account for the existence of the universe (as Creator), but the order and intelligibility
of the universe is provided by the human mind in the act of rebellion and transformation.

goods of life (such as pleasure, security, wealth, honor, virtue, salvation, or wisdom) and attempts to prove that security is the primary good or that violent death is the worst evil.[5] In place of arguments or proofs, we find weak analogies: "every man is desirous of what is good for him, and shuns what is evil, but chiefly the chiefest of natural evils, which is death; and this he doth by a certain impulsion of nature, no less than that whereby a stone moves downward" (*De Cive*,I.7). Or we find bold assertions:

> And forasmuch as a necessity of nature maketh men to will and desire *bonum sibi*, that which is good for themselves, and to avoid that which is hurtful; but most of all, the terrible enemy of Nature, death, from whom we expect both the loss of all power, and also the greatest bodily pains in the losing; it is not against reason, that a man doth all he can to preserve his own body and limbs both from death and pain. And that which is not against reason, men call *right*, or *just*, or *blameless liberty* of using our own natural power and ability. It is therefore a right of nature, that every man preserve his own life and limbs, with all the power he hath. (*Elements*, I, 14.6; Hobbes's emphasis)

In these passages Hobbes asserts without proof that the natural end of all life or being is the avoidance of violent death or its own preservation.

Hobbes's procedure in these crucial passages is not only very strange; it also is inconsistent with other statements in which Hobbes seems to suggest that one should pursue higher goals than self-preservation and that one must not forget the distinction (as Aristotle teaches) between mere life and the good life. In the Epistle to the Reader of *De Corpore*, for example, Hobbes briefly compares and judges four human activities—the accumulation of wealth, participation in politics, the enjoyment of sensual pleasure, and philosophy—in order to demonstrate that doing philosophy, although it may seem laborious, is the most desirable activity. Hobbes's criterion for judging is pleasure: the activity that brings the greatest pleasure is deemed most choiceworthy. Hobbes's argument is familiar but curious. He claims that men accumulate wealth not for its own sake but for the sake of admiring their own wisdom. Likewise, public business is done to display one's wisdom, presumably through oratory and arts of speech. Sensual pleasure, Hobbes says, is not sought for an ulterior motive but is vastly overrated because men are ignorant of the greatest pleasure, philosophy. He then describes the

---

5. Strauss, *Political Philosophy of Hobbes*, p. 152–153.

pleasure of philosophy in some of his most passionate and poetic language: it is the "pleasure of the mind to be ravished in the vigorous and perpetual embraces of the most beauteous world"—a statement that rivals Plato's *Symposium* in its description of the erotic pleasure of philosophy. Hobbes follows this remark, however, with the curious comment that even if his readers cannot feel the erotic pleasure of philosophy, they should take up philosophy to relieve the restless boredom of their leisure time instead of making trouble or getting hurt (by raising rebellions). Thus philosophy is recommended either because it is the greatest pleasure of the mind or because it is safe and harmless.

The conclusion that one can draw is that Hobbes recognizes higher activities than self-preservation, but most of them are forms of intellectual vanity (showing off one's wisdom), except for true philosophy, which is both an erotic passion *and* a way of preserving oneself. Hobbes's familiar antithesis of intellectual vanity and physical safety underlies this analysis. But a higher or more noble pursuit—an erotic passion for being intellectually "ravished and embraced" by the beauteous world—is definitely acknowledged and defended as most choiceworthy (see also *Leviathan*, Review and Conclusion, last paragraph). The ambiguity that remains is whether philosophy is an end in itself or a means to safety. Whatever is the case, mere preservation is not the primary or only human good; it must be an enjoyable or epicurean kind of preservation that involves the pursuit of wisdom.

Similarly, in the political treatises Hobbes qualifies the view that death is the greatest evil and self-preservation the greatest good by distinguishing mere life from the good life. He says in *Leviathan*, for example, that the motive for relinquishing one's natural right to all things is "nothing else but the security of a man's person, in his life, and *in the means of so preserving life, as not to be weary of it*" (ch. 14, p. 102; emphasis added). In another passage of *Leviathan* he states that the reason men establish commonwealths is "the foresight of their own preservation, *and of a more contented life thereby*" (ch. 17, p. 128; emphasis added). While generally asserting the preservation of one's life as the primary right, Hobbes acknowledges other goals that suggest a legitimate human striving for something more fulfilling than mere avoidance of death.

In one of his strangest formulations about the goods of life, Hobbes says the following:

Moreover, the greatest good for each is his own preservation. For nature is so arranged that all desire good for themselves. Insofar as it is within their capacities, it is necessary to desire life, health, and further, insofar as it can be done, security of future time. *On the other hand, though death is the greatest of all evils (especially when accompanied by torture), the pains of life can be so great that, unless their quick end is foreseen, they may lead men to number death among the goods.* (*De Homine,* XI.6; emphasis added)

Here Hobbes seems to contradict himself on the most fundamental point: self-preservation is by nature the greatest good and death the greatest evil, except when staying alive is so painful that death by suicide seems to be a good thing. How can Hobbes say apparently contradictory things about the greatest good and the greatest evil?

I propose the following interpretation. Hobbes's emphasis on avoiding death and preserving one's life is a hypothetical truth. The passion for self-preservation, arising from fear of violent death, should be conceived as the strongest passion in most men *if* one wants the certainty of building a lasting political order. But this hypothetical or conditional assertion does not make the passion of fear 'natural' or 'naturally right.' Only after the process of enlightenment frees men from certain illusions does this passion become a 'natural' fact.[6] And only when asserted against the claims of traditional higher law teachings (divine law, natural law, common law) does this natural fact become a natural right. By borrowing 'moral capital' from the tradition he seeks to overthrow, Hobbes is able to turn a hypothetical observation about human nature into a right of nature.

In other words, self-preservation was the dominant passion in the earliest stages of human history, in the condition of savagery or barbarism; but it has been repressed by artificial civilization, during which time intellectual vanity has become more powerful than fear of death. At a later and more advanced stage in human history (about the seventeenth century), enlightenment recovers the effectual truth of human behavior by liberating the mind from vanity and asserting the 'naturalness' of the passion for self-preservation. Yet this is no more than a hypothetical statement about the effectual truth of human nature. For self-preservation is hardly the dominant concern in the contemporary world and becomes primary only through enlightenment.

6. Thus Hobbes acknowledges that "most men would rather lose their lives (that I say not, their peace) than suffer slander" (*De Cive,* 3.12). Here Hobbes tries to bridge the gap between actual behavior and right behavior by asserting that to die for honor is not to deny the deeper desire for peace.

Once fear of death reemerges as the dominant passion, the 'naturalness' of self-preservation becomes a scientific doctrine. Hobbes's metaphysics and physics suggest that, although superhuman Providence has abandoned man and left his distinctive capacity for speech wholly unsupported, something 'out there' of an utterly mysterious 'nature' still cares for man. Nature still cares enough for man to reveal itself to the senses: the appearance of appearances in the mind is the most amazing, the truly miraculous phenomenon of the mysterious universe (*De Corpore*, 25.1). But the miracle of sense appearances is possible only because motion or change occurs. Thus "motion" is the last act of providence, so to speak, because it permits some access to the external world of nature by the human mind.[7]

From the statement that motion is all the mind knows about nature, however, Hobbes makes the metaphysical leap of asserting that nature is nothing else but motion and that motion is identical to life: for "life itself is but motion, and can never be without desire, nor without fear, no more than without sense" (*Leviathan*, ch. 6, p. 48). The cessation of motion is death, which means that death is "the terrible enemy of Nature." Conversely, the continuation of motion is life, which means that life is the benevolent friend of nature. Motion permits nature to live or to exist, and it permits the mind to know of nature's existence. Both history and physics concur, then, that the desire for the preservation of life or the continuation of motion is the tendency most in accordance with human nature and with nature as a whole.

As I previously argued earlier, however, this statement is a hypothetical observation about the effectual truth of things; it describes the necessary and most powerful tendency followed by men and natural objects, once artificial civilization and 'vain' philosophy have been overcome by enlightenment science. A problem still remains: merely identifying self-preservation as the strongest tendency does not thereby make it morally right or wrong, just or unjust. Indeed, Hobbes's own remarks about the pleasures and superiority of the theoretical life suggest that philosophy is truly the right life according to nature. But the corruption of philosophy by the doctrinal politics of civilization leads Hobbes to deny this point. And even though this denial seems to place undue emphasis on a historical contin-

7. Thus, as Richard Tuck points out, Hobbes is saved from the abyss of radical doubt by his belief in "motion" rather than by belief in the "non-deceiving" God of Descartes: "Hobbes and Descartes," in *Perspectives on Thomas Hobbes*, ed. Rogers and Ryan, pp. 38–41.

gency, it creates the polemical thrust against traditional natural law that is necessary to convert a hypothesis about effectual truth to an objective moral truth—to a teaching about natural right and natural law.

This step is precisely what takes place in Hobbes's most important statement about the status of justice, the state-of-nature teaching. There Hobbes says two apparently contradictory things. On the one hand, he argues that nothing is naturally right or wrong because the struggle to survive negates all moral rules and traditional hierarchies. Right is nonexistent because it is without effect against the necessities of survival. Hence men are naturally free from moral duties (they possess natural liberty) and are naturally equal (without obligations to moral superiors). On the other hand, Hobbes asserts that right exists in the form of self-preservation. Indeed, men actually have an 'obligation' to preserve themselves by seeking peace and by quitting the state of nature. Hobbes has performed a sleight of hand; having abolished natural right, he then resurrects it in a new form; he collapses it into a necessity and then turns it into a moral duty.

Like the movement from conceptual certainty to metaphysical truth in natural science, hypothetical truth becomes absolute dogma in moral and political science by the act of rebellion against traditional morality. The amoral passion of self-preservation negates the traditional claims of higher law (wisdom, virtue, holiness, age, hereditary title, etc.) simply by being so powerful or undeniable. Natural inclinations are thus freed from shame and restraint: "The desires, and other passions of man, are in themselves no sin," Hobbes says (*Leviathan*, ch. 13, p. 101). In rebelling against such moral restraints in the name of self-preservation, however, Hobbes draws upon the moral capital of the tradition. Self-preservation thereby acquires a moral status it otherwise would not possess: it creates a right in defeating a right.

If it did not have traditional morality to rebel against, self-preservation would remain a historical fact or a natural fact but would never become a right. Arising against its polemical adversaries, self-preservation is transformed into a right, an altogether new and different kind of right. Instead of obligating the will to obedience, deference, and restraint, it frees the will to follow its own necessary inclinations. Self-preservation thus gives birth to individual natural rights—to claims of enjoyment by a multiplicity of desires (for peace, comfort, property, happiness, self-respect, welfare) that may no longer be restrained by traditional higher law or that must be discovered by those who are not yet enlightened.

In sum, we can say that Hobbes betrays the hidden dogmatism of the Enlightenment in both metaphysics and morals: after severing the tie between the mind and the external world, he reconnects the two in a willful act of rebellion and transformation, turning conceptual certainties into truths about nature and natural right.

The Liberal and Illiberal Pathologies of the Enlightenment

Having seen the emergence of a new kind of dogmatism in Hobbes's thought, we can now turn to an assessment of his legacy. This issue is usually posed as the question whether Hobbes's doctrine is the precursor of modern liberalism or modern totalitarianism. Some scholars argue that Hobbes, despite his preference for absolute monarchy, paves the way for bourgeois liberalism. He asserts a natural right to self-preservation, an ethic of "possessive individualism," a theory of the neutral state, and a notion of popular sovereignty or representation, which are the essential ingredients of what later became known as liberalism (and undoubtedly influenced Locke, the acknowledged founder of liberalism).[8] Other scholars contend that Hobbes's political philosophy is decidedly illiberal. His defense of absolute sovereignty, with its special emphasis on the sovereign's right to define words arbitrarily and to impose his definitions by force, seems like a precursor of Orwellian thought control (and undoubtedly influenced Rousseau, the philosopher of the "general will," who is often blamed for the French Revolution and the rise of modern totalitarianism).[9] Although the preponderance of scholarly opinion seems to support the judgment that Hobbes is more liberal than totalitarian, this debate fails to get to the bottom of things. It is based on a false dichotomy that obscures the common root of both liberalism and totalitarianism in the modern enlightenment and its paradoxical combination of freedom and dogmatism.[10]

8. For this view see Hanna Pitkin, *The Concept of Representation* (Berkeley: University of California Press, 1967); Macpherson, *Political Theory of Possessive Individualism;* Strauss, *Political Philosophy of Hobbes* and "Modern Natural Right: Hobbes and Locke," ch. 5 of *Natural Right and History;* Eisenach, *Two Worlds of Liberalism;* Coleman, *Hobbes and America: Exploring the Constitutional Foundations.*

9. For this view see R. G. Collingwood, *The New Leviathan* (Oxford: Clarendon, 1942); Eugene J. Roesch, *The Totalitarian Threat: The Fruition of Modern Individualism as Seen in Hobbes and Rousseau* (New York: Philosophical Library, 1963); and G. P. Gooch, "Hobbes and the Absolute State," in *Studies in Statecraft and Diplomacy* (London: Longmans, Green, 1942).

10. In two previously published articles I failed to see this point and was led to an impasse on the question of Hobbes's legacy. In one article I claimed that Hobbes's 'absolutism' was really the beginning of 'liberalism.' In another article I argued that

If we take the claims of liberalism at face value, it appears to be the embodiment of the highest aspirations of the Enlightenment. Whatever form it may take—Locke's theory of natural rights, Kant's ideas of moral autonomy and human dignity, Mill's utilitarianism and notion of individuality, the principles of Madisonian pluralism or Jeffersonian democracy—liberalism upholds an idea of freedom which pertains not only to political and social life but also to intellectual life, to the life of the mind. For liberals, political freedom is inseparable from freedom of conscience, speech, and thought. Indeed, it is precisely this connection that makes liberalism a *doctrine* rather than a set of institutions or practices and distinguishes it from ancient and Renaissance examples of free city-states (which may have been influenced by Socrates, Cicero, and other philosophers, as Hobbes argues in his historical writings, but existed independently of their ideas). Liberalism is a product of the modern enlightenment because it rests on a theoretical conception of the human mind and its ability to free itself from the shackles of higher authorities, whether religious, philosophical, customary, or paternal. As Guido de Ruggiero notes in his magisterial *History of European Liberalism:*

> The principle of free examination . . . [is] the source not only of religious liberty but of all modern liberalism. No interpreter [can] come between man and the Scriptures; no ecclesiastical mediation [can] come between the believer and God. From the very solitude of his consciousness, the individual gains an intimate sense of trust and responsibility. This same attitude is found in modern philosophy, rejecting as it does all authority and tradition interposed between reason and the proper object of its speculation, and reconstructing its own ideal world for itself.[11]

Because liberalism is ultimately defined by a theoretical doctrine about the freedom of the human mind and its capacity to triumph

Locke's 'liberalism' is the same in principle as the 'absolutism' of his early *Two Tracts on Government* (written in defense of the Restoration of Charles II and bearing the imprint of Hobbes). The way out of this impasse, I now realize, is to see the common root of both positions in the Enlightenment and to see the Enlightenment itself as a paradoxical combination of freedom and dogmatism. See Robert P. Kraynak, "Hobbes's *Behemoth* and the Argument for Absolutism," *American Political Science Review,* 76 (1982), 837–847; and "John Locke: From Absolutism to Toleration," *American Political Science Review,* 74 (1980), 53–69.

11. Guido de Ruggiero, *The History of European Liberalism,* trans. R. G. Collingwood (1927; Boston: Beacon, 1959), pp. 20–23.

over the historical kingdom of darkness, its roots and origins can be traced to Hobbes. As soon as this debt is acknowledged, however, one must add an important qualification. Hobbes is far from embracing the idea of political freedom which is so important for liberal politics. He emphatically rejects the connection between the self-reliant thinking of the people who consent to a sovereign and the institutions of self-government required for the genuine exercise of political freedom—the accountability of elected representatives, legal constraints on power, the separation of powers, and decentralized government or federalism. Hobbes argues unequivocally for absolute and arbitrary power and unified sovereignty, particularly that of an absolute monarch who displays the prowess of a military conqueror. Although his defense of absolute sovereignty shares an important characteristic with the political freedom of liberalism—it demystifies the sovereign and limits the scope of government to secular or civil matters—Hobbes remains distrustful of the whole notion of self-government which is so vital to the liberal idea of political freedom.

Full-fledged liberalism, therefore, has other sources besides the doctrine of Hobbes. As noted above, enlightenment philosophers who saw a more direct connection between the theory of enlightenment and the political freedom Hobbes denigrates have been more immediately influential. In addition to these philosophers, cultural influences from Protestant Christianity and classical antiquity, as well as the practical experience of self-government itself, have played important roles in the development of liberalism. But this complicated blend of factors, so admirably described by Tocqueville in his study of America, should not blind us to the fact, also acknowledged by Tocqueville, that enlightenment thought is the dominant intellectual and cultural force in liberal societies.

Because of this fact, liberal societies enjoy many of the benefits of the enlightenment project; but they also suffer from its defects. For modern liberalism, despite its great achievements in political freedom and the art of self-government, cannot escape from the problems of the Enlightenment. The chief problems—or pathologies as I shall call them—are the new kinds of dogmatism and doctrinal politics that are inherent in the Enlightenment's radical project of reshaping the human mind and transforming the world.

These pathologies are the dominant theme of the most thoughtful critics of liberalism and modernity, the critics of mass society, as they are sometimes called—Tocqueville, Nietzsche, and Ortega y Gasset. They argue (as I have argued) that the driving force of modernity is the imperative to liberate human beings from the demands of higher authority—not only from religious authority but also from every form of social and political hierarchy. They warn that this attempt at liberation or emancipation, instead of freeing and ennobling us, creates the potential for new kinds of despotism and degradation. Their central point is that the newly emancipated individuals, claiming to stand self-reliantly on their own and to think for themselves, are agents of a new mass conformism—a new ethos of equality, materialism, and security.

What disturbs these critics is not merely the pettiness, vulgarity, and unheroic character of the new ethos but the complacency with which it is imposed. It seems to triumph without feeling any need to justify itself—as if it were self-evident. The proponents of the new ethos, among the intellectual elites as well as the ordinary people, are completely self-satisfied in the belief that they are the culmination of progress or the peak of human history. They stand without reverence or shame before every claim of moral, philosophical, or spiritual superiority, absolutely convinced that such claims have been refuted or consigned to the dustbin of history. The result is a withering of the human spirit, a suffocation of the mind and enervation of the will, which subverts the ideals of freedom and critical inquiry from which it arose.

In describing this new ethos, the critics of mass society coin new phrases to express their contempt—"the tyranny of the majority" and "soft despotism" (Tocqueville), "herd morality" and the morality of the "last man" (Nietzsche), "the revolt of the masses" (Ortega).[12] Such phrases, of course, are meant to shake us from our complacency about modernity and to make us ashamed of the kind of creatures we have become. They also provide us with a new perspective on Hobbes. For the creatures in question are none other than the new Hobbesians, the enlightened individuals who are utterly dogmatic in the belief that history has been overcome and that equality, materialism, and self-preservation are the only self-evident truths. Although many people would argue that these individuals are es-

12. These phrases and the arguments above are taken from the well-known works of the authors. See Alexis de Tocqueville, *Democracy in America*, ed. Phillips Bradley, trans. Henry Reeve, 2 vols. (New York: Vintage, 1945), especially vol. 1, chs. 15–17; vol. 2, bk. 1, chs. 1–2; bk. 2, chs. 1–20; bk. 4, chs. 1–7. Friedrich Nietzsche, *Beyond Good and Evil*, especially nos. 199–203; *The Use and Abuse of History*, trans. Adrian Collins (Indianapolis: Bobbs-Merrill, 1949), pp. 47–57; *Thus Spoke Zarathustra*, in *The Portable Nietzsche*, trans. Walter Kaufmann (New York: Viking, 1954), pt. 1, sec. 5, pp. 128–131. José Ortega y Gasset, *The Revolt of the Masses* (New York: Norton, 1957), especially chs. 1, 6–8, 11–12.

sentially benign, the critics of mass society contend that it is precisely this benevolence—this desire to abolish everything danger-ous, harsh, and demanding—that makes such creatures so con-temptible. And they fear that this enlightened and peaceful attitude will eventually produce such a weakening of character that the ex-ercise and defense of political freedom will become an unbearable burden; or it will so enervate the soul and impoverish the mind that all higher forms of life—philosophy, art, profound spirituality—will become extinct.

The Enlightenment has another side, of course, a more violent pathology that needs to be discussed. As I suggested earlier, the very claims of the Enlightenment to begin an era of everlasting peace and to establish the 'rights of man' have the potential to create a new kind of warfare—the ideological utopianism of the revolution-ary intelligentsia. In the modern world this cruel irony was grasped most clearly by Edmund Burke, who exposed and denounced it with passionate eloquence. Like Hobbes, Burke reflected deeply on the phenomenon of doctrinal politics; but whereas Hobbes thought about the old doctrinal politics, Burke reflected on the new doctri-nal politics of the Enlightenment.

Burke's whole outlook on politics was formed by a reaction to the rationalism of the Enlightenment. Although his most immediate tar-gets were Rousseau and the *philosophes*, Burke recognized Hobbes as one of the founders or forerunners of this movement, and his most potent criticisms can be directly applied to Hobbes's doctrine.[13] For the central idea of Burke's political thought is the contrast be-tween two possible foundations for civilization: tradition (embodied in authoritative opinions, beliefs, prejudices, and customs) versus ab-stract reason (the speculative principles of enlightenment science). This opposition is identical to the choice posed by Hobbes—between the kingdom of darkness and the world of enlightenment. Both Hobbes and Burke regarded the choice between these alterna-tives as a unique or unprecedented event in human history, but they took different stands on this great issue.

Burke rejects the Enlightenment because it injects theoretical rea-son into the practical world of politics. Instead of leaving politics to men of prudence—statesmen guided by tradition and custom—the Enlightenment brings forth "intriguing philosophers," "metaphysi-cal speculators," and "political men of letters" who use abstract rea-

13. See Peter J. Stanlis, "Edmund Burke and the Scientific Rationalism of the En-lightenment," in *Edmund Burke: The Enlightenment and the Modern World*, ed. Stanlis (Detroit: University of Detroit Press, 1967), pp. 81–116.

son—theoretical speculation detached from concrete experience—
to direct political action. The use of abstract reason transforms
politics into an experimental laboratory, a testing ground where intellectuals may try their doctrines. The leading doctrines are those
developed and publicized by all the enlightenment thinkers from
Hobbes to Voltaire to Rousseau: the rights of man or the natural
rights of abstract individuals in the state of nature, and the social
contract or the doctrine of popular sovereignty.

From the beginning of his career, Burke was concerned with the
political influence of these "speculative" ideas.[14] In his first published work, *A Vindication of Natural Society* (1756), he attacked the
state-of-nature doctrine for creating a false antithesis between "natural society" and "artificial society" which could lead to the subver-
sion of civilization. Through satire and polemical exaggeration,
Burke showed that this doctrine undermined existing institutions by
attributing all human ills—war, oppression, corruption—to the or-
ganized religion and government of civil society. And he exposed its
implicit assumption that the ills of civil society could be overcome
because they were merely artificial perversions of an original state
of natural freedom. Burke clearly recognized that this doctrine
arose from the new kind of rationalism of the Enlightenment, the
self-evident propositions of autonomous reason. "What would become of the world," he asked, "if the practice of all moral duties,
and the foundations of society, rested upon having their reasons
made clear and demonstrable to every individual?"[15]

When he expressed these criticisms in 1756, Burke could not have
been certain that such doctrines might someday be used to destroy
existing civilized society. They aroused his deepest suspicions but
did not necessarily prejudice him against all political movements
that appealed to natural rights or popular sovereignty. Hence in the
1770s Burke supported the American colonists in their protests
against Great Britain and eventually in their movement for indepen-

14. As Strauss notes in *Natural Right and History*, p. 303, "the 'speculatist' approach
to politics came to [Burke's] critical attention a considerable time before the French
Revolution. Years before 1798, [Burke] spoke of 'the speculatists of our speculating
age.' It was the increased political significance of speculation which, very early in his
career, most forcefully turned Burke's attention to 'the old quarrel between speculation and practice.'"

15. "A Vindication of Nature Society; or, A View of the Miseries and Evils arising
to Mankind from every Species of Artificial Society" in *The Works of Edmund Burke*, 9
vols. (Boston: Little, Brown, 1839), I, 4, 8–12. In this work Burke specifically mentions Hobbes as a proponent of the sweeping indictment of preexisting civilization:
"A meditation on the conduct of political societies made old Hobbes imagine, that
war was the state of nature" (I, 12).

dence. He did so because he believed that the American colonists were motivated not by a desire to realize abstract rights but by a desire to restore their "ancient condition"—the practice of self-government in the colonial assemblies which had been taken away by the British policy of "taxation without representation."[16] With the outbreak of the French Revolution in 1789, Burke saw his criticisms of Enlightenment rationalism fully vindicated. Unlike the American Revolution, he thought, the French Revolution was an attempt to implement fully the abstract ideas of the enlightenment program. Its driving force was an "armed doctrine" that sought to destroy all existing institutions through revolutionary violence and to create a utopian society through reeducation and forceful imposition.[17]

In attempting to understand the "armed doctrine" of the French Revolution, Burke looked for historical precedents. In his essay "Thoughts on French Affairs" (1791) he provides a brief history of doctrinal warfare which in many ways is reminiscent of Hobbes's historical writings. Burke begins by describing the French Revolution as "a revolution of doctrine and theoretic dogma" whose "spirit of proselytism" takes it beyond national boundaries and makes it universal in scope. He then searches for historical comparisons among the doctrinal wars of the past, citing religious wars as the closest analogies but also mentioning cases of political wars as possible precedents. In recent history, the Reformation was a "revolution of doctrine and theory" that produced religious parties, factions, and sects in the countries of Europe and wars between alliances of Catholic and Protestant nations. In the ancient world, a "spirit of general political faction" as powerful and destructive as religious factions excited all the Greek states, dividing them into aristocratic parties (led by Lacedemonians) and democratic parties (led by the Athenians); this was a conflict of "political dogmas." In the Middle Ages, political factions in favor of the pope and the emperor, Guelphs and Ghibellines, divided the city-states of Italy; but they had in them little or no "mixture of religious dogma," despite their universal appeals. Having discovered these historical parallels, Burke nevertheless maintains that "the present revolution in France seems to be quite of another character and description, and to bear little resemblance

16. "Speech on Conciliation with America" (1775), in *Works*, II, 33, 39–40, 70–75, 82–83; "Letter to the Sheriffs of Bristol (1777)," in ibid., pp. 119–125; also stated in hindsight in an "Appeal from the New to the Old Whigs" (1791), in ibid., III, 363–367.
17. "Letters on a Regicide Peace," First Letter, in ibid., IV, 344.

or analogy to any of those which have been brought about in Europe." The French Revolution, in other words, was a unique and unprecedented event.[18]

What made the French Revolution unique? According to Burke, it had the zeal and missionary impulse of a religious crusade but it was antireligious or atheistic in principle. It was purely political, but it originated in a "theoretic dogma" that was abstracted from politics and political experience. It was unique, then, because it was the first revolution made solely by secular philosophers or enlightened intellectuals whose dogma sought to achieve a *"complete* revolution . . . [a] revolution . . . extended even to the constitution of the mind of man."[19] And even though it was driven by abstract theory, it relied on political power and violent coercion. This was a new kind of doctrinal politics: a revolution guided by the theoretical dogma of intellectuals, united with the coercive power of the state; an armed doctrine that sought to remake the human mind and create a completely new society.

Burke's criticism of the new doctrinal politics builds upon his early insights and develops their full implications. The new doctrine posits the existence of abstract liberty, the liberty of individuals in a state of nature, devoid of social controls and sacred restraints, beholden to no authority. In the *Reflections on the Revolution in France,* Burke criticizes this idea of liberty because it "stands stripped of every relation, in all the nakedness and solitude of metaphysical abstraction." It ignores the "circumstances (which with some gentlemen pass for nothing)" but which "in reality [give] to every political principle its distinguishing color and discriminating effect."[20] Burke's objection, however, is not simply that such an abstraction is false (he even allows that the state-of-nature doctrine may be a probable historical truth). His objection is that the philosophers and political advocates of abstract liberty are not satisfied with calling it a mental construct or even a probable description of primitive times. They insist that this idea describes man's "nature" and should become a living reality in the modern world. But they have no grounds for asserting the reality or metaphysical truth of this idea, other than its self-evidence as an abstract principle. Hence they are perfect dogmatists, demanding that mere mental ideas be treated as liv-

18. "Thoughts on French Affairs," in ibid., pp. 10–13; "Reflections on the Revolution in France," in ibid., III, 28.

19. "A Letter to a Noble Lord," in ibid., IV, 284; Burke's emphasis.

20. *Works,* III, 25. Also Sir Ernest Barker, "Burke on the French Revolution," in *Essays on Government* (Oxford: Clarendon, 1965), p. 219.

ing realities. They are pseudo-metaphysicians, followers of "the metaphysic knight of the sorrowful countenance."[21]

Burke denies that the state of nature and the rights of man are natural or real or metaphysically true. These doctrines cannot be real because they are in conflict with reality. The effort to bring them into being requires the most violent acts against the existing world, the physical destruction of existing institutions, such as monarchy, aristocracy, church and clergy, property relations, established legal structures. The revolutionary violence unleashed by such abstract ideas shows that they are unnatural—dogmatic assertions that have no reality of their own, that cannot prevail except by forceful imposition. Burke's conclusion is that the existing world, the world so disdainfully dismissed by enlightened intellectuals as mere art or convention, is the real or natural world. "The state of civil society . . . is a state of nature; and much more truly so than a savage and incoherent mode of life. . . . Art is man's Nature," Burke replies to pseudo-metaphysicians of the Enlightenment.[22]

Burke's conclusion, of course, contains a profound irony. All of the philosophers of the Enlightenment claim to have discovered the *real* nature of human beings—the nature that has been corrupted by artificial civilization and hidden or suppressed by traditional philosophy and theology. But the Enlightenment philosophers' description of that real nature, precisely because it is constructed in opposition to the appearances of the existing world, seems like an arbitrary assertion. Not only is it asserted without proof, it seems to vary according to the philosopher's personal idiosyncrasies. Hobbes describes our real nature as fearful and rationally selfish. Locke softens the picture by describing the natural individual as an accumulator of property. The utilitarians say we are creatures of pleasure and pain, utility maximizers. Rousseau discovers our natural indolent selfishness and pity. The Scottish Enlightenment philosophers find some middle ground between the two, a natural social sympathy or benevolence. Marx asserts that our true nature is our "species being," a social feeling for humanity as a whole. The problem with abstract reason is that, after rejecting the world of appearances as artificial, it has no necessary rules for determining what original human beings really were or naturally are. Hence it is governed far more by the idiosyncrasies of the particular philosopher than was the dialectical reason of classical philosophers, whose trust in appearances checked their personal biases. The reason of the En-

21. "Reflections," in *Works*, III, 26, 81–83.
22. "Appeal from the New to the Old Whigs," in ibid., p. 425.

lightenment philosophers—"stripped of every relation, in all the nakedness and solitude of abstraction"—merely posits a mental image
from introspection and then insists that it is real or demands that it
be brought into existence.[23]

After positing a view of human nature, the Enlightenment philosophers claim to build a political science that can be realized without
reliance on wishful thinking or chance; they claim to be more realistic than the ancients and to be more concerned with actualizing
their principles.[24] Hence Hobbes posits the abstract individual in the
state of nature in order to create a doctrine of sovereignty that will
strengthen existing institutions because it accords with a realistic view
of human nature. Locke also uses a state-of-nature teaching and a
doctrine of popular sovereignty to legitimize authority, in his early
Two Tracts on Government supporting the Restoration of King Charles
II and in his later *Second Treatise* supporting the settlement of the
Glorious Revolution.[25] Even Rousseau develops a doctrine of sovereignty to perfect Hobbesian realism—to legitimize the "chains" of
government by articulating a doctrine of the general will that cannot err or be disputed because it unites interest and duty.[26] But
Burke argues that the practical effect of such doctrines is exactly the
reverse of their authors' intention: Hobbes, Locke, and Rousseau
are subversives and revolutionaries rather than upholders and legit-
imizers of authority. Far from being realists, they are the greatest
utopians that ever lived.

They have been more devastating in their effect than Socrates,
who merely raised critical questions about received opinions and
sketched in speech the perfectly just society that admittedly could be
realized only by chance, if at all. The hidden dogmatism latent in
the scientific constructs of the Enlightenment becomes a revolutionary and destructive force rather than an instrument for providing a
more secure foundation for civilization. For the vaunted 'realism'
about human nature is so different from existing civilized behavior
that the whole world of appearances must be destroyed. And the
doctrine of sovereignty is so far from legitimizing authority that it

23. This criticism, implicit in Burke, is a central point of Hegel's critique of the
Enlightenment. See Lewis P. Hinchman, *Hegel's Critique of the Enlightenment* (Tampa:
University of South Florida Press, 1984), pp. 78–81.

24. See Strauss, *What is Political Philosophy?* pp. 40–55.

25. John Locke, *Two Tracts on Government,* ed. Phillip Abrams (Cambridge: Cambridge University Press, 1967), pp. 120, 123; and Preface to the Reader, in *Two Treatises on Government,* ed. Peter Laslett (New York: Cambridge University Press, 1963),
p. 171.

26. See Arthur M. Melzer, "Rousseau's Moral Realism: Replacing Natural Law with
the General Will," *American Political Science Review,* 77 (1983), 633–651.

leads to utopianism. The result is either anarchy or tyranny—revolutionary violence to destroy existing institutions or unconstrained power in the name of utopian construction.

In his last work on the French Revolution, *Letters on a Regicide Peace* (1796), Burke warns in ominous words of the "dreadful energy" that has been released by the revolutionary doctrines of the Enlightenment. Pocock has described this phenomenon as the energy of

> the human intellect set free from all social restraints, so that it is free to be constructive or destructive as it chooses, and it frequently chooses the latter in sheer assertion of its own power. A revolutionary intelligentsia is still the main vehicle of this energy, but its allies are less the "monied interest" of the *Reflections* . . . than the bureaucrats and technocrats of national power. . . . This confederate *trahison des clercs* has erected a state which has no purpose but the assertion of its own power and will readily lay waste the very provinces it is supposed to govern.[27]

Reflecting on this statement, we can see the ultimate irony of the Enlightenment. Its struggle against the kingdom of darkness is directed against the authoritative wisdom of priests, scholars, and philosophers who (allegedly) dominate others by disguising their own opinions as the wisdom of superhuman powers. The Enlightenment seeks to liberate the mind from such (alleged) hypocrisy by exposing all claims of higher insight as mere vanity or pretexts for persecution. But, as Burke shows, the Enlightenment does not free the mind from slavery to other men. It creates a new class of self-appointed wise men—the modern intelligentsia—who also seek to impose their opinions on others while disguising their impositions with a new and more brazen form of hypocrisy. As educators, enlightened intellectuals dominate by teaching the people to discard traditional authority and to listen to themselves as the authentic voice of the people. As political demagogues and allies of political leaders, enlightened intellectuals dominate in the name of liberating people from false consciousness (the 'dark ages') and have few inhibitions about using political power to transform human nature. The Enlightenment, then, does not free the world from authoritative wisdom; it creates a new kind that has abandoned the ideal of theoretical detachment and lacks the moderation or restraint of the old kind.

27. J. G. A. Pocock, Introduction to Edmund Burke, *Reflections on the Revolution in France* (Indianapolis: Hackett, 1987), p. xxxvii.

Burke was aware, of course, that not every modern nation or intellectual accepted the Enlightenment or carried its new form of doctrinal warfare to the logical conclusion. Thus he could hope that by attacking abstract reason and reaffirming (genuine) authoritative wisdom—opinion, prejudice, convention, custom, tradition, common law, religious faith, and the established church—he could help preserve a basis for ordered and virtuous liberty. In the case of England, Burke felt that trust in authoritative wisdom, embodied in the ancient constitutional order, had never been abandoned. The speculative ideas of the Enlightenment, he contended, had no great appeal to the English people (despite the efforts of Hobbes and Locke). The English mind instinctively preferred tradition to novelty, reform to revolution, common sense to metaphysical speculation, history to abstract science, practical experience to theory. It was only a matter of reminding the English people of their traditional national character.[28]

In younger and less traditional nations such as America, Burke simply denied the influence of Locke, Paine, Jefferson, and the philosophers of the 'rights of man.' He traced the American love of liberty not to philosophical ideas but to "its temper and character . . . [in which] a love of freedom is the predominating feature. . . . This fierce spirit of liberty is stronger in the English colonies, probably, than in any other people of the earth . . . [but it is] liberty according to English ideas and English principles. Abstract liberty, like other mere abstractions, is not to be found." The American attachment to liberty is a matter of character, Burke argues, shaped by a variety of causes—English descent, the Protestant Reformation, a predominance of lawyers, habits of self-government, the haughty pride of southern slave owners, the vast distance from the mother countries of Europe—but in no case is it attributable to abstract ideas.[29]

Burke's most important message, therefore, is that political freedom cannot be based on the Enlightenment. For the Enlightenment subverts the authoritative traditions that are necessary for the proper exercise of political freedom; and it leads to new forms of oppression, either the soft despotism of mass society or the hard despotism of ideological utopianism and modern totalitarianism. But Burke, unfortunately, does not escape completely from the intellectual revolution brought about by the Enlightenment. He certainly rejects the most important premise of the Enlightenment: the existence of the self-reliant mind or reason separated from trust in

28. "Reflections," in *Works*, III, 106–110.
29. "Speech on Conciliation with America," in ibid., II, 32–38.

authoritative wisdom. Burke rejects this premise because of its impiety: it suggests that the human mind has been abandoned by nature and by God, that Providence and superhuman support for justice do not exist. In the face of such denials, Burke reaffirms faith in Providence and trust in the wisdom of authority. But he does so by accepting the crucial secondary premise of the Enlightenment.

Burke accepts the argument that authoritative wisdom cannot be found in the utterances of human authorities, such as priests, prophets, philosophers, and wise men. Instead, he finds it in the impersonal forces of history. For Burke, history operates by gradual evolution and comprises a thousand impersonal accidents and contingent decisions that mysteriously add up to a coherent pattern or spirit of a nation. This pattern, which Burke calls "prescription," is "the happy effect of following nature, which is wisdom without reflection," and reveals "the known march of the ordinary providence of God."[30] Through prescription the wisdom of the natural and divinely created order is revealed, supplanting conscious reason and moving history unconsciously toward the beneficent end of ordered and virtuous liberty. By insisting that the authoritative wisdom of society inheres in prescription rather than in a human author, Burke is at one with the Enlightenment in its distrust of self-appointed wise men.

Burke's attempt to overcome the Enlightenment is therefore unsatisfactory. He may have reaffirmed faith in Providence, reestablished trust in authoritative wisdom, and restored the historical realm that was expunged by Hobbes and the Enlightenment. But his extreme aversion to theoretical speculation and to doctrinal politics of any kind prevented him from seeing the philosopher or the prophet as the guiding light of knowledge. This blindness makes his escape from the Enlightenment incomplete.

If we accept Burke's challenge to overcome the Enlightenment, then two additional insights are necessary. One is the observation that we can never abolish doctrinal politics by denying the need for self-appointed wise men. Hobbes thought he could overcome the need for such authorities by finding an impersonal repository of wisdom in the self-reliant mind and its exact sciences or methodologies; but he simply created a new kind of doctrinal politics. Burke was more conscious than Hobbes of the inconsistency of attacking

30. "Speech on the Representation of the Commons in Parliament," in ibid., v, 405; "Reflections," in ibid., III, 52–54. See also Peter J. Stanlis, *Burke and the Natural Law* (Ann Arbor: University of Michigan Press, 1958), pp. 44, 74–75, 98, 113, 167; and Harvey C. Mansfield, Jr., *Statesmanship and Party Government: A Study of Burke and Bolingbroke* (Chicago: University of Chicago Press, 1965), pp. 227–228.

doctrinal politics with a new doctrine. Hence Burke never developed a systematic philosophy, even though he implicitly relied on a metaphysical teaching in his notion of prescription and appealed frequently to divine and natural law. But his trust in the impersonal forces of history is almost as bad as the use of an impersonal method. For without the mediation of self-appointed authorities (such as Burke himself), history is blind. By acknowledging the failure of Hobbes and the limitations of Burke, we see the necessity once again for philosophers and prophets as the mediators for superhuman wisdom and accept the fact that deadly conflict over first principles can never be eliminated.

But this admission raises the old question: Who shall be the judge of wisdom and how can we distinguish the truly wise from the impostors? The simple answer is that only the wise can recognize true wisdom, a statement that seems like an empty tautology to modern intellectuals who have not freed themselves from the spell of the Enlightenment and its illusion of impersonal certainty. For others, however, this statement is not a tautology but a profound insight about human imperfection and the intimate connection between wisdom and self-knowledge. It means that truth will always coexist with error because, as Pascal says, "We know too little to be dogmatists, but we know too much to be skeptics." Pascal's thought is that nature's intelligibility and God's Providence will never be clear and distinct; but they are not so obscure that the human mind is utterly without guidance and support. The truly wise recognize this predicament. They feel a sense of humble awe, knowing that truth is hidden; yet they also feel specially chosen to speak authoritatively about the things that have been uncovered by them or revealed to them. Mixing humble awe and bold self-appointment, they embrace neither dogmatism nor skepticism nor that hybrid monster of the Enlightenment, dogmatism built on radical skepticism. They recognize instead our dual nature, our imperfection and longing for perfection. And they live within the two realms of human responsibility—the practical and theoretical, the temporal and the spiritual—without forgetting that the human soul needs theoretical detachment and divine illumination to be complete. This truth, known to the ancients and medievalists, but deliberately destroyed by modern philosophers and apparently forgotten even by Edmund Burke, is the truth to which we must return if we are to free ourselves from the darkness of the Enlightenment.

Selected Bibliography

Ashcraft, Richard. "Ideology and Class in Hobbes' Political Theory." *Political Theory*, 6 (1978), 27–62.
——. "Political Theory and Practical Action: A Reconsideration of Hobbes's State of Nature Doctrine." *Hobbes Studies*, 1 (1988); 63–88.
Barker, Sir Ernest. *Essays on Government*. Oxford: Clarendon, 1965.
Barnouw, Jeffrey. "Persuasion in Hobbes's *Leviathan*." *Hobbes Studies*, 1 (1988); 3–25.
Baumgold, Deborah. *Hobbes's Political Theory*. Cambridge: Cambridge University Press, 1988.
Brandt, Frithiof. *Thomas Hobbes's Mechanical Conception of Nature*. Copenhagen: Levin & Munksgaard, 1928.
Burke, Edmund. *The Works of Edmund Burke*. 9 vols. Boston: Little, Brown, 1839.
Burtt, Edwin A. *The Metaphysical Foundations of Modern Physical Science*. Garden City, N.Y.: Doubleday, 1954.
Cassirer, Ernst. *The Philosophy of the Enlightenment*. Boston: Beacon, 1955.
Coleman, Frank M. *Hobbes and America: Exploring the Constitutional Foundations*. Toronto: University of Toronto Press, 1977.
Collingwood, R. G. *The New Leviathan*. Oxford: Clarendon, 1942.
Collins, James. *Descartes' Philosophy of Nature*. Oxford: Blackwell, 1971.
Cropsey, Joseph. "Hobbes and the Transition to Modernity." In *Ancients and Moderns*, 213–237. New York: Basic Books, 1964.
Descartes, René. *The Philosophical Works of Descartes*. Trans. Elizabeth S. Haldane and G. R. T. Ross. 2 vols. Cambridge: Cambridge University Press, 1969.
Dewey, John. "The Motivation of Hobbes's Political Philosophy." In *Thomas Hobbes in His Time*, ed. Ralph Ross, Herbert Schneider, and Theodore Waldman, pp. 8–30. Minneapolis: University of Minnesota Press, 1974.

Diodorus Siculus. *Diodorus of Sicily.* Trans. C. H. Oldfather. 10 vols. Loeb Classical Library. London: William Heinemann, 1933.

Eisenach, Eldon. *Two Worlds of Liberalism: Religion and Politics in Hobbes, Locke, and Mill.* Chicago: University of Chicago Press, 1981.

Figgis, J. N. *The Theory of the Divine Right of Kings.* 2d ed. Cambridge: Cambridge University Press, 1914.

Gavre, Mark. "Hobbes and His Audience: The Dynamics of Theorizing." *American Political Science Review,* 68 (1974); 1542–1556.

Goldsmith, Maurice M. *Hobbes's Science of Politics.* New York: Columbia University Press, 1966.

Gooch, G. P. "Hobbes and the Absolute State." In *Studies in Statecraft and Diplomacy.* London: Longmans, Green, 1942.

Hampton, Jean. *Hobbes and the Social Contract Tradition.* Cambridge: Cambridge University Press, 1986.

Hinchman, Lewis P. *Hegel's Critique of the Enlightenment.* Tampa: University of South Florida Press, 1984.

Hobbes, Thomas. *Behemoth.* In *The English Works of Thomas Hobbes of Malmesbury,* ed. Sir William Molesworth, vol. 6. London: John Bohn, 1841.

———. *Behemoth or The Long Parliament.* Ed. Ferdinand Tönnies. 2d ed. Introduction by Maurice M. Goldsmith. New York: Barnes & Noble, 1969.

———. *De Cive.* In *The English Works of Thomas Hobbes of Malmesbury,* ed. Sir William Molesworth, vol. 2. London: John Bohn, 1841.

———. *De Corpore.* In *The English Works of Thomas Hobbes of Malmesbury,* ed. Sir William Molesworth, vol. 1. London: John Bohn, 1839.

———. *De Homine.* In *Man and Citizen,* ed. Bernard Gert, trans. Charles T. Wood, T. S. K. Scott-Craig, and Bernard Gert. Garden City, N.Y.: Doubleday, 1972.

———. *A Dialogue between a Philosopher and a Student of the Common Laws of England.* Ed. Joseph Cropsey. Chicago: University of Chicago Press, 1971.

———. *The Elements of Law Natural and Politic.* In *The English Works of Thomas Hobbes of Malmesbury,* ed. Sir William Molesworth, vol. 4. London: John Bohn, 1840.

———. "An Historical Narration on Heresy and the Punishment Thereof." In *The English Works of Thomas Hobbes of Malmesbury,* ed. Sir William Molesworth, vol. 4. London: John Bohn, 1840.

———. Introduction to the translation of Thucydides. In *The English Works of Thomas Hobbes of Malmesbury,* ed. Sir William Molesworth, vol. 8. London: John Bohn, 1843.

———. *The Leviathan.* In *The English Works of Thomas Hobbes of Malmesbury.* ed. Sir William Molesworth, vol. 3. London: John Bohn, 1840.

———. *The Whole Art of Rhetoric.* In *The English Works of Thomas Hobbes of Malmesbury,* ed. Sir William Molesworth, vol. 7. London: John Bohn, 1845.

Hoffding, Harold. *A History of Modern Philosophy.* Trans. B. E. Meyer. 2 vols. London: Macmillan, 1900.

Hood, F. C. *The Divine Politics of Thomas Hobbes.* Oxford: Clarendon, 1964.

Johnston, David. *The Rhetoric of "Leviathan": Thomas Hobbes and the Politics of Cultural Transformation.* Princeton: Princeton University Press, 1986.

Kant, Immanuel. "What Is Enlightenment?" In *On History,* trans. Lewis White Beck. Indianapolis: Bobbs-Merrill, 1963.

Kavka, Gregory. *Hobbesian Moral and Political Theory.* Princeton: Princeton University Press, 1986.

Kennington, Richard. "The 'Teaching of Nature' in Descartes' Soul Doctrine." *Review of Metaphysics,* 26 (1972), 86–117.

King, Preston. *The Ideology of Order: A Comparative Analysis of Jean Bodin and Thomas Hobbes.* London: Allen & Unwin, 1974.

Kirkpatrick, Jeane. *Dictatorships and Double Standards.* New York: American Enterprise Institute and Simon & Schuster, 1982.

MacGillivray, Royce. "Thomas Hobbes's History of the English Civil War: A Study of *Behemoth.*" *Journal of the History of Ideas,* 31 (1970); 179–198.

McNeilly, F. S. *The Anatomy of "Leviathan."* London: Macmillan, 1968.

Macpherson, C. B. *The Political Theory of Possessive Individualism.* London: Oxford University Press, 1962.

Mansfield, Harvey C., Jr. "Hobbes and the Science of Indirect Government." *American Political Science Review,* 65 (1971), 97–110.

———. "Machiavelli's New Regime." *Italian Quarterly,* 13 (1970), 68–80.

———. *Statesmanship and Party Government: A Study of Burke and Bolingbroke.* Chicago: University of Chicago Press, 1965.

Melzer, Arthur M. "Rousseau's Moral Realism: Replacing Natural Law with the General Will." *American Political Science Review,* 77 (1983), 633–651.

Orwin, Clifford. "On Sovereign Authorization." *Political Theory,* 3 (1975), 26–44.

———. "Stasis and Plague: Thucydides on the Dissolution of Society." *Journal of Politics,* 50 (1988), 833–846.

Pacchi, Arrigo. "Hobbes and the Problem of God." In *Perspectives on Thomas Hobbes,* ed. G. A. J. Rogers and Alan Ryan, pp. 171–188. Oxford: Clarendon, 1988.

Peters, Richard. *Hobbes.* Baltimore: Penguin, 1956.

Pitkin, Hanna. *The Concept of Representation.* Berkeley: University of California Press, 1967.

Pocock, J. G. A. Introduction to Edmund Burke, *Reflections on the Revolution in France.* Indianapolis: Hackett, 1987.

———. "Time, History, and Eschatology in the Thought of Thomas Hobbes." In *Politics, Language, and Time.* New York: Atheneum, 1971.

Polin, Raymond. *Politique et philosophie chez Thomas Hobbes.* Paris: Presses Universitaires de France, 1953.

Rapaczynski, Andrzej. *Nature and Politics: Liberalism in the Philosophies of Hobbes, Locke, and Rousseau.* Ithaca: Cornell University Press, 1987.

Reik, Miriam. *The Golden Lands of Thomas Hobbes.* Detroit: Wayne State University Press, 1977.

Reventlow, Henning G. *The Authority of the Bible and the Rise of the Modern World.* Trans. John Bowden. Philadelphia: Fortress Press, 1985.

Roesch, Eugene J. *The Totalitarian Threat: The Fruition of Modern Individualism as Seen in Hobbes and Rousseau.* New York: Philosophical Library, 1963.

Ruggiero, Guido de. *The History of European Liberalism.* Trans. R. G. Collingwood. Boston: Beacon, 1959.

Schochet, Gordon. "Thomas Hobbes on the Family and the State of Nature." *Political Science Quarterly,* 82 (1967); 427–445.

Sorrell, Tom. *Hobbes.* London: Routledge & Kegan Paul, 1986.

Spragens, Thomas A., Jr. *The Politics of Motion: The World of Thomas Hobbes.* Lexington: University Press of Kentucky, 1973.

Stanlis, Peter J. *Burke and the Natural Law.* Ann Arbor: University of Michigan Press, 1958.

——. "Edmund Burke and the Scientific Rationalism of the Enlightenment." In *Edmund Burke: The Enlightenment and the Modern World,* ed. Stanlis. Detroit: University of Detroit Press, 1967.

Stephen, Sir Leslie. *Hobbes.* London: Macmillan, 1904.

Strauss, Leo. *Natural Right and History.* Chicago: University of Chicago Press, 1953.

——. "On the Basis of Hobbes's Political Philosophy." In *What Is Political Philosophy?* New York: Free Press, 1959.

——. *The Political Philosophy of Hobbes.* Trans. E. M. Sinclair. Chicago: University of Chicago Press, 1936.

——. *Spinoza's Critique of Religion.* Trans. E. M. Sinclair. New York: Schocken, 1965.

Taylor, A. E. "The Ethical Doctrine of Hobbes." In *Hobbes Studies,* ed. Keith C. Brown, pp. 35–55. Cambridge: Harvard University Press, 1965.

Tuck, Richard. "Hobbes and Descartes." In *Perspectives on Thomas Hobbes,* ed. G. A. J. Rogers and Alan Ryan, pp. 11–43. Oxford: Clarendon, 1988.

Watkins, J. W. N. *Hobbes's System of Ideas: A Study in the Political Significance of Philosophical Theories.* London: Hutchinson, 1965.

——. "Philosophy and Politics in Hobbes." In *Hobbes Studies,* ed. Keith C. Brown, pp. 237–262. Cambridge: Harvard University Press, 1965.

Weber, Max. *The Theory of Social and Economic Organization.* Trans. A. M. Henderson and Talcott Parsons. New York: Free Press, 1947.

Weinberger, Jerry. "Hobbes's Doctrine of Method." *American Political Science Review,* 69 (1975), 1338–1353.

Whelan, Frederick. "Language and Its Abuses in Hobbes's Political Philosophy." *American Political Science Review,* 75 (1981), 59–74.

Wolin, Sheldon. *Politics and Vision.* Boston: Little, Brown, 1960.

Index

Absolute sovereignty, 6, 36, 56; analyzed, 166–186

Arbitrary will, 111–112, 120; in language, 117, 126; in opinions, 73, 88; in sovereign, 167, 169–170

Aristotle, 11, 48, 57, 68, 90, 105, 157–158, 198; defends civilization, 15–16; metaphysics, 128; source of democratic opinions, 48–55; use of dialectics, 82, 160

Ashcraft, Richard, 10n, 32n, 38–39

Authoritative opinion, 17; definition of, 70; distinguishes civilization from barbarism, 27–28; in Plato, 29. *See also* Opinion

Authority, 26, 70, 73, 99; cause of trust in, 85–94, 100–108

Autonomous reason, 6, 28, 98, 111–112, 117, 154

Barbarian princes, 66, 175–177

Barbarism, 12, 65; Hobbes's definition of, 12–17; in state of nature, 142

Behemoth: analyzed, 32–68; Marxist interpretation of, 38–40. *See also* English Civil War

Brandt, Frithiof, 120n, 125, 135–137, 159n

Burke, Edmund, 6; analysis of new doctrinal politics, 207–214; failure to overcome Enlightenment, 214–216

Cassirer, Ernst, 97n

Certainty, 103, 124–125, 216; conceptual, vs. metaphysical truth, 130–131, 192–203

Charles I, 36, 54, 174

Charles II, 62–65, 174–175

Christianity: disputes and wars, 24–27, 40–47; and individual conscience, 117

Christian politics, Hobbes's view of, 45–47

Civilization: ancient, 4; final state of, 27–31; Hobbes's ambivalence about, 27–28; Hobbes's definition of, 11–16; three historical stages of, 17–27

Common law: and dialectical reasoning, 83–84; and rebellion, 55–60. *See also* Custom

Conquest, 59–60; right of, 63–65, 174. *See also* Natural force

Consent or contract, 67, 173, 178–180; not a historical event, 183–184

Cromwell, Oliver, 54, 65–67, 174, 176

Cropsey, Joseph, 49n, 52n, 6on

Custom, 57–60, 160, 207

Democracy, 26, 47–55, 116

Democratical gentlemen, 47–55, 115

Modernity, 1–6, 216
Moses, Hobbes's view of, 20–21

Natural force, 13, 145; in orgin of state, 173–178
Naturalistic fallacy, 152–153, 184
Natural justice: in classical philosophy, 30, 49; in Hobbes, 140
Natural law, 14, 178, 183, 216
Natural reason, 31
Natural right: and natural necessity, 151–153; of self-preservation, 167, 183, 197–203
Nietzsche, Friedrich Wilhelm, 193, 206

Obligation, 153, 179, 184
Opinion, 34, 39, 47; freedom from, 31, 192; methodical analysis of, 69–94; in political treatises, 158; precise definition of, 76–78; replaces force, 16, 60; resolved into speech, thoughts, and passions, 74–84. See also Authoritative opinion
Orthodoxy, 40–43, 114, 168, 181–182; vs. uniformity, 172
Orwin, Clifford, 23n, 180n

Papacy, 40–42, 67
Parliament, 14, 62; Long, 47–55
Pascal, Blaise, 216
Patriarchy, 13, 17
Peace, immortal or perpetual, 6, 26–31, 62, 113, 185–186, 189
People, 37, 44; and enlightenment, 111–118
Peters, Richard, 9n, 120n, 123, 125n, 135, 139n, 153n
Philosophical politics, 21–25
Philosophy, 18; before and after enlightenment, 187–191; for Hobbes, 199
Physics, 132–138
Plato, 29–30, 52, 100, 123, 185, 188n, 199
Political science, Hobbes's, 139–141
Positivism, 124–125; in law, 172; and metaphysics, 130; in physics, 134; in Weber, 182–183
Postmodernity, 1
Prerogatives, 58–59, 62, 176
Prophecy, 18–22; false, 115

Protestant Reformation, 26–27, 42–47, 115–116
Providence, 72, 110, 168–169, 190; and Burke, 215; and enlightenment, 195–196

Representation, 180–184
Republicanism, 11, 21–25. See also Democracy; Liberty
Resolutive-compositive method, 7–8, 71, 120
Rhetoric, 26, 54, 80–81
Rhetorical strategies of political treatises, 154–164
Right reason, 70, 82, 84, 111, 151, 168
Rousseau, Jean-Jacques, 28, 45, 46n, 47n, 144, 151, 203, 212

Savagery. See Barbarism
Scholasticism, 26, 42, 83, 156
Science: dialectical vs. introspective, 122–127; Enlightenment, 101–103, 122; Hobbes's natural, 127–137
Self-preservation, 139, 167, 185, 197–203
Socrates, 18, 22–25, 29, 49–50, 53, 123, 212
Soldiers, 58–59, 66
Sovereign, 167–172; origins of, 173–185
Speech, 26; metaphysical assumptions of, 88–94; misuses of, 78–84
Spinoza, Benedict, 92, 103
State of nature: as historical teaching, 142–145; as logical construction, 148–151; as psychological teaching, 145–148; scholarly interpretations of, 141–142
Strauss, Leo, 8n, 23n, 28n, 90n, 93n, 102, 106, 109n, 125n, 141n, 164n, 197, 208n

Taxation, 59–60
Taylor-Warrender thesis, 153n, 184n
Thucydides, 11, 22–23, 34
Tocqueville, Alexis de, 205–206
Totalitarianism, 203, 214
Tribes, 12–13, 143

Universities, 41, 26; and enlightenment, 62, 99, 185; and rebellion, 55

Library of Congress Cataloging-in-Publication Data

Kraynak, Robert P., 1949–
    History and modernity in the thought of Thomas Hobbes / Robert P.
Kraynak.
        p.   cm.
    Includes bibliographical references and index.
    ISBN 0–8014–2427–5 (alk. paper)
    1. Hobbes, Thomas, 1588–1679.   Behemoth.   2. Hobbes, Thomas.
1588–1679—Views on modern history.   3. Great Britain—History—
Puritan Revolution, 1642–1660—Historiography.   4. Great Britain—
History—Civil War, 1642–1649—Historiography.   5. Historiography—
Great Britain—History—17th century.   I. Title.
DA400.H63K73   1990
941.06′2—dc20   90–36301